BEYOND MADRID
See pp118–141

CENTRAL SPAIN

Sigüenza

Guadalajara

San Martin

MADRID

Torrijos

Aranjuez

Toledo

FURTHER AFIELD
See pp106–115

Around La Castellana

Bourbon Madrid

BOURBON MADRID
See pp62–89
Street Finder maps 7, 8

EYEWITNESS TRAVEL GUIDES

MADRID

EYEWITNESS TRAVEL GUIDES

MADRID

Main contributor: MICHAEL LEAPMAN

LONDON, NEW YORK,
MELBOURNE, MUNICH AND DELHI
www.dk.com

Project Editor Helen Townsend
Art Editor Gillian Andrews
Editors Elizabeth Atherton, Sophie Warne
Designers Carolyn Hewitson, Nicola Rodway
Map Co-ordinator David Pugh
DTP Designer Pamela Shiels
Picture Researcher Monica Allende

Main Contributors
Adam Hopkins, Mark Little,
Edward Owen

Photographers
Peter Wilson and Kim Sayer

Illustrators
Richard Bonson, Stephen Gyapay, Claire Littlejohn,
Isidoro González-Adalid Cabezas (Acanto, Arquitectura y
Urbanismo S.L.), Maltings Partnership, Chris Orr & Associates

Reproduced by Colourscan (Singapore)
Printed and bound by South China Printing Co. Ltd., China

First published in Great Britain in 1999
by Dorling Kindersley Limited
80 Strand, London WC2R 0RL

Copyright 1999, 2005 © Dorling Kindersley Limited, London
A Penguin Company

Reprinted with revisions 2000, 2001, 2002, 2003, 2004, 2005

Contents

Winged Victory on the dome of
the Edificio Metrópolis (see p74)

Introducing Madrid

Madrileños enjoying the May-time
Fiesta de San Isidro (see p34)

Restaurant inside the historic Hotel Reina Victoria *(see p47)*

Selection of Madrid's cakes

The 13th-century church of San
Esteban in Segovia *(see p128)*

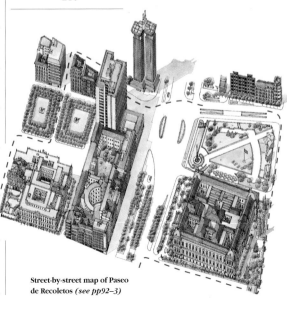

Street-by-street map of Paseo
de Recoletos *(see pp92–3)*

INTRODUCING MADRID

Putting Spain on the Map

Spain, in southwestern Europe, covers the greater part of the Iberian Peninsula. The third largest country in Europe, it includes the Canary Islands in the Atlantic and the Balearics in the Mediterranean, and two small territories in North Africa. Its capital, Madrid, lies geographically in the centre of the country, some 650 m (2,130 ft) above sea level.

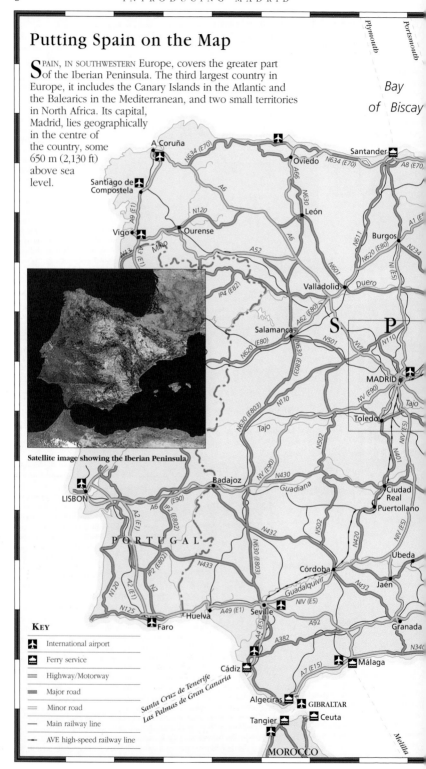

Plymouth

Portsmouth

Bay of Biscay

A Coruña

Santiago de Compostela

Vigo

Ourense

Oviedo

Santander

León

Burgos

Valladolid

Duero

Salamanca

S **P**

MADRID

Toledo

Tajo

Badajoz

Guadiana

LISBON

Ciudad Real

Puertollano

PORTUGAL

Tajo

Córdoba

Guadalquivir

Ubeda

Jaén

Faro

Huelva

Seville

Granada

Cádiz

Málaga

Santa Cruz de Tenerife
Las Palmas de Gran Canaria

Algeciras

GIBRALTAR

Ceuta

Tangier

Melilla

MOROCCO

Satellite image showing the Iberian Peninsula

Key

🛩 International airport

⚓ Ferry service

═══ Highway/Motorway

━━━ Major road

═══ Minor road

── Main railway line

►── AVE high-speed railway line

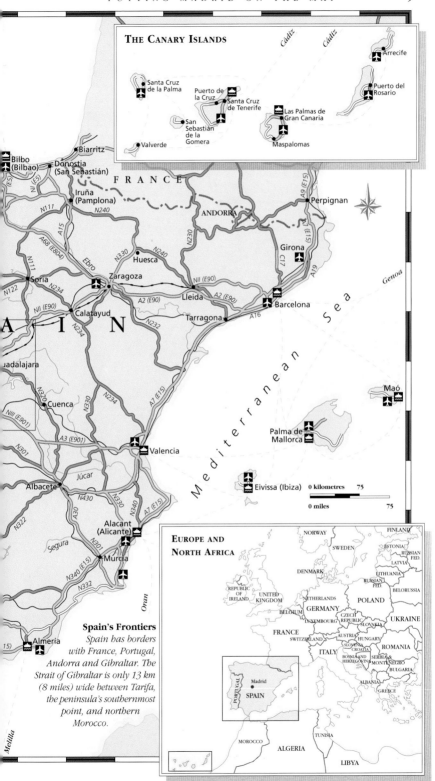

THE CANARY ISLANDS

Santa Cruz de la Palma

Puerto de la Cruz
Santa Cruz de Tenerife

San Sebastián de la Gomera

Valverde

Las Palmas de Gran Canaria

Maspalomas

Arrecife

Puerto del Rosario

Cádiz *Cádiz*

Bilbo (Bilbao)
Donostia (San Sebastián)
Biarritz

FRANCE

Iruña (Pamplona)

ANDORRA

Perpignan

Huesca

Zaragoza

Soria

Lleida

Girona

Calatayud

Tarragona

Barcelona

Genoa

AIN

uadalajara

Cuenca

Mediterranean Sea

Maó

Valencia

Palma de Mallorca

Albacete

Alacant (Alicante)

Eivissa (Ibiza)

0 kilometres   75

0 miles   75

Murcia

Almería

Oran

Spain's Frontiers
*Spain has borders
with France, Portugal,
Andorra and Gibraltar. The
Strait of Gibraltar is only 13 km
(8 miles) wide between Tarifa,
the peninsula's southernmost
point, and northern
Morocco.*

Melilla

EUROPE AND NORTH AFRICA

NORWAY SWEDEN FINLAND

REPUBLIC OF IRELAND UNITED KINGDOM DENMARK

ESTONIA RUSSIAN FED. LATVIA LITHUANIA

RUSSIAN FED. BELORUSSIA

NETHERLANDS GERMANY POLAND

BELGIUM LUXEMBOURG CZECH REPUBLIC SLOVAKIA UKRAINE

FRANCE SWITZERLAND AUSTRIA HUNGARY SLOVENIA CROATIA ROMANIA

ITALY BOSNIA AND HERZEGOVINA SERBIA & MONTENEGRO BULGARIA

ALBANIA GREECE

PORTUGAL SPAIN Madrid

MOROCCO ALGERIA TUNISIA LIBYA

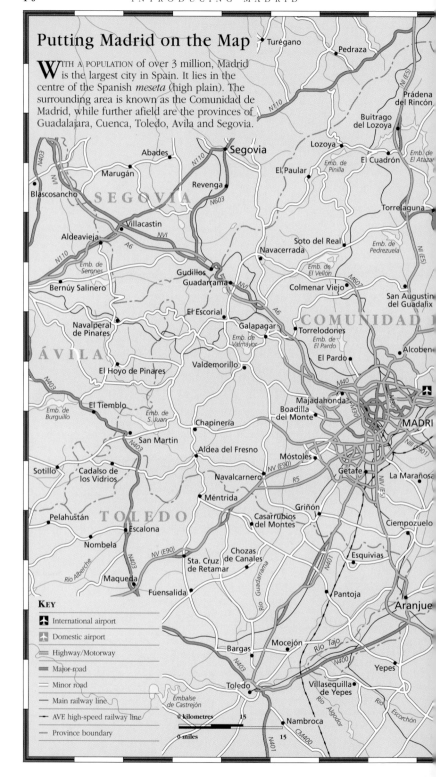

Putting Madrid on the Map

With a population of over 3 million, Madrid is the largest city in Spain. It lies in the centre of the Spanish *meseta* (high plain). The surrounding area is known as the Comunidad de Madrid, while further afield are the provinces of Guadalajara, Cuenca, Toledo, Ávila and Segovia.

Turégano
Pedraza
Prádena del Rincón
Buitrago del Lozoya
Lozoya
El Cuadrón
Emb. de El Atazar
Segovia
El Paular
Emb. de Pinilla
Abades
Marugán
Revenga
Torrelaguna
Blascosancho
SEGOVIA
Villacastin
Soto del Real
Emb. de Pedrezuela
Aldeavieja
Navacerrada
Emb. de Serones
Emb. de El Vellón
San Augustin del Guadalix
Bernúy Salinero
Gudillos
Guadarrama
Colmenar Viejo
El Escorial
COMUNIDAD
Navalperal de Pinares
Galapagar
Torrelodones
Alcoben
ÁVILA
Emb. de Valmayor
Emb. de El Pardo
El Hoyo de Pinares
Valdemorillo
El Pardo
MADRID
Majadahonda
El Tiemblo
Boadilla del Monte
Emb. de Burguillo
Emb. de S. Juan
Chapinería
San Martin
Móstoles
Aldea del Fresno
Getafe
La Marañosa
Sotillo
Cadalso de los Vidrios
Navalcarnero
Griñón
Ciempozuelo
Méntrida
Casarrubios del Montes
Pelahustán
Escalona
TOLEDO
Esquivias
Nombela
Chozas de Canales
Sta. Cruz de Retamar
Pantoja
Aranjue
Maqueda
Río Alberche
Fuensalida
Río Guadarrama
Bargas
Mocejón
Río Tajo
Yepes
Toledo
Villasequilla de Yepes
Río Algodor
Embalse de Castrejón
Nambroca
Río Escorhón

KEY

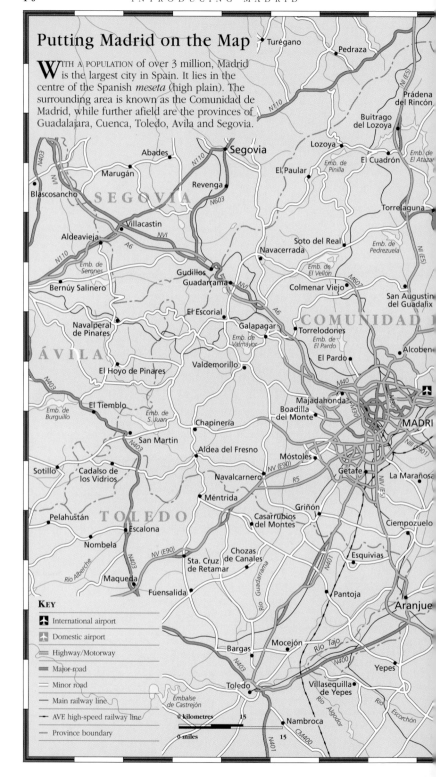 International airport

 Domestic airport

Highway/Motorway

Major road

Minor road

Main railway line

AVE high-speed railway line

Province boundary

0 kilometres 15

0 miles 15

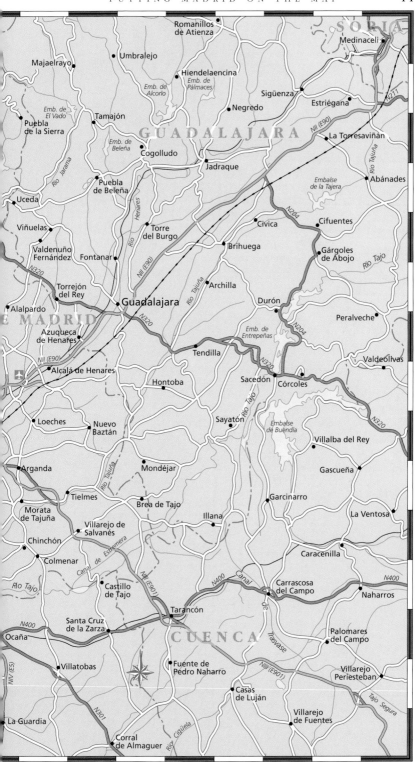

THE HISTORY OF MADRID

ALTHOUGH ARCHEOLOGICAL EVIDENCE *suggests that humans were attracted to the area in prehistoric times, the story of Madrid doesn't begin until 852, when the Moors built a fortress near the Manzanares river. By Spanish standards, the city is a mere adolescent – it was born 21 centuries after the Phoenicians founded Cádiz and six centuries after the Romans constructed Itálica near Seville.*

In the early 8th century, a Moorish army from North Africa landed at Gibraltar and, within a few years, conquered most of the Iberian peninsula. The Moors established an independent emirate based in Córdoba, southern Spain and, in 852, under Emir Mohamed I, they built a fortress (alcázar) to protect the northern approach to Toledo; it stood on the site of Madrid's present-day royal palace. Named Mayrit (later corrupted to Magerit, then Madrid), a small community arose around the alcázar.

Ornate Moorish warrior helmet

CHRISTIAN CONQUEST

Timidly at first, then with gathering strength, the Christians to the north rallied against the Moorish invaders, pushing southward in the so-called Reconquest. By the middle of the 11th century, the kingdom of Castile had arisen as the major Christian power, its territory extending as far south as the Cordillera central mountain range, within sight of Mayrit. In 1085, the Castilians under Alfonso VI mustered for the decisive thrust against Toledo. Mayrit stood in the path of the advancing army. According to one story, the troops mistook it for the much larger Toledo, which is why they bothered laying siege to it. Another legend has it that the Christian attackers subdued the town after some of the more intrepid soldiers clambered up the defence walls.

Once all the excitement was over, the town of Madrid settled back into its sleepy rural existence. Many of its earliest inhabitants were monks, encouraged by the Spanish rulers to establish monasteries there and thus breathe new life into the community. Before long, Madrid had 13 churches, more than enough to serve the spiritual needs of its small population.

Among the first *Madrileños* was San Isidro Labrador, a local farmer who founded a *cofradía* (religious brotherhood). It is also said he performed miracles, but little else is known about Madrid's rustic patron saint.

In the 13th century a dispute arose over hunting rights on land owned by the Church. It was agreed that, while the Church owned the soil, *Madrileños* had rights to all that was above it, namely, game. Thus Madrid acquired its symbol – a bear (the Church's emblem) sniffing a tree.

TIMELINE

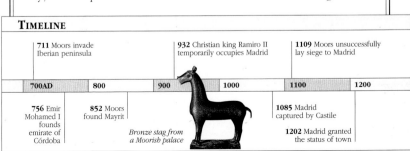

711 Moors invade Iberian peninsula		**932** Christian king Ramiro II temporarily occupies Madrid	**1109** Moors unsuccessfully lay siege to Madrid

700AD	**800**	**900**	**1000**	**1100**	**1200**

756 Emir Mohamed I founds emirate of Córdoba	**852** Moors found Mayrit	*Bronze stag from a Moorish palace*	**1085** Madrid captured by Castile **1202** Madrid granted the status of town

◁ **Tiled mural showing San Isidro Labrador, Madrid's patron saint, and another farmer tilling the soil**

Columbus setting foot in the Americas in the late 15th century

ROYAL HUNTING GROUND

Madrid's reputation as a hunting paradise attracted the attention of Castilian royals, whose visits became increasingly frequent. The city was especially favoured by Enrique IV de Trastamara who was, by all accounts, physically repellent, politically inept and morally perverted. Enrique was married to Juana of Portugal, but most people doubted that their daughter, Juana, was actually the king's; it was assumed her real father was the queen's lover, Beltrán de la Cueva, thus earning her the sobriquet, La Beltraneja (Beltrán's little one). On Enrique's death in 1474, a dynastic struggle ensued between supporters of La Beltraneja and those of Enrique's half-sister, Isabel, who went down in history as Isabel la Católica. Madrid's nobility threw its support behind La Beltraneja, and the forces of Isabel and her husband Fernando of Aragón laid siege, conquering Madrid with the help of supporters within the town. Although

Fernando of Aragón, the Catholic Monarch

Isabel and Fernando visited often, most of the momentous events of the age, such as the final war against the Moors and Columbus' encounter with the queen, took place elsewhere.

When Isabel died in 1504, her daughter Juana *"la Loca"* ("the Mad") was deemed unfit to rule. She and her husband, the Archduke of Austria, who were living in Burgundy, returned to Spain to reassert their rights. But the archduke soon died, leaving Juana to slip further into dementia. Fernando of Aragón acted as regent until the couple's son, Charles of Ghent, acceded to the throne in 1517 as Carlos I, the first of the Spanish Habsburgs (later Holy Roman Emperor Charles V).

Carlos I (1516–56)

Carlos I ruled over a European empire that included the Low Countries, parts of Italy and Germany, and Spain's newly conquered possessions in the Americas. But he had been brought up in France, spoke no Spanish when he arrived to claim the throne and, although his reign lasted 40 years, he spent only 16 of them in Spain. The European wars and the Counter-Reformation kept him busy elsewhere. Finally, spiritually exhausted and plagued with gout, Carlos I retired to the monastery of Yuste in western Spain, where he died at the age of 58.

TIMELINE

1309 First royal Cortes (parliament) held in Madrid

1361 Pogroms sweep through Madrid's Jewish quarter

1498 Pigs banned from roaming freely in Madrid streets

1492 Moorish Granada falls; Columbus reaches America; Jews are expelled from Spain

1300	1350	1400	1450	1500

1339 Alfonso XI holds Cortes in Madrid

1434 Madrid buffeted by rain, hailstorms and floods for nine weeks

1474 Supporters of Queen Isabel besiege Madrid

1478 Start of Spanish Inquisition

Brotherhood of Death

A City is Born

Since the beginnings of the kingdom of Castile, its rulers travelled ceaselessly from one part of the realm to another, with the entire court tagging along. Fed up with this migrant existence, Carlos I's successor, Felipe II, established a permanent capital in Madrid in 1561. It was centrally located in the Iberian Peninsula and small enough to lack the complex web of loyalties and intrigues of larger cities, such as Toledo.

Felipe V, the first Bourbon king

Artisans, cooks, poets, soldiers, thieves and hangers-on from around the peninsula flocked to the new capital. Within four decades, the population swelled from some 20,000 to 85,000.

Unlike his father, Felipe II spent most of his reign in Spain. Under him, the Inquisition became a major force, and the unsuccessful Spanish Armada was launched against England. The "Black Legend" has painted a dark picture of Felipe II, yet whatever his shortcomings, laziness and dishonesty were not among them and, during his reign, Spain's world power was virtually unchallenged.

Due to its sudden rise to prominence, Madrid's growth was haphazard. Yet under the Habsburgs the city acquired some of its most notable constructions. The best examples were built in the reigns of Felipe's successors, a period when the country enjoyed an age of cultural brilliance (the *Siglo de Oro*) just as Spain's military and political strength was declining. The Plaza Mayor *(see p44)*, the epitome of Habsburg Madrid, was built during the reign of Felipe III. His successor, Felipe IV, built a stylish new palace at El Retiro. At the same time, Cervantes, Lope de Vega, Velázquez, Zurbarán and Murillo *(see pp26–7)* were active in Madrid. Money poured in from the New World and, although most of it financed Spain's foreign wars and increasing debt, enough was left to fuel an artistic boom.

The Bourbon Zenith

It was too good to last. The inbred Habsburg dynasty produced the gentle but dim-witted Carlos II who died without an heir in 1700, leaving the Spanish throne in dispute. France favoured Philippe of Anjou, the grandson of Louis XIV. Alarmed at the implications of a French-Spanish alliance, England, Austria and Holland supported the Archduke Charles of Austria. This dispute led to the 14-year-long War of Spanish Succession. At the end of the conflict Philippe was crowned as Felipe V – the first Bourbon king – and Spain was securely in the French orbit.

Bullfighting in Madrid's Plaza Mayor in the 17th century

1561 Felipe II establishes capital of Spain in Madrid

1600 Felipe III moves Spanish capital to Valladolid

1605 Publication of *Don Quixote* by Cervantes

1621 Felipe III dies, succeeded by Felipe IV

1701 Felipe V arrives in Madrid as first Bourbon king

1550   1600   1650   1700

1520 Madrid joins *Comunero* rebellion of Castilian towns against Carlos I

1563 Work starts on El Escorial *(see pp122–5)*

1588 Spanish Armada fails to reach Britain

1606 Madrid reinstated as capital

1632 Real Sitio del Buen Retiro palace *(see p77)* is completed

Felipe III

1734 Fire destroys Madrid's Moorish alcázar

1746 Fernando VI becomes king

The Bourbons were able administrators, availing themselves of French and Italian advisers who introduced modern improvements to Spain. Felipe V spoke little Spanish and his main concern was making Madrid look as French as possible. When the alcázar burned down in 1734, he ordered the construction of a royal palace *(see pp54–7)* modelled on Versailles, but died before it was completed. The first occupant was Carlos III, under whose rule the Bourbon dynasty, and Madrid, reached their greatest splendour. At this time the centre of the city shifted from the old Plaza Mayor to the new Paseo del Prado, and many new buildings were constructed. Such was Carlos's urbanistic zeal that he is still cited as the best "mayor" Madrid ever had.

Carlos III

The presence of foreign advisers did not sit well with *Madrileños*, however, and the Church encouraged sentiment against interloping outsiders. The most famous incident was the 1766 Esquilache affair in which the Marqués de Esquilache, adviser to the king, banned the traditional broad-brimmed hat and long cape, as they enabled weapons to be concealed. His men roamed the streets armed with scissors to trim the offending garb. The people took this as an attempt to make them conform to foreign fashions, and fierce riots ensued. The Jesuits were thought to be behind the disturbances, and the order was expelled from Spain.

On his death in 1788, Carlos was succeeded by his vacillating son, Carlos IV, who ushered in the decline of the monarchy. The real power sat with his domineering wife, María Luisa of Parma, and chief minister, Manuel Godoy.

A City in Arms

Godoy struck a deal with the France of Napoleon (who had declared himself emperor in 1804) to allow French troops to cross Spain to conquer Portugal. In the end, however, the French occupied Spain itself. *Madrileños* blamed the royals and their hated counsellor, Godoy, and riots broke out in March 1808. The king was forced to abdicate in favour of his son, Fernando VII, though with the French occupying Madrid he ruled in name only.

On 2 May, *Madrileños* turned on the occupying troops in front of the Palacio Real. This popular uprising was met with bloody reprisals by the French the following day.

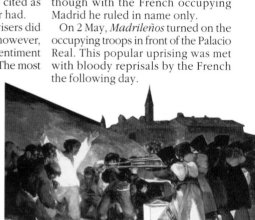

Goya's *The 3rd of May* (1814) with the French executing Spanish patriots

TIMELINE

1764 Palacio Real is completed	**1769** Work on Puerta de Alcalá *(see p66)* starts	**1790** Plaza Mayor severely damaged by fire	**1805** Nelson defeats combined Spanish-French fleet at Trafalgar	**1808** French soldiers occupy Spain; riots in Madrid; Joseph Bonaparte becomes king	**1835** Church property seized

1750	1770	1790	1810	1830

1759 Carlos III becomes king		**1788** Carlos III dies, succeeded by Carlos IV		**1820** Liberal *coup* led by General Riego
1763 Birth of Spanish National Lottery	**1767** Jesuits expelled from Spain	*Joseph Bonaparte*	**1812** Wellington enters Madrid	**1813** Fernando VII becomes king

After the May riots Napoleon, increasingly impatient with events in Spain, installed his brother Joseph Bonaparte (José I) on the Spanish throne. Spanish sentiment against the occupying French could not be stopped, however, and the country rose up in arms. In the face of organized, well-armed French troops, Spaniards resorted to terrorist tactics, with small bands mounting surprise attacks on the enemy before vanishing into mountain hiding places.

In 1810, the army of the British Duke of Wellington landed in Portugal and started the two-year campaign to drive the French from the Iberian Peninsula.

LIBERALS VERSUS CONSERVATIVES

A century of close contact with the French left its mark on Spain. Liberal ideas found fertile soil among the Spanish enlightened classes and, while the war was at its peak, delegates in Cádiz drafted Spain's first constitution. Yet when Fernando VII was restored to the throne in 1813, he rejected the Cádiz document and ruled as an absolute monarch. This rift between reactionary and progressive sides would plague the country for the next century and a half. When an army uprising headed by the liberal Rafael de Riego in 1820 forced the king to accept the constitution, the exercise ended with Riego's execution.

After Fernando VII's death in 1833, Spanish politics became a complicated succession of *coups d'état* and uprisings. To make matters worse, the choice of his young daughter Isabel II as successor angered supporters of his brother Carlos, leading to a civil war in which 140,000 died. During Isabel's 38-year reign, Spanish politics were dominated by military brass, conservative or liberal.

Isabel II

Against this background of instability, Madrid was slowly becoming a modern European capital with a growing middle class. It was expanding relentlessly with the *Ensanche* (widening), with fashionable residential areas replacing overcrowded working-class districts.

In 1868 liberals joined forces with disgruntled military to oust Isabel II under the pretext of her corrupt and lascivious behaviour. But Spaniards still favoured a monarchy, and placed Amadeo of Savoy, son of Italy's King Victor Emmanuel, on the throne. The king received the cold shoulder from *Madrileños*, however, and abdicated after two years, at which point the Cortes (parliament) proclaimed a republic. The First Republic lasted only 11 months. In 1874, General Manuel Pavia ended it all by riding up the steps of the Cortes, declaring support for Isabel II's son, Alfonso. Under Alfonso XII (1875–85) and, later, the regency of his wife, María Cristina, who reigned on behalf of her son Alfonso XIII until 1902, Madrid enjoyed a period of prosperity and unstoppable growth, culminating with the inauguration of the Gran Vía *(see p48)* by Alfonso XIII in 1908.

THE BATTLE OF MADRID

Alfonso XIII felt it his duty to meddle in political affairs. Ministers were sacked by the dozen, and there were 33 governments between 1902 and 1923. Finally, the king resorted to General Miguel Primo de Rivera, who installed a dictatorship. It was relatively benign and had support among much of the working class. Spain underwent a flurry of public works, but Primo de Rivera was a disaster when it came to economics.

1840 Radical *coup* by General Espartero	1868 *Coup* by General Prim ends reign of Isabel II; the peseta becomes the Spanish monetary unit	1876 New Spanish constitution		1885 Alfonso XII dies	1906 Ritz hotel opens	1908 Work starts on Gran Vía
	1850	1870		1890		1910
	1850 Inauguration of Cortes building and Teatro Real *(see p58)*	1873 First Spanish Republic			1897 Prime minister Cánovas del Castillo assassinated by Italian anarchist	
1843 Conservative *coup* by General Narváez		1875 Bourbon monarchy restored under Alfonso XII	Alfonso XII			

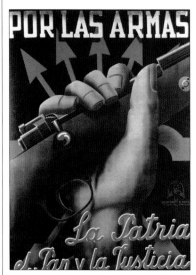

Poster for the Nationalist cause in the Civil War

increasing territory, and by November 1936 the Nationalists had reached the outskirts of Madrid. The city was to be on the front line for the duration of the Civil War, suffering severe bombardment, until it finally fell in March 1939.

General Franco, who had manoeuvred himself into position as the uprising's *generalísimo*, was installed as dictator. Although Spain had remained nominally neutral during World War II, Franco's sympathies for Hitler and Mussolini were not forgotten, and for more than a decade the country was ostracized from the community of nations.

Farms suffered a devastating drought, the black market thrived and Franco taught "autarchy" – his extreme form of isolationism and self-sufficiency. Yet the nation was starving, and millions were forced to emigrate to work in factories in France and Germany.

By the 1950s geopolitics came to the rescue. The US forgave Franco's past sins in return for support in the Cold War against the Soviet Union, in the form of US military bases in Spain. The door was open to foreign aid and investment. The first adventurous travellers soon followed.

General Francisco Franco

Within six years the country was bankrupt. After the dictator stepped down in 1930, Republicans forced Alfonso XIII to call elections. The vote went overwhelmingly to the Republicans, and the king headed for exile after an angry Madrid crowd demanded his abdication.

During the brief Second Republic, the bourgeoisie, landowners and military were increasingly alarmed by the spread of left-wing ideas. The assassination of conservative member of parliament, José Calvo Sotelo, in July 1936 precipitated events. On 18 July news reached Madrid that a military uprising had taken several Andalusian cities, including Seville. *Madrileños* flocked to the army barracks, demanding arms to defend the Republic, and within a day the working-class militia controlled the city. But, with much of the Spanish army's troops and weapons in the hands of insurgent Nationalists, the rebellion gathered

DICTATORSHIP TO DEMOCRACY

Franco's twilight years were devoted to securing the continuity of his regime. Alfonso XIII's grandson Juan Carlos was groomed as his nominal successor, while the real power was to be wielded by the hard-line prime minister, Admiral Luis Carrero Blanco. But in 1973, the militant wing of the Basque separatist group ETA assassinated Carrero Blanco.

TIMELINE

1921 Madrid Metro opens

1923 Primo de Rivera establishes dictatorship

Primo de Rivera

1929 Telefónica building *(see p49)* completed

1931 Second Republic established; Alfonso XIII goes into exile

1936 Civil War starts; Nationalists lay siege to Madrid

1939 Franco's troops enter Madrid; Civil War ends

1953 Spain agrees to allow building of US bases on its soil; Edificio de España *(see p53)* inaugurated

1955 Spain joins United Nations

1910	1920	1930	1940	1950

The Cortes being held at gunpoint in the *coup d'état* on 23 February 1981

When Franco died in November 1975, all eyes turned on his heir apparent, who was sworn in as king. Juan Carlos had been planning for Spain's reunion with the modern world while lending lip service to the Franco regime, and in a series of bold moves, he manoeuvred the country into its first post-Franco democratic elections in 1977. When die-hard supporters of the old regime seized the Cortes in 1981, the *coup* failed largely due to Juan Carlos's intervention.

The next year the government passed bloodlessly from the centrists to the social democratic PSOE, under long-serving prime minister Felipe González. The first half of his tenure coincided with a period of economic buoyancy, crowned in 1992 with the Olympic Games in Barcelona, a world fair in Seville and Madrid's stint as the "European Capital of Culture". The 1980s were a time of euphoria and cultural

ferment, especially in Madrid. Under mayor Enrique Tierno Galván, the arts experienced a flurry of creativity, and the city revelled in a spirit of optimism and confidence, known as *La Movida (see p104)*.

The party couldn't last forever. Creative verve can only go so far, and a series of scandals involving some people serving in high offices chipped away at the public's faith in the governing powers, ultimately costing the PSOE the 1996 elections.

Like their counterparts in other European capitals, *Madrileños* complain about traffic, never-ending public works and pollution. Yet despite this they retain a fiercely individualistic spirit, a refusal to conform to European hours and, above all, a sardonic sense of humour that sets them apart from other Spaniards. They are living in one of the world's most lively and attractive cities… and they know it.

Aerial image of present-day Madrid, a thriving metropolis

Rulers of Spain

S PAIN BECAME A NATION-STATE under Isabel and Fernando, whose marriage eventually united Castile and Aragón. With their daughter Juana's marriage, the kingdom was delivered into Habsburg hands. Carlos I and Felipe II were both capable rulers, but in 1700 Carlos II died without leaving an heir. After the War of the Spanish Succession, Spain came under the French Bourbons, who have ruled ever since – apart from an interregnum, two republics and Franco's dictatorship. The current Bourbon king, Juan Carlos I, a constitutional monarch, is respected for his support of democracy.

1665–1700
Carlos II

1479–1516
Fernando, King of Aragón

1474–1504 Isabel, Queen of Castile

1516–56 Carlos I of Spain (Holy Roman Emperor Charles V)

1598–1621 Felipe III

1400	1450	1500	1550	1600	1650
INDEPENDENT KINGDOMS		**HABSBURG DYNASTY**			
1400	1450	1500	1550	1600	1650

1469 Marriage of Isabel and Fernando leads to unification of Spain

1504–16 Juana la Loca (with Fernando as regent)

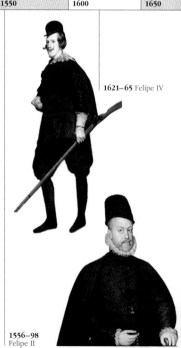

1621–65 Felipe IV

Fernando and Isabel, the Catholic Monarchs

UNIFICATION OF SPAIN

In the late 15th century the two largest kingdoms in developing Christian Spain – Castile, with its military might, and Aragón (including Barcelona and a Mediterranean empire) – were united. The marriage of Isabel of Castile and Fernando of Aragón in 1469 joined these powerful kingdoms. Together the so-called Catholic Monarchs defeated the Nasrid Kingdom of Granada, the last stronghold of the Moors (see p14). With the addition of Navarra in 1512, Spain was finally unified.

1556–98
Felipe II

1843–68 Isabel II reigns following the regency of her mother María Cristina (1833–41) and General Espartero (1841–3)

1814–33 First Bourbon restoration, following French rule – Fernando VII

1871–3 Break in Bourbon rule – Amadeo I of Savoy

1939–75 General Franco Head of State

1724 Luis I reigns after Felipe V's abdication, but dies within a year

1759–88 Carlos III

1931–9 Second Republic

1875–85 Second Bourbon restoration – Alfonso XII

1700	1750	1800	1850	1900	1950
BOURBON DYNASTY		**BOURBON**		**BOURBON**	
1700	1750	1800	1850	1900	1950

1808–13 Break in Bourbon rule – Napoleon's brother, Joseph Bonaparte, rules as José I

1746–59 Fernando VI

1724–46 Felipe V reinstated as king upon the death of his son, Luis I

1788–1808 Carlos IV

1902–31 Alfonso XIII

1886–1902 María Cristina of Habsburg-Lorraine as regent for Alfonso XIII

1700–24 Felipe V

1873–4 First Republic

1868–70 The Septembrina Revolution

1975 Third Bourbon restoration – Juan Carlos I

MADRID AT A GLANCE

OVER 100 PLACES OF interest are described in the *Madrid Area by Area* and *Beyond Madrid* sections of this book. The detailed catalogue of significant buildings and monuments traces the history of the city – beginning with the 16th- and 17th-century Habsburg Madrid ("Madrid de los Austrias"), as exemplified by the medieval Plaza de la Villa *(see p45)* and the Colegiata de San Isidro *(see p46)*. From here, it follows the development of Madrid from the Bourbon city of the 18th century with its Parque del Retiro and Plaza de Cibeles *(see p67)*, to the upmarket 19th-century Barrio de Salamanca and the modern skyscrapers in the Azca area. The list also includes recreational sights, such as Casa de Campo *(see p114)*. Pictured below are some attractions no visitor should miss.

MADRID'S TOP TOURIST ATTRACTIONS

Plaza Mayor
See p44.

Plaza de Toros de Las Ventas
See p110.

Museo Lázaro Galdiano
See pp100–101.

Parque del Retiro
See p77.

Museo Thyssen-Bornemisza
See pp70–73.

Museo Arqueológico Nacional
See pp96–7.

Centro de Arte Reina Sofía
See pp86–9.

Palacio Real
See pp54–7.

Museo del Prado
See pp80–83.

◁ **The Art Deco Capitol building along the Gran Vía**

Madrid's Best: Museums and Galleries

For a city of its size, Madrid boasts an exceptional number of world-class museums and galleries. Heading the list are the Prado, with the world's largest collection of Spanish art, the Thyssen-Bornemisza, which traces the development of Western art from the 14th century, and Reina Sofía, with its outstanding display of modern art. But there are many smaller, more intimate museums, too. Some, such as the Museo Lázaro Galdiano, are gems both for the sumptuous mansions housing the collections and for the untold treasures within. Note that many museums are closed on Mondays when planning your itinerary.

Museo Municipal
Anyone with an interest in Madrid's evolution, from prehistoric to present times, will be fascinated by this museum, which features a captivating scale model of 19th-century Madrid (see p103).

Museo Cerralbo
Entering this 19th-century mansion, with its eclectic array of artifacts, paintings and sculptures, gives an uncanny sense of stepping back in time and experiencing aristocratic life in Madrid at the turn of the 20th century (see p52).

Old Madrid

Real Academia de Bellas Artes
Goya's Entierro de la Sardina *is one of more than 1,000 paintings and sculptures, from the 16th–20th centuries, which can be seen at this arts academy (see p47).*

Museo Thyssen-Bornemisza
Sold to the nation in 1993, this vast private art collection traces Western art through the ages, with major works by Titian, Goya, Picasso and Rubens (see pp70–73).

Museo Lázaro Galdiano

The collection of the late José Lázaro Galdiano includes paintings, sculptures, jewellery, archeological finds and ceramics in his recently renovated Neo-Renaissance mansion (see pp100–1).

Around La Castellana

Museo Arqueológico Nacional

This museum, situated at the back of the Biblioteca Nacional, is second only to the Prado in terms of the importance of its collection. Exhibits date from prehistoric times to the 19th century (see pp96–7).

Museo del Prado

Recognized as one of the world's greatest art galleries, the Prado is particularly notable for its collections by Velázquez and Goya (see pp80–83).

Bourbon Madrid

Centro de Arte Reina Sofía

A former hospital, the Reina Sofía now houses an out-standing collection of 20th-century art (see pp86–9), including Retrato de Josette, *by the Spanish Cubist Juan Gris (pictured), and* Guernica, *Picasso's famous depiction of the horrors of the Civil War.*

| 0 kilometres | 0.5 |
| 0 miles | 0.5 |

Famous People of Madrid

EVER SINCE Felipe II made Madrid the capital of Spain in 1561 *(see p15)*, the city has attracted the best artistic and literary talent in the country. Painters, writers, composers and architects in search of fame and fortune left behind their rural dwellings and migrated to Madrid, where they could take advantage of royal sponsorships and subsidies, publish their works and sell their wares to the city's ever-growing population. Thus Madrid became the cultural centre of Spain, a distinction that grew in times of political and economic stability, and flourished – as great art usually does – following times of turmoil and strife.

The prolific Golden Age dramatist, Félix Lope de Vega (1562–1635)

WRITERS

SPANISH WRITERS were the first to make their mark in Madrid, and throughout the 17th century the city acted as a magnet for the country's most famous scribes. The Barrio de los Literatos (Writers' Quarter), or Huertas district, was where Spain's greatest literary figure, Miguel de Cervantes Saavedra (1547–1616), produced his comic masterpiece, *Don Quixote*. In the local taverns he would argue with his rival, Félix Lope de Vega (1562–1635), Spain's most prolific dramatist. The Huertas area was also home to Cervantes' and Lope's 17th-century contemporaries, writer Francisco de Quevedo

José Zorrilla (1817–93)

y Villegas (1580–1645) and dramatist Pedro Calderón de la Barca (1600–81).

In the following centuries, this small area of Madrid continued to be the haunt of famous writers. The 18th-century Madrid native Leandro Fernández de Moratín was influenced by the French Enlightenment, as evidenced by his popular comedy *El Sí de las Niñas*. José Zorrilla y Moral (1817–93) was raised in the Huertas area, and his world-famous Romantic play, *Don Juan Tenorio* (1844), had its first showing in Madrid. In the same century, Madrid's most beloved writer, Benito Pérez Galdós (1843–1920), wrote his famous novel, *Miau* – a literary masterpiece that takes the reader on a journey through the streets and society of the Spanish capital during the city's most vibrant years. Madrid was at the centre of the "Generation of [19]27" writers that included poet and playwright Federico García Lorca (1899–1936) who, during his student years in Madrid, found inspiration as well as the theatres he needed to showcase his creations. The 20th century also produced Nobel Prize-winning novelist Camilo José Cela (born 1916), whose novel *La Colmena* depicted

Novelist Camilo José Cela (born 1916), painted by Alvaro Delgado

everyday life in hungry, postwar Madrid. And while 20th-century American writer Ernest Hemingway could not be mistaken for a *Madrileño*, his novels helped the world fall in love with Spain, and his antics in the city after long nights of sipping gin at the Ritz hotel *(see p68)* made him a local favourite. Today it is difficult to walk through Madrid's Plaza Mayor without imagining the writer swaggering down the narrow steps of the Arco de Cuchilleros on his way to a roast suckling pig dinner at El Sobrino del Botín *(see p28)*.

PAINTERS

ALL OF SPAIN'S most famous artists had an impact, one way or another, on Madrid. But it was 17th-century artist Diego de Velázquez (1599–1660) and 18th-century painter Francisco de Goya (1746–1828) who actually formed part of the city's history. Both were Spanish court painters whose works were inspired by their surroundings in the capital. Each weekend *Madrileños* brave traffic jams to escape the grey city in search of the blue skies made famous by Velázquez, whose complete collection of works has been brought together by Madrid's Museo del Prado *(see pp80–83)*. There you can see his 1656 masterpiece, *Las Meninas*. Goya began his stint at the Spanish court in 1763 at the age of 17, and stayed on until 1826, two years before his death. He depicted life during

Velázquez Bosco's Palacio de Cristal

one of the city's most violent times and was the painter of four kings – Carlos III, Carlos IV, José I (Joseph Bonaparte) and Fernando VII. While his works can be seen at several museums in Madrid, his masterpieces *The 3rd of May*, *Saturn Devouring One of his Sons* and *Naked Maja* are all displayed at the Prado.

Las Meninas **(1656) by Diego de Velázquez**

ARCHITECTS

ARCHITECTURE IS AN art form of which *Madrileños* are especially proud. Some of the best architects in the world have contributed to turning the capital into the "City of a Thousand Faces". Francesco Sabatini designed the Palacio Real *(see pp54–7)*, the grand Puerta de Alcalá *(see p66)* and the 18th-century extension wing to the Palacio de El Pardo *(see p134)*. Juan Gómez de la Mora was the architect responsible for the Plaza Mayor *(see p44)*, which was

completed in 1619. Mora learned his trade from the masterful Juan de Herrera, the designer of Felipe II's monasterial palace El Escorial *(see pp122–5)*. In the 1640s, Mora designed the Monasterio de la Encarnación *(see p53)* and the *Ayuntamiento* (town hall) in the Plaza de la Villa. A balcony was added to the town hall by Juan de Villanueva, the architect of the Prado museum. In 1781 Villanueva, along with botanist Gómez Ortega, designed the Real Jardín Botánico, or Royal Botanical Gardens *(see p84)*. In the Parque del Retiro *(see p77)* there are two beautiful palaces built by architect Velázquez Bosco in 1887: the Neo-Classical Palacio de Velázquez and the Palacio de Cristal, constructed of glass and iron. Noteworthy contemporary architects include José Rafael Moneo Valles, who redesigned the 18th-century Palacio de Villahermosa, home to the Museo Thyssen-Bornemisza *(see pp70–73)*. Also notable are Luis Gutiérrez Soto for the Ministerio del Aire in the Plaza de la Moncloa, Antonio Lamela for the Torres de Colón in the Plaza de Colón *(see p98)* and Francisco Saenz de Oiza for the Torres Blancas on Avenida de América.

Although not an architect, the Marqués de Salamanca, a flamboyant banker and speculator, had a profound effect

on the design of the upmarket Barrio de Salamanca *(see p99)*. When investors shied away from much-needed expansion plans in the 1860s, the Marqués stepped in and began work on what is today a fashionable line of housing blocks along Calle de Serrano.

POLITICIANS

SINCE MADRID IS the Spanish capital, there is a tendency here to claim or disclaim national figures as the city's own. Kings, dictators and prime ministers, while ruling from Madrid, did not always have a popular impact on the city. Felipe II *(see p15)*, for example, made Madrid the capital but then promptly left for his palace at El Escorial.

One of the best-loved political figures was the 18th-century *rey-alcalde* (king-mayor) Carlos III *(see p16)*. He took a personal interest in the city and set out to improve it with monuments, fountains, arches, street lighting and sewers. Another favourite politician was 20th-century (civilian) Socialist Mayor Enrique Tierno Galván, who became mayor in 1979, and died in 1986. He helped bring Madrid out of the grey dictatorial years by throwing his full support behind cultural events and progressive causes. He was instrumental in making Madrid's San Isidro festival *(see p34)* the popular cultural event it is today.

Enrique Tierno Galván, mayor of Madrid in the post-Franco era

Madrid's Best: Tabernas

IT COULD BE ASSUMED that the first business establishment in Madrid was a *taberna* (tavern). In the 14th century, the area around Plaza Mayor and Plaza de la Villa was home to over 50 *tabernas*. Two hundred years later, their number had risen to 800. But, of the classical *tabernas* that took shape in the early to mid-19th century, only about a hundred remain. Although each is unique, they share common features, such as a large clock standing guard over a carved wooden bar with a zinc counter, and wine flasks cooled by water running through a polished filter on the bar. Table tops tend to be of marble, and ceramic tiles often line the façade or interior. To find out more about traditional *tapas* and the locations of these popular classical *tabernas*, see pages 30–31.

Taberna del Foro
While more modern than most, this taberna *has gone to fantastic lengths to recreate a feeling of "Old Madrid". Its bar is an authentic example of genuine* taberna *craftsmanship.*

La Bola
This small, bright red taberna *was founded nearly 200 years ago. It has a beautifully carved wooden bar and, since 1873, it has been serving some of Madrid's best* cocido *(see p155).*

Old Madrid

El Sobrino del Botín
Established in 1725, this is one of the city's oldest tabernas *and is considered by many to be one of Madrid's finest restaurants. It serves traditional Castilian fare, including roast suckling pig, and was, at one time, favoured by the writer Ernest Hemingway.*

Taberna Antonio Sanchez
Madrid's tabernas *take their cue from this classical, 200-year-old watering hole, where the character of the place is just as important as the service. Many later* tabernas *have emulated its decor.*

```
0 kilometres  0.5
0 miles          0.5
```

Casa Carmencita
This mid-19th-century taberna *was famous in the early 1920s as a hang-out of writers, artists and politicians. Its wooden façade, elegant tiling and gas lamps add to its character.*

Casa Domingo
Almost 80 years ago this elegant taberna *was turned into a select restaurant for upmarket* Madrileños. *Today it serves local and international cuisine in an inviting, warm atmosphere.*

Around La Castellana

Los Gabrieles
The astonishing tile work of ceramics artist Enrique Guijo covers the walls of this museum-like taberna. *Los Gabrieles comes at the top of the list for most* taberna-*hoppers.*

Bourbon Madrid

Viva Madrid
Famous for its fine ceramic work, both inside and out, this taberna *has been adopted by the younger* Madrileño *crowd that gathers nightly around the lively Plaza de Santa Ana area.*

Casa del Abuelo
This diminutive taberna *more than makes up for its lack of size with its larger-than-life atmosphere. Founded in 1906, it specializes in sweet red wine and prawns cooked in four different ways.*

Choosing Tapas

Dry *fino* sherry

MORE THAN A MORSEL of food, *tapas* are a way of life – part of a ritual which involves drink, good company and lively conversation. The custom of serving a tasty snack with each drink originated in Andalusia, but Madrid soon adopted it with gusto and is now a *tapa*-crawler's paradise. A *tapa* is any small portion of food – a brace of anchovies, a meatball, a few olives, a sliver of cheese or a steaming dollop of stew. Small *tapas*, chosen by the waiter, are often served free with a drink; larger portions (*raciones*) are ordered separately.

Chorizo, *a popular sausage that is flavoured with garlic and paprika, is usually eaten cold; but some kinds are fried and served hot.*

Jamón serrano, *salt-cured ham dried in mountain* (serrano) *air, can be served unadorned in chunks* (tacos) *or in thin slices* (lonchas). *This basic tapas dish is often accompanied by bread.*

Tortilla a la española *is the ubiquitous thick Spanish omelette, a tasty dish of onion and potato, bound together with seasoned egg. It is served in wedges or small squares.*

Queso manchego (see p166) *is sheep's cheese from La Mancha and Spain's most popular cheese. It is served with bread in a mild, semi-soft form* (semicurado) *or, when left to age, a tangy mature form* (curado).

Albondigas *(meatballs) are a hearty* tapa *and may be served with a zesty tomato sauce.*

Aceitunas *(olives) are common* tapas, *and come in several varieties. Gordals are fat Seville olives. Manzanillas may be pitted and stuffed with anchovies, almonds or pimientos. Some olives are marinated in herbs and oil.*

Prawn   Hard-boiled egg

Olive

Gherkin

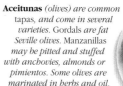

Mejillones a la marinera *is a dish of mussels cooked in a tasty sauce of sautéed onion and garlic, white wine, olive oil, lemon juice and parsley.*

Banderillas *are canapés skewered on toothpicks. Popular ingredients include marinated fish and vegetables, egg and olives. The entire canapé should be eaten at once, to blend the flavours.*

Patatas bravas *is a piquant dish of potatoes fried in oil and coated in a spicy tomato sauce flavoured with onion, garlic, white wine, parsley and red chilli peppers. The bite-sized morsels are both delicious and filling.*

Salpicón de mariscos *is a luxurious cold salad consisting of an assortment of fresh seafood, including lobster, crab and prawn, with chopped tomatoes. The salad is coated in a zesty vinaigrette flavoured with onion and peppers.*

Calamares fritos *are squid rings which have been dusted with flour before being deep fried in olive or vegetable oil. They are served garnished with a slice of lemon.*

Gambas a la plancha *is a simple but flavourful dish of whole grilled unpeeled prawns.*

Fritura de pescado *is a mixture of fried fish and seafood served with lemon. It includes red mullet, squid and baby hake or other available fresh fish.*

Ensalada de pimientos rojos *is a colourful cold salad of roasted red peppers and tomatoes. The juices from the roasting are combined with olive oil and vinegar to make a delicious dressing for the salad.*

Almendras fritas, *or fried salted almonds, are a common snack throughout the whole of Spain. Pistachios* (pistachos), *salted peanuts* (cacahuetes) *and sunflower seeds* (pipas) *can also be ordered to accompany a drink.*

GOOD TABERNAS FOR TAPAS AND DRINKS

La Bola
Calle de la Bola 5. **Map** 4 D1.
91 547 69 30.

Casa del Abuelo
Calle de la Victoria 12. **Map** 7 A2.
91 521 23 19.

Casa Domingo
Calle de Alcalá 99. **Map** 8 F1.
91 576 01 37.

Los Gabrieles
Calle de Echegaray 17. **Map** 7 A3.
91 429 62 61.

El Sobrino del Botín
Calle de los Cuchilleros 17.
Map 4 E3.
91 366 42 17.

Taberna del Alabardero
Calle Felipe V 6. **Map** 4 D2.
91 541 46 70.

Taberna Antonio Sanchez
Calle del Mesón de Paredes 13.
Map 4 F4.
91 539 78 26.

Taberna de Conspiradores
Calle Moratin 33. **Map** 7 B3.
91 369 47 41.

Taberna del Foro
Calle de San Andrés 38. **Map** 2 F4.
91 445 37 52.

Madrid's Best: Architecture

MADRID HAS BEEN DESCRIBED as the "city of a thousand faces", an image reflected in the diversity of its architectural styles. Among these are the rich and highly ostentatious buildings that mark the 16th-century areas of Old Madrid around the Plaza Mayor and the Plaza de la Villa. Northwest of Madrid, in El Escorial *(see pp122–5)*, the architecture of Felipe II's palace is characterized by unornamented severity of style. The 18th century brought with it the Bourbon urge to break with the previous mould, introducing new, ornate styles of Baroque architecture. In the mid-18th century, with the arrival of Carlos III *(see p16)*, more sedate Neo-Classical lines became fashionable. And, as the city expanded outwards, so did its love for new styles of architecture. Today Madrid's architects continue to experiment with adventurous building styles and techniques.

Modernism
The Puerta de Europa twin towers survived a financial scandal and now seem to defy gravity as they lean over Paseo de la Castellana.

Art Deco
The huge Palacio de la Música cinema on Gran Vía (see p48) *seats some 2,600 people. It is seen as a jewel of Art Deco architecture.*

Old Madrid

Habsburg
Since 1560 the red brick and granite Monasterio de las Descalzas Reales (see p52) *has been home to a society of cloistered nuns – the Royal Barefoot Sisters.*

| 0 kilometres | 0.5 |
| 0 miles | 0.5 |

Baroque
Built in the 1720s by baroque architect Jose de Churriguera, this residence was acquired by the Real Academia de Bellas Artes in 1774 and stripped of its eloborate baroque detail.

Art Nouveau
*An eyecatching
example of Madrid's
version of this art form
is the Sociedad General
de Autores de España.*

Neo-Mudéjar
*The Antiguas Escuelas
Aguirre is a good example
of this late 19th-century
Moorish style,
characterized by
its extensive use
of fine brick-
work, balconies
and row of
vantage points
along its bevel.*

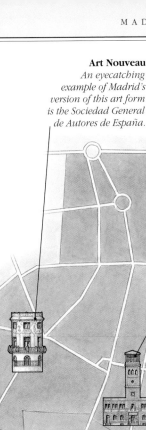

*Around La
Castellana*

Bourbon
*Influenced by French
architecture, the grand
Puerta de Alcalá (see
p66) was erected by
Carlos III as part of
his plan to improve
eastern Madrid. He
effectively moved the
centre of the city from
the Plaza Mayor to the
Paseo del Prado.*

Bourbon Madrid

Francoesque
*The Instituto de Crédito Oficial
is in the Neo-Herrerismo style,
invented in the Franco years
and named after 16th-century
architect, Juan de Herrera.*

Neo-Classical
*Designed in 1785 by
Juan de Villanueva, the
Museo del Prado (see
pp80–83) illustrates the
Neo-Classical move
towards dignity and
away from the excesses
of Baroque architecture.*

MADRID THROUGH THE YEAR

A WIDE SELECTION of fiestas, sports competitions and cultural events crowds the calendar in Madrid. Every neighbouring district, town and village also has its own fiestas, especially during the summer, with hair-raising bull runs, music and dancing until the early hours and spectacular fireworks which rank among the best in the world. There are vibrant street processions to celebrate Christmas and Easter, and at other times the capital's roads are completely taken over by bicycles, marathon runners and even sheep. Check with the tourist information office to see if your visit coincides with any public holidays, local festivals or special fairs.

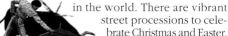

Matador with a cape playing a bull

Colourful tulips in a park, signalling the start of spring

SPRING

IN LATE MARCH the boulevards of the capital are lined with tulips, and on the first warm day in April the cafés open up their terraces. But the weather is changeable, and it may be warm one day and snowing the next. May's San Isidro fiestas, which herald the start of the bullfighting season, are often marred by rain, but the countryside also looks its best at this time. Many *Madrileños* leave town for the Easter Semana Santa holiday, and the half-deserted streets of Madrid resound with solemn religious processions.

MARCH

Cristo de Medinaceli *(first Fri)*, Iglesia de Medinaceli, Calle del Duque de Medinaceli. Thousands of people come to this church to make three wishes before the image of Christ, one of which will hopefully come true.
Expo/Ocio, Feria del Tiempo Libre *(second or third week)*, Parque Ferial Juan Carlos I. This annual exhibition is dedicated to sports and hobbies.

APRIL

Semana Santa *(Easter week)*. On Holy Thursday and Good Friday evening processions are held in Toledo *(see pp136–41)* and all over Madrid. On Easter Saturday there are church services and a passion play in Chinchón *(see p135)*. Easter Sunday is marked in Tiermes by the symbolic burning of a tree and an effigy of Judas at noon.
Artisans & Ceramic Fair *(Easter week)*, Plaza de las Comendadoras.
El Día de Cervantes *(23 April)*, Alcalá de Henares. Commemorates the death of Cervantes with a book fair and literary discussions.
Madrid Marathon *(last Sun)*.

MAY

Labour Day *(1 May)*. Public holiday and rally held in the Puerta del Sol *(see p44)*.
Fiestas de Mayo *(1 May)*, Ajalvir, Casarrubuelos, Fresno de Torote and Torrelaguna. Local fiestas celebrating May.
Las Mayas *(first Sun)*, around Iglesia de San Lorenzo in the Lavapiés district *(see p61)*. Each street elects a May Queen *(maya)* who sits in her best clothes surrounded by flowers in a spring fertility ritual.
La Maya *(2 May)*, Colmenar Viejo. Similar fiesta to above.
Día de la Comunidad *(2 May)*. Public holiday in Madrid with a military parade in the Puerta del Sol, a festival in Malasaña's Plaza del Dos de Mayo *(see p103)* and Móstoles.
Fiestas de San Isidro *(15 May)*. Public holiday in Madrid and the feast of the region's patron saint. For a week either side of 15 May, the city vibrates with fiestas, music and dance, including the *chotis*. Bands play nightly in the Jardines de las Vistillas, Calle de Bailén.
San Isidro Corridas *(15 May–end Jun)*. Daily bullfight fiesta at Plaza de Toros de Las Ventas *(see p110)*.
Corpus Christi *(end May)*. Religious holiday with processions in Madrid and Toledo.
Romería Alpina *(last Sun)*, Lozoya. Country procession with La Virgen de la Fuensanta.
Feria del Libro *(end May–mid-Jun)*, Parque del Retiro *(see p77)*. Book fair.

Semana Santa *(Easter Week)* observed with solemn religious processions

AVERAGE DAILY HOURS OF SUNSHINE

Sunshine Chart
Madrid is a sunny place and, even in the depths of winter when temperatures plummet, there are usually a few hours of sunshine to brighten the skies. At the height of the Madrid summer you can expect an average of 12 hours of blistering sun a day, so come prepared with a hat and a high-factor sun cream, and avoid the midday sun.

SUMMER

MADRID'S OUTDOOR swimming pools and aqua parks open in June *(see p180).* By August, the fierce dry heat settles in and entire families escape to the cool of the mountains, the coast or out lying villages to visit relatives. Most offices work intensively from 8am to 3pm. Many bars and restaurants close in August, but those that stay open are thronged until the early hours. With a fraction of the usual traffic on the roads, it is a pleasant month in Madrid.

Madrid's terrace bars, great for cooling down in the summer heat

JUNE

Fiesta de San Antonio de la Florida *(13 Jun),* Ermita de San Antonio, Paseo de la Florida. *Señoritas* throw pins in a font, dip in their hands and ask St Anthony for a boyfriend. If any pins stick to their hands they will have that many boyfriends in the year ahead.

JULY

Fiestas de la Virgen del Carmen *(around 16 Jul).* District fiestas in Chamberí.
Concierto de las Velas *(9 Jul),* Pedraza, Segovia. Candlelit fiesta with music.

Madrileños in traditional **castizo** costume at the Fiesta de San Isidro

Fiestas de Santiago Apóstol *(25 Jul).* Public holiday for Spain's patron saint.
Romería Celestial *(26 Jul),* Alameda del Valle, Lozoya. Procession climbs 3 km (2 miles) to La Ermita de Santa Ana. Bring your own picnic.

AUGUST

Castizo Fiestas *(6–15 Aug).* Traditional *castizo (see p105)* fiestas in La Latina and Lavapiés. Traditional *Madrileño* fiestas of San Cayetano *(3 Aug),* San Lorenzo *(5 Aug)* and La Virgen de la Paloma *(15 Aug).*
Fiesta de San Lorenzo *(10 Aug),* El Escorial *(see pp122–5).*
Fiesta de San Roque, *(12–18 Aug),* Chinchón. A bullfight in Plaza Mayor and *anís* tastings.
Asunción *(15 Aug).* Assumption Day national holiday.
Encierros *(end Aug).* Bull runs in San Sebastián de los Reyes.

Fiestas de San Bartolomé *(24 Aug),* Alcalá de Henares. Fiestas with giants, classical theatre and bullfights.
Encierros *(last week),* Cuellar, Segovia. Spain's oldest known bull run, dating back to 1546.
El Motín de Aranjuez *(end Aug or early Sep),* Aranjuez. Carlos IV's abdication (1808), commemorated with bullfights, outdoor concerts and fireworks.

Decorations for La Virgen de la Paloma fiesta

Average Monthly Rainfall

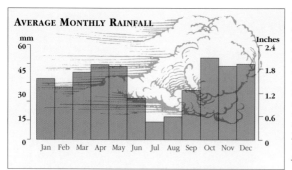

Rainfall Chart
Madrid has two main rainy periods – one from March to May, and the other from October to December. During the autumn, the skies tend to open in short thundery bursts, bringing the year's highest rainfall. Summers are dry and hot, and you are very unlikely to see much rain from June to September.

View of the Plaza de España *(see p53)* in autumn

Virgen de la Fuencisla *(27 Sep)*. Segovia fiesta.
Procesión de San Andrés *(30 Sep)*, Rascafría. Procession in honour of the local saint.

October

Festival Taurino *(around 12 Oct)*, Chinchón. Bullfights.
Día de la Hispanidad *(12 Oct)*. Spanish National Day.
Virgen de Pilar *(around 12 Oct)*, Plaza Dalí, Salamanca. Various district fiestas are held.
Festival de Otoño *(mid-Oct to mid-Nov)*. Annual drama, ballet and opera festival.

November

Todos los Santos *(1 Nov)*. On All Saints' Day flowers are taken to graves of relatives for 2 November, the Day of the Dead. Bakeries sell *Huesos de Santo* (Saints' Bones).
La Almudena *(9 Nov)*. Old Madrid honours its patron saint La Virgen de la Almudena.
Romería de San Eugenio *(14 Nov)*. *Castizo* procession in open carriages to El Monte de El Pardo for picnics, collecting acorns, singing and dancing.

Autumn

With the onset of autumn, the first rains for months relieve the parched countryside and begin to replenish depleted reservoirs. *Madrileños* love foraging in pine forests for the wild mushrooms produced by damp nights. The hunting season begins in October, and wild *níscalos* (fungi), boar, partridge and pheasant begin to appear on restaurant menus.

Wild mushrooms

September

Encierros *(first 12 days)*, Torrelaguna. Exciting bull runs and local celebrations.
Procesión Marítima *(first Sun)*, Fuentidueña de Tajo. Maritime procession with illuminated barges.

Procesión de la Virgen de la Cigüeña *(6 Sep)*, Fuente de Saz de Jarama. Procession honouring the Virgin of the Stork amid burning scrub.
Romería Panorámica *(second Sun)*, San Lorenzo de El Escorial. Procession with La Virgen de la Gracia (Grace) to a picnic in La Herrería woods.
Romería de la Virgen de los Hontanares *(10 Sep)*, Riaza, Segovia. Local pilgrimage and fiesta of the Virgin of Springs.

Celebration of Mass in Plaza Mayor to honour La Virgen de la Almudena

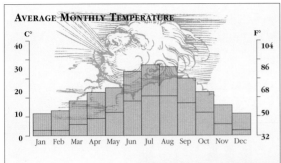

AVERAGE MONTHLY TEMPERATURE

Temperature Chart
Scorching hot summers and freezing winters make Madrid a place of extremes, with averages giving scant indication of the heights and depths of temperature the city can achieve. For many people, the most comfortable months to visit Madrid, in terms of milder temperatures, are June and October.

WINTER

THE FIRST SNOW usually falls in the Sierra de Guadarrama *(see p126)*, heralding the start of the skiing season, and traffic jams form on the way up to its small resorts. Madrid, and the higher parts of central Spain, can become very cold. Christmas is a special time of celebration – an occasion for families to reunite, share food and attend religious services. On New Year's Eve, crowds gather in the Puerta del Sol.

Skiers in the Sierra de Guadarrama, north of Madrid *(see p126)*

DECEMBER

Día de la Constitución *(6 Dec)*. Constitution Day.
Inmaculada Concepción *(8 Dec)*. Immaculate Conception.
Christmas Fair *(mid-Dec–5 Jan)*, Madrid's Plaza Mayor.
Noche Buena *(24 Dec)*. Christmas Eve – an important night of family celebrations.
Día de Navidad *(25 Dec)*. Christmas Day celebration.
Belén Viviente *(last eves Dec)*, Buitrago del Lozoya. Nativity play on horseback.
Noche Vieja *(31 Dec)*. New Year's Eve. Crowds in Puerta del Sol eat a grape and make a wish at each midnight chime.

JANUARY

Cabalgata de Reyes *(5 Jan)*. Twelfth Night procession from Parque del Retiro *(see p77)* to the Plaza Mayor *(see p44)* with floats, animals and celebrities.
Los Reyes Magos *(6 Jan)*. Epiphany is celebrated with the giving of gifts.
San Antón *(17 Jan)*, Calle de Hortaleza 63, Madrid. Animals blessed at Iglesia de San Antón.

Cabalgata de Cercedilla *(19 Jan)*, Cercedilla. Winter procession with horse-drawn sleighs.
Vaquillas *(20 Jan)*, Pedrezuela and Fresnedillas. Fiesta in which youths dress up as bulls.
San Sebastián *(20 Jan)*, Villaviciosa de Odón. Procession, fiestas and dancing.
FITUR Tourist Fair *(end Jan)*, Parque Ferial Juan Carlos I.

FEBRUARY

La Vaquilla Premiada *(2 Feb)*, Colmenar Viejo. Amateur bullfighting contest and fiesta.
La Romería de San Blas *(3 Feb)*, Madrid and Miraflores. Costumed celebrations.
Alcadesas de Zamarramala *(around first Sun)*, Segovia. For a week village women boss their men around.
Semana Internacional de la Moda *(mid-Feb)*, Parque Ferial Juan Carlos I. International fashion week.
ARCO *(mid-Feb)*, Parque Ferial Juan Carlos I. International contemporary art fair.
Carnaval *(run up to Lent)*. Fancy-dress parties; parade from Plaza de Colón *(see p98)* to Plaza de Cibeles *(see p67)*.

Entierro de la Sardina *(Shrove Tue)*, Casa de Campo. "Burial of the Sardine" parade to mark the changeover from *Carnaval* to Lent.

NATIONAL PUBLIC HOLIDAYS

Año Nuevo *(New Year's Day)* (1 Jan)
Los Reyes Magos *(Epiphany)* (6 Jan)
Jueves Santo *(Maundy Thursday)* (Mar/Apr)
Viernes Santo *(Good Friday)* (Mar/Apr)
Domingo de Pascua *(Easter Sunday)* (Mar/Apr)
Día del Trabajo *(Labour Day)* (1 May)
Asunción *(Assumption Day)* (15 Aug)
Día de la Hispanidad *(National Day)* (12 Oct)
Todos los Santos *(All Saints' Day)* (1 Nov)
Día de la Constitución *(Constitution Day)* (6 Dec)
Inmaculada Concepción *(Immaculate Conception)* (8 Dec)
Día de Navidad *(Christmas Day)* (25 Dec)

MADRID AREA
BY AREA

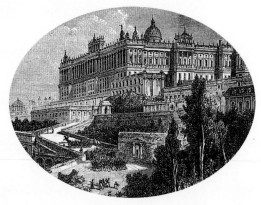

OLD MADRID

WHEN FELIPE II chose Madrid as his capital in 1561, it was a small Castilian town with a population of barely 20,000. In the following years, it was to grow into the nerve centre of a mighty empire. Narrow streets with houses and medieval churches began to grow up behind the old Moorish fortress (see p13), which was later replaced by a Gothic palace and eventually by the present-day Bourbon palace, the Palacio Real. By the end of the century the population had more than trebled.

The 16th-century city is known as the "Madrid de los Austrias", after the Habsburg dynasty. At this time, monasteries were endowed and churches and palaces were built. In the 17th century, the Plaza Mayor was added and the Puerta del Sol became the spiritual and geographical heart of Spain.

SIGHTS AT A GLANCE

Historic Buildings
Edificio Grassy **11**
Muralla Arabe **26**
Palacio de Santa Cruz **7**
Palacio del Senado **18**
Palacio Real pp54–7 **20**
Teatro Real **22**
Telefónica **12**

Museums and Galleries
Museo Cerralbo **16**
Real Academia de
  Bellas Artes **9**

Churches and Convents
Basílica Pontificia de
  San Miguel **5**
Catedral de la
  Almudena **24**
Colegiata de San Isidro **6**
Iglesia de San Nicolás **23**
Monasterio de la
  Encarnación **19**

Monasterio de las
  Descalzas Reales **14**
San Francisco
  el Grande **27**

**Streets, Squares, Parks
and Districts**
Calle de Preciados **15**
Campo del Moro **25**
Gran Vía **10**
La Latina **29**
Plaza de España **17**
Plaza de la Paja **28**
Plaza de la Villa **4**
Plaza de Oriente **21**
Plaza de Santa Ana **8**
Plaza del Callao **13**

Plaza Mayor **2**
Puerta del Sol **1**

Markets
El Rastro **30**
Mercado de San Miguel **3**

GETTING THERE
Line 1 on the Metro goes to Gran Vía and Sol, while 2, 3, 5 and 10 are good for getting to the main sights. Useful buses include the 51, 52, 150 and 153 to the Puerta del Sol.

KEY

	Street-by-Street map *pp42–3*
Ⓜ	Metro station
🚌	Main bus stop
ℹ	Tourist information
P	Parking

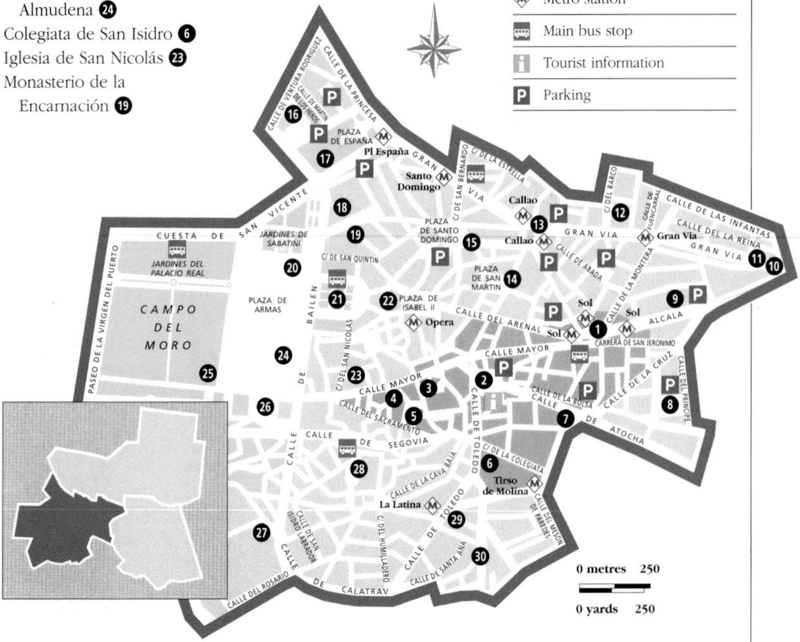

◁ **Equestrian statue of Felipe III in the centre of the Plaza Mayor** *(see p44)*

Street-by-Street: Old Madrid

Stretching from the charming Plaza de la Villa to the busy Puerta del Sol, the compact heart of Old Madrid is steeped in history and full of interesting sights. Trials by the Inquisition and executions were once held in the Plaza Mayor. This porticoed square is Old Madrid's finest piece of architecture, a legacy of the Habsburgs *(see p14)*. Other noteworthy buildings include the Colegiata de San Isidro and the Palacio de Santa Cruz. For a more relaxing way of enjoying Old Madrid, sit in one of the area's numerous cafés or browse among the colourful stalls of the Mercado de San Miguel.

★ Plaza Mayor
This beautiful 17th-century square competes with the Puerta del Sol as the focus of Old Madrid. The arcades at the base of the impressive buildings are filled with cafés and craft shops ❷

Mercado de San Miguel
Housed in a 19th-century iron structure, the market sells a variety of fresh food ❸

Palacio Real

PLAZA DE LA VILLA

CALLE MAYOR

PLAZA MORENAS

CALLE DE SACRAMENTO

CORDÓN

PUÑONROSTRO

CUCHILLEROS

Town hall (ayuntamiento)

Casa de Cisneros

Arco de Cuchilleros

★ Plaza de la Villa
The 15th-century Torre de los Lujanes is the oldest of several historic buildings standing on this square ❹

0 metres	100
0 yards	100

Basílica Pontificia de San Miguel
This imposing 18th-century church has a beautiful façade and a graceful Baroque interior ❺

STAR SIGHTS

★ Plaza Mayor

★ Plaza de la Villa

★ Puerta del Sol

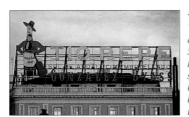

★ Puerta del Sol

With its shops and cafés, the Puerta del Sol is one of the city's liveliest areas. This sign for Tío Pepe, a brand of sherry, has become synonymous with the square ❶

LOCATOR MAP
See Street Finder map 4

AROUND LA CASTELLANA

OLD MADRID

BOURBON MADRID

Iglesia de San Ginés

Sol Metro

Casa de Correos

Equestrian statue of Carlos III

Bourbon Madrid

CALLE DEL ARENAL

BORDADORE

PUERTA DEL SOL

CALLE DE ALCALÁ

CALLE MAYOR

CALLE DE POSTAS

CALLE PAZ

CALLE DE CARRETAS

ESPOZ Y MINA

BARCELONA

PLAZA MAYOR

PLAZA PROVINCIA

PLAZA DE JACINTO BENAVENTE

SALVADOR

DUQUE DE RIVAS

CALLE DE TOLEDO

CALLE DE LA COLEGIATA

Tirso de Molina Metro

Palacio de Santa Cruz
Built as the court prison in the 17th-century, this Baroque palace is now occupied by the Foreign Ministry ❼

Colegiata de San Isidro
Named after the city's 12th-century patron saint, this was Madrid's provisional cathedral until the Catedral de la Almudena was completed (see p59) ❻

KEY

– – – Suggested route

Kilometre Zero, the centre of Spain's road network, at the Puerta del Sol

Puerta del Sol ●

Map 4 F2. ● *Sol*.

Noisy with traffic, chatter and policemen's whistles, the Puerta del Sol ("Gateway of the Sun") makes a fitting centre for Madrid. It is one of the city's most popular meeting places; huge crowds converge on this famous square on their way to the shops and sights in the old part of the city. Restoration work will affect the area from mid-2004 to 2007.

The square marks the site of the original eastern entrance to Madrid, once occupied by a gatehouse and castle. These disappeared long ago and in their place came a succession of churches. In the late 19th century the area was turned into a square and became the centre of café society.

Today the "square" is shaped like a half moon. The equestrian statue of Carlos III in its centre is a recent addition. The square's southern side is occupied by the austere red-brick Casa de Correos, once the city's post office, built in the 1760s under Carlos III. In 1847 it became the headquarters of the Ministry of the Interior. In 1866 the clocktower, which gives the building much of its identity, was added. During the Franco regime *(see p18)*, the police cells beneath the building were the site of many human rights abuses. In 1963, Julián Grimau, a member of the underground Communist party, allegedly fell from an upstairs window and miraculously survived, only to be executed shortly afterwards.

The building is now home to the regional government and

is the focus of many festive events. At midnight on New Year's Eve dense crowds fill the square and people swallow a grape on each stroke of the clock, a tradition supposed to bring good luck for the rest of the year. Outside the building, a symbol on the ground marks Kilometre Zero, considered the centre of Spain's road network.

The buildings opposite are arranged in a semicircle and contain modern shops and cafés. On the corner of Calle del Carmen is a bronze statue of the symbol of Madrid – a bear reaching for the fruit of a *madroño* (strawberry tree).

The Puerta del Sol has witnessed many important historical events. On 2 May 1808 the uprising against the occupying French forces began here, but the crowd was crushed *(see p16)*. In 1912 the liberal prime minister José Canalejas was assassinated in the square and, in 1931, the Second Republic *(see p18)* was proclaimed from the balcony of the Ministry of the Interior.

Plaza Mayor ●

Map 4 E3. ● *Sol*.

The Plaza Mayor forms a splendid rectangular square, complete with balconies, pinnacles, dormer

Allegorical paintings on the Casa de la Panadería, Plaza Mayor

windows and steep slate roofs. The square, with its theatrical atmosphere, has a noticeably Castilian character. Much was expected to happen here and a great deal did – bullfights, executions, pageants and trials by the Inquisition *(see p15)* – all watched by crowds, often in the presence of the reigning king and queen.

The first great public scene in the Plaza Mayor was the beatification of Madrid's patron, San Isidro, in 1621. During the same year, the execution of Rodrigo Calderón, secretary to Felipe III, was held here. Although hated by the Madrid populace, Calderón bore himself with such dignity on the day of his death that the phrase "proud as Rodrigo on the scaffold" survives to this day. Perhaps the greatest occasion of all, however, was the arrival here – from Italy – of Carlos III in 1760.

Construction of the square started in 1617, and was completed in just two years, replacing slum houses on the site. Its architect, Juan Gómez de la Mora, was successor to Juan de Herrera, designer of El Escorial *(see pp122–5)*, Felipe II's austere monastery-palace. Mora echoed the style of his master, softening it slightly. The fanciest part of the arcaded construction is the **Casa de la Panadería** (bakery). Its façade, which has undergone restoration, is decorated with allegorical paintings.

The **equestrian statue** in the centre is of Felipe III, who ordered the square to be built. Begun by the Italian Giovanni de Bologna and finished by his pupil Pietro Tacca in 1616, the statue was moved here in 1848 from the Casa de Campo *(see p114)*. Nowadays the square is lined with outdoor cafés and is the venue for a collectors' market on Sundays. The southern exit leads into the Calle de Toledo towards the streets where El Rastro, Madrid's famous flea-market *(see p61)*, is held. A flight of steps in the southwest corner of the square takes you under the Arco de Cuchilleros to the Calle de Cuchilleros, where there are a number of *mesones*, traditional restaurants.

Colourful food stalls in the 19th-century Mercado de San Miguel

Mercado de San Miguel ❸

Plaza de San Miguel. **Map** 4 D3. Ⓜ *Sol.* ☐ *9am–2pm, 5–8pm Mon–Fri, 9am–2pm Sat.* ● *public hols.*

ALTHOUGH THERE ARE larger markets in Madrid, this one is the last surviving example in the capital of a marketplace constructed from iron. The unique single-level, glassed-in market was built in 1914–15. It stands on the site of the former Iglesia de San Miguel de los Octoes, which was demolished in 1810 during the reign of Joseph Bonaparte. Fresh fruit and vegetables, fish, meat and other produce are sold at individual stalls, decorated with beautiful tiles. Because of competition from modern supermarkets, several stalls are now unoccupied.

Plaza de la Villa ❹

Map 4 D3. Ⓜ *Ópera, Sol.*

THIS MUCH RESTORED and frequently remodelled square is one of Madrid's most atmospheric spots, surrounded by many historic buildings.

The oldest building is the early 15th-century **Torre de los Lujanes**, with its Gothic portal and Mudéjar-style horseshoe arches. France's François I was allegedly imprisoned in it following his defeat at the Battle of Pavia in 1525. The **Casa de Cisneros** was built in 1537 for the nephew of Cardinal Cisneros, founder of the historic University of Alcalá *(see p131)*. The façade on Calle de Sacramento is an excellent example of the Plateresque style – early Spanish Renaissance with fine detail.

Linked to this building by an enclosed bridge is the **town hall** *(ayuntamiento)*. Designed in the 1640s by Juan Gómez de la Mora, architect of the Plaza Mayor, it exhibits the same combination of steep roofs with dormer windows, steeple-like towers at the corners and an austere brick-and-stone façade. Before construction was completed, more than 30 years later, the building had acquired handsome Baroque doorways. A balcony was later added by Juan de Villanueva, architect of the Prado *(see pp80–83)*, so that the Royal Family could watch Corpus Christi processions passing by.

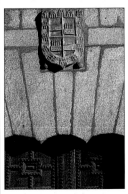

Portal of the Torre de los Lujanes

Basílica Pontificia de San Miguel ❺

Calle de San Justo 4. **Map** 4 D3. ☎ *91 548 40 11.* Ⓜ *Sol.* ⏱ *10am–2pm, 5:30–9pm Mon–Sat; 6–9pm Sun.* 🚫

STANDING ON THE SITE of an old Romanesque church dedicated to two local child-martyrs put to death by the Romans, this building is a rare example of Bourbon-inspired Baroque in the middle of old Madrid. It was built for Don Luis de Borbón y Farnesio, the youngest son of Felipe V and Archbishop of Toledo at only five years of age.

Several architects had a hand in its design and construction between 1739 and 1746. The pediment and twin bell towers topping its convex façade were, however, added later. Four allegorical statues, representing Charity, Fortitude, Faith and Hope, grace the elegant façade. There are also carvings depicting the two child-martyrs, Justo and Pastor.

Inside, there is a single nave, and the roof is supported only by the curved and crossing arches sprouting from the exterior walls. The decor is a curious mixture of old and new – the frescoes on the ceiling and the organ in the choir (above the entrance) date from the 18th century, but many of the paintings and

Statue of Charity gracing the façade of Basílica Pontífica de San Miguel

stained-glass windows are contemporary. Today the church is administered by the Catholic lay organization, Opus Dei, who use it as a base for some of their activities. One of the side chapels, which is dedicated to the organization's Spanish founder, Monsignor José María Escrivá de Balaguer (1902–75), houses an eerily lifelike statue of him.

Ornate altar in the Colegiata de San Isidro

Colegiata de San Isidro ❻

Calle de Toledo 37. **Map** 4 E3. ☎ *91 369 20 37.* Ⓜ *La Latina.* ⏱ *8am–12:45pm, 6–8:30pm Mon–Sat; 8:30am–2:30pm, 5–8:30pm Sun.*

THIS TWIN-TOWERED church was built in the Baroque style for the Jesuits in the mid-17th century. It was used as Madrid's unofficial cathedral until 1993 when Nuestra Señora de la Almudena *(see p59)* was finally completed and consecrated by the pope.

After Carlos III (1759–88) expelled the influential Jesuit order from Spain in 1767 *(see p16)*, he commissioned Ventura Rodríguez to redesign the church's interior. It was then re-dedicated to St Isidore, Madrid's patron saint and, two years later, the saint's remains were brought here from the Iglesia de San Andrés. The Colegiata was returned to the Jesuits during the reign of Fernando VII (1814–33).

Palacio de Santa Cruz ❼

Plaza de Santa Cruz. **Map** 4 E3. ☎ *91 379 97 00.* Ⓜ *Sol.* ⏱ *to the public.*

CONSTRUCTED between 1629 and 1643, this building is one of the jewels of Habsburg architecture. Since 1901 it has been the Ministry of Foreign Affairs, but has also housed the Overseas Ministry, law courts and, originally, the Carcel de la Corte (city prison). It was here that the luckless participants in the *autos de fé* (Spanish inquisition trials), held in the nearby Plaza Mayor *(see p44)*, awaited their fate. Its more famous inmates include the playwright Lope de Vega (1562– 1635), imprisoned for libelling his former lover, the actress Elena Osorio. The English writer and travelling Bible sales-man, George Borrow, who was accused of instigating liberal ideas, also spent three weeks here. General Rafael de Riego, who led an uprising against Fernando VII in 1820, and the famous bandit Luis Candelas spent their last hours in its cells. Candelas was a colourful Robin Hood-like character, educated in Greek and Latin, who rubbed shoulders with the aristocracy (and stole their jewels). He was executed on 6 November 1837; today one of Madrid's tourist restaurants, situated on nearby Cava de San Miguel, is named after him.

The palace underwent a restoration in 1846, following a fire, and again in the aftermath of the Spanish Civil War *(see p18)*, but its original architecture remains essentially intact. The style of the building is in keeping with the area around the Plaza Mayor, with spired towers on its corners and two interior courtyards. The building only became known as the Palacio de Santa Cruz

The 17th-century Palacio de Santa Cruz – a jewel of Habsburg architecture

after 1846, when it was made the headquarters of Spain's Overseas Ministry.

Plaza de Santa Ana ⑧

Map 7 A3. Ⓜ Sevilla, Antón Martín.

THIS LARGE SQUARE, just four blocks southeast of the Puerta del Sol *(see p44),* is a popular gathering place with a lively, at times rowdy, atmosphere. Built during the reign of Napoleon Bonaparte's brother Joseph (1808–13), the square took its name from the 16th-century Convent of Santa Ana that stood here. It was demolished to make way for the square.

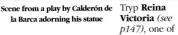

Scene from a play by Calderón de la Barca adorning his statue

Monuments to two of Spain's most famous writers testify to the square's strong literary connections. At one end, a statue of the poet Federico García Lorca *(see p26),* erected in 1998, commemorates the centenary of his birth. At the other is the older and rather more brooding marble figure of Pedro Calderón de la Barca (1600–81). Madrid-born, he was the leading playwright in the twilight years of Spain's *Siglo de Oro* (Golden Century) of arts. His best-known work is *La Vida es Sueño* (Life is a Dream). The monument, with scenes from four of Calderón's plays adorning the pedestal,

was sculpted by Juan Figueras in 1878 and faces the **Teatro Español** *(see p76).* Built in 1745, the theatre was originally known as the Teatro del Príncipe. It had to be restored in 1980 after a devastating fire.

The square's theatrical links go back even earlier, as the theatre stands on the spot of the Corral del Príncipe, one of Madrid's popular, 16th-century *corrales de comedias* (open courtyards where plays were staged). These tended to be boisterous affairs, often culminating in fights between the actors and the audience. Across from the theatre are the glassed-in balconies of Hotel Tryp **Reina Victoria** *(see p147),* one of Madrid's classic hostelries. Before the Tryp chain acquired it, the hotel's then modest lodgings were used by bullfighters who could not afford luxurious city rooms. The taurine theme has been preserved.

The other two sides of Plaza de Santa Ana and adjoining streets are home to some of the city's most popular bars and restaurants. The classic **Cervecería Alemana**, built in 1904 and once frequented by author Ernest Hemingway, is always packed with customers.

Around the corner from the theatre is the **Viva Madrid** *(see p29).* This is a popular bar with the young, fashionable and single, as is **Los Gabrieles**

(see p29). They are both worth looking in to for their extraordinary 19th-century ceramic tableaux. Tile landscapes also adorn the **Villa Rosa**, which is located on the corner of Plaza de Santa Ana and Calle de Núñez de Arce.

Real Academia de Bellas Artes ⑨

Calle de Alcalá 13. **Map** 7 A2.
📞 *91 524 08 64.* Ⓜ *Sevilla, Sol.*
🕐 *9am–7pm Tue–Fri, 10am–2:30pm Sat–Mon.* ⬤ *some public hols.* ♿ *(free Wed).* 🎫 *by appointment.* ♿
🌐 *www.rabasf.insde.es*

DALÍ AND PICASSO are among the former students of this arts academy, housed in an 18th-century building by Churriguera. Its art gallery displays a large selection of works, including drawings by Raphael and Titian. A superb collection of old masters includes paintings by Rubens and Van Dyck. Spanish artists from the 16th to the 19th centuries are particularly well represented, with magnificent works by Ribera, Murillo, El Greco and Velázquez. One of the highlights is Zurbarán's *Fray Pedro Machado,* typical of his paintings of monks.

An entire room is devoted to Goya, a former director of the academy. On show here are his painting of Carlos IV's chief minister, Manuel Godoy, the *Burial of the Sardine,* the grim *Madhouse,* and a self-portrait painted in 1815.

Fray Pedro Machado by Zurbarán

Gran Vía ❿

I N THE MID-1800s, Madrid's burgeoning middle class was pushing the city's limits outwards, destroying houses and poor districts to allow for the *Ensanche* (widening). The city fathers saw the need for a new thoroughfare – a *Gran Vía*. Departing from the haphazard growth of the past, this street was to follow a plan and be a symbol of modern Madrid. On the drawing board since 1860, with even a satirical *zarzuela (see p75)* devoted to it, the project was not approved until 1904. Inaugurated by Alfonso XIII in 1908 *(see p17)*, building was carried out

Brass detail on the Edificio Metrópolis

in three stages, each segment bearing a different name, although they are no longer used. The first, and most elegant – Avenida Conde de Peñalver (after the Mayor) – ran from Calle de Alcalá to Red de San Luis. The second phase, to the Plaza de Callao, was completed in 1922, while the final segment, ending in the Plaza de España, was built between 1925 and 1929. The new street gave architects an opportunity to prove their skill, providing a survey of early 20th-century design trends, including some of the best examples of modern architecture in the city.

The Museo Chicote cocktail bar, on the ground floor of Gran Vía No. 12, has an immaculately preserved Art Deco interior. It opened in 1932 and was patronized by Salvador Dalí, Frank Sinatra, Ava Gardner and Orson Welles.

The rounded Art Deco façade of this building, like many along the Gran Vía, displays a style and grandeur befitting the city's most impressive thoroughfare. Many Art Deco buildings were built as cinemas, several of which are clustered around Plaza del Callao.

Behind La Gran Peña's curved façade (No. 2) is a luxurious, increasingly popular men's club. In 1926, attempts to make Franco a member caused such a stir that the club was later taken over and used by the militia during the Civil War (see p18).

Edificio la Estrella (No. 10) is a good example of the eclectic mix of Neo-Classical design and ornamental touches evident in the first buildings to have appeared along Gran Vía.

Today's Gran Vía continues to be a throbbing main artery for the city of Madrid, lined with theatres and cinemas, hotels, shops and restaurants.

The two-tiered colonnade of the Edificio Grassy on Gran Vía

Edificio Grassy ⓫

Gran Vía 1. **Map** 7 B1. 🕻 91 532 10 07. ⓜ Banco de España, Sevilla. ⭘ 10am–1pm, 5–8pm Mon–Sat.

DESIGNED by Eladio Laredo on a small sliver of land between the Gran Vía and the Calle de Caballero de Gracia, the Grassy building boasts a circular end-tower similar to that of the nearby Edificio Metrópolis (see p74). It is crowned by a round, two-tiered colonnade. It was built in 1917, but became known as the Grassy building in the 1950s, after the jewellery shop that has occupied the ground floor since then. The prestigious jewellery firm, which was established in 1923, specializes in watches and, in the basement, is the **Museo de Reloj Grassy**, a collection of around 500 valuable timepieces, from the 16th to 19th centuries, including rare clocks which belonged to European royalty. The museum has recently been renovated.

Clock at the Grassy museum

Telefónica ⓬

Gran Vía 28. **Map** 4 F1, 7 A1. ⓜ Gran Vía, Callao. **Museum** 🕻 91 522 66 45. ⭘ 10am–2pm, 5–8pm Tue–Fri, 11am–8pm Sat, 10am–2pm Sun & public hols. ⬤ Aug. ⬚ 🔶 🔶 (call to arrange).

IF THE TELEFÓNICA building has an American look to it, it is because it was inspired by Manhattan's skyscrapers and designed by an American – Louis S Weeks – although the Spanish architect Ignacio de Cárdenas was made officially responsible in order to secure planning permission. Built between 1926 and 1929 to house the Spanish telephone company, it was Madrid's tallest building. Its façade consists of tapered setbacks, ending in a central tower 81 m (266 ft) tall. The little exterior ornamentation it has was added by Cárdenas so that the building would seem less out of place amid the neighbouring architecture. The clear view from the upper floors enabled the Republican defenders of the city to monitor the movements of besieging Nationalists in the Spanish Civil War (see p18).

A section of the lower floors, which is entered from Calle de Fuencarral, is used for exhibitions. There are temporary exhibitions on the ground floor and a permanent one of the evolution of telecommunications on the first floor. Displays range from old phones, including the one used by Alfonso XIII to inaugurate Madrid's automatic telephone service in 1926, to a bank of switchboards with 19 life-sized operators and sound effects. The exhibition rooms are arranged around a gallery that overlooks the main foyer. The gallery once housed a formidable collection of modern art, now on long-term loan to the Centro de Arte Reina Sofía (see pp86–9).

The Telefónica – a Manhattan-style skyscraper from the 1920s

Plaza del Callao ⓭

Plaza del Callao. **Map** 4 E1. ⓜ Callao.

THIS CITY'S PASSION for films is fed by more than 60 cinemas and Plaza del Callao, the movie mecca of Madrid, has seven of them. Situated at the junction of Gran Vía and Calle de Preciados, the square was named after a naval battle off Callao, Peru, in 1866. The cinemas are the Art Deco Cine Callao, Imperial, Avenida, Rex, Capitol, Palacio de la Música (music hall) and Palacio de la Prensa (Madrid Press Association). Films are advertised on huge, hand-painted signs.

Housed in the Capitol building is the Capitol cinema, built in 1933. A superb example of Art Deco architecture, its features include a covered entrance and a vast, box-like interior, 35 m (115 ft) wide, adorned with simple lines and curves.

The Capitol cinema, a good example of Art Deco architecture

Chapel with ornate altar in the Monasterio de las Descalzas Reales

Monasterio de las Descalzas Reales **⓮**

Plaza de las Descalzas 3. **Map** 4 E2.
☎ 91 454 88 00. **Ⓜ** Sol, Callao.
◯ 10:30am–12:45pm, 4–5:45pm
Tue–Thu & Sat, 10:30am–12:45pm Fri,
11am–1:45pm Sun & public hols. **●** 1
& 6 Jan, 16–19 Apr, 1 & 15 May, 9 Sep,
24–25 & 31 Dec. **▨** (free guided tour
Wed for EU residents).
Ⓦ www.patrimonionacional.es.

MADRID'S MOST notable
religious building is also
a rare surviving example of
16th-century architecture in the
city. Around 1560 Felipe II's
sister Doña Juana converted
the medieval palace which
stood here into a convent for
nuns and women of the royal
household. Her rank, and that
of her fellow nuns, accounts
for the vast store of art and
wealth of the Descalzas Reales
(Royal Barefoot Sisters).
The stairway has a fresco of
Felipe IV with his family, and a
fine ceiling by Claudio Coello.
It leads to a first-floor cloister,
ringed with chapels containing
paintings and precious objects.
The main chapel houses Doña
Juana's tomb. The Sala de
Tapices (Tapestries Room) contains a series of 17th-century
tapestries. There are also works
by Brueghel the Elder, Titian,
Zurbarán, Murillo and Ribera.

Calle de Preciados **⓯**

Map 4 F2. **Ⓜ** Sol, Callao.

THIS PEDESTRIAN street leading
north from Puerta del Sol
to the busy Plaza de Callao is
now the domain of shoppers.
It was originally a humble
country path from the centre of
old Madrid to the orchards and
threshing floors of the Convent
of San Martín which, until
1810, faced the Monasterio
de las Descalzas Reales. In the
17th century two brothers,
the Preciados, purchased land
from the convent to build
their homes. They were in
charge of controlling official
weights and measures used
for trade in Madrid.
Calle de Preciados acquired
its modern look during the
Ensanche (urban renewal) of
the mid-19th century. It is the
birthplace of Spain's most successful department store chain,
El Corte Inglés. Started by
Ramón Areces as a modest
clothes store in 1940, it now
occupies an eight-floor site at
the southern end of the street.
At the northern end stands a
modern building occupied by
FNAC, the local branch of a
French chain which is one of
the city's best sources for
music, videos and books.
Between the two superstores,
trendy boutiques share space
with old-fashioned shops.

Museo Cerralbo **⓰**

Calle de Ventura Rodríguez 17. **Map**
1 C5. **☎** 91 547 36 46. **Ⓜ** Plaza de
España, Ventura Rodríguez. **◯** mid-
Sep–mid-Jun: 9:30am–3pm Tue–
Sat, 10am–3pm Sun; mid-Jun–
mid-Sep 9:30am–2pm Tue–Sat,
10am–2pm Sun. **●** public hols. **▨**
(free Wed & Sun). **♿ ⓘ**
Ⓦ www.mcu.es/guia

THIS 19TH-CENTURY mansion
is a monument to Enrique
de Aguilera y Gamboa, the
17th Marquis of Cerralbo. He
bequeathed his lifetime's
collection of art and artifacts to
the nation in 1922, which
ranges from Iberian pottery to
18th-century marble busts.
One of the star exhibits is
El Greco's *The Ecstasy of Saint
Francis of Assisi*. There are also
paintings by Ribera, Zurbarán,
Alonso Cano and Goya.
The focal point of the main
floor is the ballroom, lavishly
decorated with mirrors.

Main staircase of the exuberant Museo Cerralbo

◁ **Nighttime traffic on the Gran Vía, seen from the Plaza de España**

Stone obelisk with statue of Miguel de Cervantes, Plaza de España

Plaza de España ⑰

Map 1 C5. 🚇 *Plaza de España.*

ONE OF MADRID's busiest traffic intersections and most popular meeting places is the Plaza de España. In the 18th and 19th centuries the square was occupied by military barracks, built here because of the square's proximity to the Palacio Real *(see pp54–7)*. However, further expansion of Madrid resulted in it remaining a public space.

The square acquired its present appearance during the Franco period with the construction of the massive **Edificio España**. Commissioned by the Metropolitana real estate developers, the 26-floor concrete structure was built between 1947 and 1953, when Spain was isolated from the western world and materials were scarce. It was seen as a triumph of "autarchy" *(see p18)*. The imposing main tower is flanked by two 17-floor wings. The eastern wing now houses the Holiday Inn Crowne Plaza hotel *(see p147)*.

Metropolitana also built the 33-floor **Torre de Madrid** on the corner of Plaza de España and Calle Princesa. Completed in 1957 and nicknamed La Jirafa (the Giraffe), for a time it was the tallest concrete structure in the world.

The most attractive part of the square is its centre, with a massive stone obelisk built in 1928. In front of it is a statue of Cervantes *(see p131)*. Below him, Don Quixote rides his horse while Sancho Panza trots alongside on his donkey.

Palacio del Senado ⑱

Plaza de la Marina Española. **Map** 3 C1.
📞 91 538 10 00. 🚇 *Plaza de España, Ópera.* ⬜ *tours by appointment (91 538 1441).* 🚫 ♿
Ⓦ www.senado.es

THE UPPER HOUSE of the Cortes (Spanish parliament) is installed in a 16th-century monastery, adapted in 1814 for the purpose. It became the Senate headquarters when a two-chamber system was introduced 23 years later.

The monastery's courtyards were covered to create more meeting rooms. Some, such as the Salón de los Pasos Perdidos (Hall of the Lost Footsteps), contain enormous paintings depicting great moments in Spanish history. Among these are the surrender of Granada and Queen Regent María Cristina swearing to uphold the Constitution in 1897.

The library is a magnificent example of English Gothic style, dating from the turn of the 20th century. Ornate tiers of black metal bookcases contain 14,000 volumes, including a copy of Nebrija's *Gramática*, the first Spanish grammar.

In 1991 a modern granite-and-glass circular wing was added at the back of the building to create more space.

The Palacio del Senado is open to the public for three days, free of charge, in early December each year, to mark the establishment of the Constitution on 6 December.

Old assembly hall of the Palacio del Senado, housed in the church of the monastery

Imposing entrance to the Monasterio de la Encarnación

Monasterio de la Encarnación ⑲

Plaza de la Encarnación 1. **Map** 3 C1.
📞 91 454 88 00. 🚇 *Ópera, Santo Domingo.* ⬜ *10:30am–12:45pm, 4–5:45pm Tue–Thu & Sat, 10:30am–12:45pm Fri, 11am–1:45pm Sun & public hols.* ⬛ *1 & 6 Jan, 16–19 Apr, 1 & 15 May, 27 Jul, 9 Sep, 24–25 & 31 Dec.* 🎫 *(free Wed for EU residents).* ♿ Ⓦ www.patrimonionacional.es

SET IN A lovely tree-shaded square, this Augustinian convent was founded in 1611 for Margaret of Austria, wife of Felipe III. The architect, Juan Gómez de la Mora, also built the Plaza Mayor *(see p44)*.

Still inhabited by nuns, the convent has the atmosphere of old Castile, with its Talavera tiles, exposed beams and portraits of royal benefactors. It also contains a collection of 17th-century art, with paintings by José de Ribera and Vincente Carducho and a polychrome wooden statue *Cristo Yacente* (*Lying Christ*) by Gregorio Fernández. The main attraction is the reliquary chamber which is used to store the bones of saints. There is also a phial of St Pantaleon's dried blood which, according to legend, liquifies each year on 27 July, the anniversary of the saint's death. The church, rebuilt by Ventura Rodríguez after a fire in 1767, has paintings by Francisco Bayeu and frescoes by González Velázquez.

Palacio Real ⓴

Statue of Carlos III

Madrid's vast and lavish royal palace was built to impress. The site, on a high bluff overlooking the Río Manzanares, had been occupied for centuries by a royal fortress but, after a fire in 1734, Felipe V commissioned a truly palatial replacement. Construction lasted 26 years, spanning the reign of two Bourbon monarchs, and much of the exuberant decor reflects the tastes of Carlos III and Carlos IV *(see p16)*. The palace was used by the royal family until the abdication of Alfonso XIII in 1931. The present king, Juan Carlos I, lives in the more modest Zarzuela Palace outside Madrid, but the Royal Palace is still used for state occasions.

★ Dining Room
This gallery was decorated in 1879. Its chandeliers, ceiling paintings and tapestries evoke the grandeur of Bourbon and Habsburg entertaining.

★ Porcelain Room
The walls and ceiling of this room, built on the orders of Carlos III, are entirely covered in royal porcelain from the Buen Retiro factory. Most of the porcelain is green and white, and depicts cherubs and wreaths.

First floor

The Hall of Columns, once used for royal banquets, is decorated with 16th-century bronzes and Roman imperial busts.

Star Features

★ Dining Room

★ Porcelain Room

★ Gasparini Rooms

★ Throne Room

★ Gasparini Room
Named after its Neapolitan designer, the Gasparini Room is decorated with lavish Rococo chinoiserie. The adjacent antechamber, with painted ceiling and ornate chandelier, houses Goya's portrait of Carlos IV.

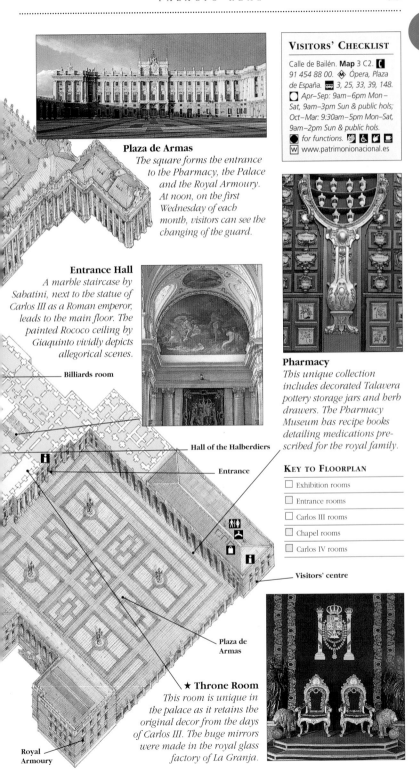

Plaza de Armas
The square forms the entrance to the Pharmacy, the Palace and the Royal Armoury. At noon, on the first Wednesday of each month, visitors can see the changing of the guard.

Entrance Hall
A marble staircase by Sabatini, next to the statue of Carlos III as a Roman emperor, leads to the main floor. The painted Rococo ceiling by Giaquinto vividly depicts allegorical scenes.

Billiards room

Hall of the Halberdiers

Entrance

Plaza de Armas

★ Throne Room
This room is unique in the palace as it retains the original decor from the days of Carlos III. The huge mirrors were made in the royal glass factory of La Granja.

Royal Armoury

Visitors' centre

VISITORS' CHECKLIST

Calle de Bailén. **Map** 3 C2.
91 454 88 00. Ópera, Plaza de España. 3, 25, 33, 39, 148.
Apr–Sep: 9am–6pm Mon–Sat, 9am–3pm Sun & public hols; Oct–Mar: 9:30am–5pm Mon–Sat, 9am–2pm Sun & public hols.
for functions.
w www.patrimonionacional.es

Pharmacy
This unique collection includes decorated Talavera pottery storage jars and herb drawers. The Pharmacy Museum has recipe books detailing medications prescribed for the royal family.

KEY TO FLOORPLAN

☐ Exhibition rooms
☐ Entrance rooms
☐ Carlos III rooms
☐ Chapel rooms
☐ Carlos IV rooms

Exploring the Palacio Real

THIS SPLENDID ROYAL PALACE stands on the site of the original Moorish fortress, or alcázar, which served as a residence for visiting royals after the Christian conquest of Madrid in 1085 *(see p13)*. Following extensive modifications in 1561, it became the residence of Felipe II until the completion of El Escorial *(see pp122–5)* in 1584. The alcázar was destroyed by fire on Christmas Eve, 1734, during the reign of Felipe V. This suited Spain's first Bourbon king well – his idea of a royal palace was the Versailles of his childhood, and so he commissioned a new royal palace decorated in the French style.

Grand entrance stairway with 72 steps in Toledo marble

Stately façade of the Palacio Real, seen from the Plaza de Armas

THE PALACE

MOST OF THE massive lime-stone and granite building is the work of Italian Giovanni Battista Sachetti, with later modifications by other architects. So vast was the plan that construction lasted from 1738 to 1764, by which time Felipe V

was dead. His son, Carlos III, became the first royal resident. The palace remained the official home of the Spanish royal family until Alfonso XIII left for exile in 1931. The distribution of rooms and the interior decoration were altered by successive monarchs.

General Franco *(see p18)* also used the palace – known at the time as the Palacio de Oriente – for official business, and would address crowds of sympathizers from its eastern balcony overlooking the Plaza de Oriente *(see p58)*. Today it is used for state functions.

Visitors enter the palace from the **Plaza de Armas**. The main entrance is crowned by a pediment with a clock and two bells, one of which dates from 1637 and is a survivor of the fire which destroyed the old alcázar. The interior is remarkable for its size and for the exuberant decor, carpets, tapestries and antique furnishings in many of the rooms.

ENTRANCE ROOMS

THE TOLEDO MARBLE in the main stairway, presided over by ceiling frescoes by Corrado Gialquinto, provides a regal taste of what is to follow. The first port of call is the **Salón de los Alabarderos** (Hall of the Halberdiers, or palace guards), decorated with a fresco by Tiépolo. Adjoining it is the **Salón de Columnas** (Hall of Columns), which served as the banquet hall until the new dining hall was incorporated in the 19th century. Today it is used for receptions and functions – the charter by which Spain joined the EU was signed here, on the 19th-century table supported by sphinxes. There are five tapestries of the Deeds of the Apostles, based on cartoons by Raphael and originally commissioned by the Vatican.

Finally, visitors enter the Carlos III rooms through the 18th-century Rococo **Salón del Trono** (Throne Room), whose decor has remained constant throughout generations of rulers. Completed in 1772, it has two rock crystal chandeliers, numerous candelabra and mirrors, and walls of crimson velvet with silver embroidery. The twin thrones are recent (1977), while the bronze lions that guard them date from 1651. The room is used for functions, such as the royal reception on 12 October (the Día de la Hispanidad) or the yearly reception for the diplomatic corps posted in Madrid.

Regal crimson-and-gold Throne Room with a rock crystal chandelier

CARLOS III ROOMS

LEADING OFF from the throne room are three smaller halls named after Mattia Gasparini, the original decorator. These were the king's private chambers. He would take his meals in the **Sala de Gasparini** – lonely affairs considering the queen had her own dining room. The **Antecámara de Gasparini** contains four paintings by Goya of Carlos IV and María Luisa de Parma. In the **Cámara de Gasparini** the king would be dressed, usually in the presence of courtiers. This is the only room to retain its original decor – Rococo and oriental, with a stucco ceiling and embroidered silk walls.

A small room, the **Tranvía de Carlos III**, leads into the former bedroom of Carlos III. In the Baroque **Sala de Porcelana** (Porcelain Room), 18th-century porcelain from the Buen Retiro factory covers the walls. The **Salita Amarilla** (Yellow Room), named after the tapestry covering the walls, leads to the Gala Dining Hall.

Portrait of *Carlos IV* by Goya in the Antecámara de Gasparini

DINING ROOM

THIS 400-SQ M (4,300-sq ft) banquet hall was formed in 1879 when the queen's private chambers were joined together, during the reign of Alfonso XII. It is richly adorned with gold plate decoration on the ceiling and walls, frescoes, chandeliers, Flemish tapestries, Chinese vases and embroidered curtains. The table can accommodate up to 160 diners.

The rooms leading off from the dining room house exhibits of royal household possessions. The room immediately off the dining hall is devoted to commemorative medals, and also contains the elaborate centrepiece used during banquets. Other rooms contain the silverware, china, crystal, and an extraordinary collection of musical instruments, including unique Stradivarius examples.

CHAPEL ROOMS

BUILT IN 1749–57, the chapel is still used for religious services, and also for musical soirées. While the decor is luxurious, it is the dome, with its murals by Giaquinto, that immediately catches the eye.

Next, visitors pass through the **Salón de Paso** and into María Cristina's chambers (originally Carlos IV rooms). During the reign of Alfonso XII these four small rooms served as an American-style billiards room, Oriental-style smoking room, the **Salón de Estucos** (queen's bedroom), and the **Gabinete de Maderas de Indias**, used as an office.

The lavish dining room, formerly the queen's private chambers

PHARMACY AND ARMOURY

RETURNING TO THE PLAZA de Armas, near the ticket office is the **Real Farmacia** (Royal Pharmacy) founded by Felipe II in 1594. The pharmacy is a warren of rooms, with jars and vials bearing the names of different potions and medicinal plants.

On the other side of the plaza is the **Real Armería** (Royal Armoury), housed in a pavilion built in 1897 after the original armoury was destroyed by fire. It contains weapons and royal suits of armour. On display is an elaborate suit of armour which once belonged to Carlos I, the Holy Roman Emperor Charles V. The armoury could be considered as Madrid's first museum because it has been open to the public since Felipe II inherited the collection from his father. It originally contained weapons used by Spanish kings and those from defeated enemy armies.

Armour of
Carlos I

Equestrian statue of Felipe IV, by Pietro Tacca, Plaza de Oriente

Plaza de Oriente ㉑

Map 3 C2. Ópera.

DURING HIS DAYS as king of Spain, Joseph Bonaparte (José I) carved out this stirrup-shaped space from the jumble of buildings to the east of the Palacio Real *(see pp54–7)*, providing the view of the palace enjoyed today.

The square was once an important meeting place for state occasions: kings, queens and dictators all made public appearances on the palace balcony facing the plaza. The many statues of early kings

which stand here were originally intended to adorn the roofline of the Palacio Real, but proved to be too heavy. The equestrian statue of Felipe IV in the centre of the square is by Italian sculptor Pietro Tacca, and is based on drawings by Velázquez.

In the southeast corner of the plaza is the **Café de Oriente** *(see p158)*, with outdoor tables for enjoying the view.

Teatro Real ㉒

Plaza de Oriente. **Map** 4 D2. 91 516 06 00 (info); 90 224 48 48 (tickets). Ópera. 10:30am–1pm Mon, Wed–Fri, 11am–1:30pm Sat–Sun & some public hols. Aug. www.teatro-real.com

MADRID'S OPERA HOUSE stands opposite the Palacio Real *(see pp54–7)* on the Plaza de Oriente. It is an imposing six-sided grey building, made all the more impressive by the six floors below street level as well as the nine floors visible above ground.

It was originally built around 1850. However, much of the structure that exists today is the result of a massive project to renovate the theatre, which took place between 1991 and 1997. The horseshoe-shaped main theatre area, decorated

in red and gold with seating on five levels, holds 1,630 spectators and the stage area measures 1,430 sq m (15,400 sq ft). This, together with the curtain and the magnificent crystal chandelier weighing 2.5 tonnes, are among the theatre's noteworthy features.

On the second floor, there are four large foyers arranged around the main hall. They contain tapestries, paintings, mirrors, chandeliers and antiques. All of them are laid with carpets produced especially for the theatre by the Manuel Morón workshop in Ciudad Real, south of Madrid.

The second-floor restaurant is also worth seeing. It has a ceiling representing Madrid's starlit sky as it was on the night of the theatre's inauguration. It is open from Tuesday to Sunday for tea (at 6:30pm) and dinner (at 9pm), but is reserved for theatre-goers on nights when there are perfor-mances. The

Costume used in Anne Boleyn

restaurant is located in what was originally the ballroom, where Isabel II would often throw lively parties. On display are costumes from the operas *Aïda* and *Anne Boleyn*.

On the sixth floor there is a pleasant cafeteria which has a good view overlooking the Plaza de Oriente and the Palacio Real *(see pp54–7)*.

The site has always been associated with the stage. In 1708, an Italian company built a small theatre here, which was demolished in 1735 to be replaced by a more ambitious building. However, due to the presence of underground streams, this theatre suffered severe structural problems. In 1816, it was torn down to make way for a modern opera house instigated by Fernando VII. Construction dragged on in fits and starts for 32 years. The theatre was finally inaugur-ated in 1850 by Isabel II on her 20th birthday. A production

Awe-inspiring interior of Madrid's opera house, the Teatro Real

of Gaetano Donizetti's *La Favorita* marked the occasion, and the theatre became a centre of Madrid culture until the late 1920s. It appeared, however, that the new building was beset with problems just like its predecessor, and needed constant repair work to keep it upright. In the Spanish Civil War *(see p18)* it was used as a weapons depot and suffered further damage from an explosion. It was finally closed in 1988.

In 1991, an ambitious project to renovate the building was also plagued with problems. The architect died of a heart attack while inspecting the works and, when the theatre finally opened in October 1997 with a performance of Falla's *The Three-Cornered Hat*, it was way over budget and five years behind schedule.

Iglesia de San Nicolás ❷

Plaza de San Nicolás 1. **Map** 3 C2.
☎ *91 559 40 64.* Ⓜ *Ópera.*
⭘ *8:30am–1:30pm, 5:30–8:30pm Mon, 6:30–8:30pm Tue–Sat, 10am–2pm, 6:30–8:30pm Sun.* 🎟 *by appointment.*

THE FIRST MENTION of the church of San Nicolás is in a document written in 1202. Its striking brick tower, decorated with horseshoe arches, is

12th-century Mudéjar-style brick tower of the Iglesia de San Nicolás

View of the Catedral de la Almudena and the Palacio Real

the oldest surviving religious structure in Madrid. Thought to date from the 12th century, it is Mudéjar in style, and may originally have been the minaret of a Moorish mosque.

Catedral de la Almudena ❷

Calle de Bailén 8–10. **Map** 3 C2.
☎ *91 542 22 00.* Ⓜ *Ópera.*
⭘ *9am–9pm daily.* ♿

THE BUILDING OF Madrid's cathedral began in 1879, but it was not until as late as 1993 that it was completed and subsequently inaugurated by the Pope. The slow construction, which ceased completely during the Spanish Civil War, involved several architects. The cathedral's Neo-Gothic grey and white façade resembles that of the Palacio Real, which stands opposite. The crypt houses a 16th-century image of the *Virgen de la Almudena.* Further along, the Calle Mayor is the site of excavations which have unearthed remains of Moorish and medieval city walls.

Campo del Moro ❷

Map 3 A2. Ⓜ *Príncipe Pío.*
⭘ *Oct–Mar: 10am–6pm Mon–Sat, 9am–6pm Sun & public hols; Apr–Sep: 10am–8pm Mon–Sat, 9am–8pm Sun & public hols.* ● *1 & 6 Jan,1 & 15 May, 12 Oct, 9 Nov, 24–25 & 31 Dec.*

THE CAMPO DEL MORO (Field of the Moor) is a pleasing park, rising steeply from the Río Manzanares to offer one of the finest views of the Palacio Real *(see pp54–7).* The park has a varied history. In 1109, a Moorish army, led by Ali ben Yusuf, set up camp here – hence the name. The park later became a jousting ground for Christian knights.

In the late 19th century, it was used as a playground for royal children and landscaped in what is described as the English style – with winding paths, grass and woodland, as well as fountains and statues.

In 1931, under the Second Republic *(see p18),* the Campo del Moro was opened to the public. Under Franco it was closed again and was not reopened until 1983.

The Muralla Arabe – archeological remains of Madrid's Moorish heritage

Muralla Arabe 26

Parque del Emir Mohamed I, Cuesta de la Vega. **Map** 3 C3. ✺ *Opera.* ◯ *dawn–sunset.*

Other than the city's name, which comes from the Arabic *Mayrit*, a small stretch of outer defence wall is all that is left of Madrid's Moorish heritage. The Muralla Arabe (Arab Wall) stands to the south of the Catedral de Nuestra Señora de la Almudena, down the steep Cuesta de la Vega street. It is believed that one of the main gateways to the Moorish town stood near this site *(see p13)*. The wall, constructed from flintstone blocks of various shapes and sizes, rises over 3 m (10 ft) along one side of the Parque del Emir Mohamed I. The park is named after the Moorish leader who founded Madrid.

The site was discovered while excavations were being carried out in 1953. As well as Moorish ruins dating from the ninth century, there is also a segment of a 12th-century Christian wall. On the other side of the wall, and visible from Cuesta de la Vega, are examples of typically Moorish brick horseshoe arches.

Across the street, a plaque and an image of the Virgin identify this as the spot where the statue of the Virgen de la Almudena was discovered in 1085 (*almudena* is from the Arabic for "outer wall"), possibly hidden from the Moors.

During the summer, outdoor concerts are occasionally held in Parque del Emir Mohamed I.

At other times, this treeless area is not well patrolled, and you should not visit the park on your own or after dark.

San Francisco el Grande 27

Plaza de San Francisco. **Map** 3 B4. ◖ *91 365 38 00.* ✺ *La Latina, Puerta de Toledo.* **Museum** ◯ *11am– 12:30pm, 4–6:30pm Tue–Fri.* **Capilla del Cristo de los Dolores** ◯ *11am–1pm Sat.* ◪ ◪

The site of this basilica was previously occupied by a Franciscan convent founded, according to legend, by St Francis of Assisi in 1217. When Felipe II made Madrid the capital of Spain in 1561 *(see p15)*,

Interior of San Francisco el Grande, a church richly endowed with the work of great artists

the convent's wealth and status grew, and it was made custodian of the "Holy Places" conquered by the crusaders.

In 1760 Carlos III ordained that the convent be replaced by a Neo-Classical basilica. The architect, Francesco Cabezas, designed a dome to measure over 33 m (108 ft) in diameter. However, in 1768, work had to be halted due to complications with the size. It was finally completed in 1784 by Francesco Sabatini.

The basilica was taken over by the Foreign Ministry in 1835 and used as an army barracks. A few years later it was made into a national pantheon. The Franciscan friars were forced to leave, and were only able to return to the basilica in 1926.

In 1878, a renovation project was initiated and the church decorated extravagantly. The façade is dominated by the dome and twin towers, which house 19 bells, 11 of which form the church's carillon.

The seven main doors were carved in walnut by Juan Guas, under the direction of sculptor Antonio Varela. The central image above the doors is of Christ crucified with Faith and Hope at his feet. On either side are the two thieves who were crucified with him. The panels on the doors show biblical scenes. Just inside the basilica, supported by bronze angels, are huge scallop-shaped marble bowls containing holy water. The scaffolding inside the church has been in place since 1973 due to problems with the restoration of the roof and frescoes.

The main chapel contains five large paintings executed by Manuel Domínguez and Alejandro Ferrant depicting the life of St Francis. The Four Evangelists, made from wood and plaster but imitating bronze, are by Sanmartí and Molinelli.

On each side of the basilica are three chapels, the most famous being the one just to the left of the main entrance. This chapel boasts an early painting by Goya of San Bernardino de Siena, with the painter himself appearing on the right of the picture. Work by Andrés de la Calleja and Antonio González Velázquez is also featured here. As well as the chapels, the sacristy and old cloisters can be visited.

The adjoining Capilla del Cristo de los Dolores, dating from 1162, was designed by architect Hermano Francisco Bautista. In it is the remarkable sculpture of *Cristo de los Dolores*, with bleeding holes in Christ's hands from the nails on the cross. This polychrome statue was created in 1643 by Diego Rodríguez but is, in fact, a copy of Domingo de la Rioja's original sculpture. This statue, now in Serradilla, was venerated for its association with miracles and spent some time in the alcázar, taken there by Felipe IV *(see p20)*.

Plaza de la Paja 28

Map 4 D3. *La Latina.*

ONCE THE FOCUS of medieval Madrid, the area around the Plaza de la Paja – literally Straw Square – is still atmospheric. Despite its location, in a less than affluent district, many interesting buildings are located around the square.

Climbing upwards from the Calle de Segovia, a glimpse left along Calle del Príncipe Anglona yields a view of the

Mudéjar-style brick tower of the **Iglesia de San Pedro**, dating from the 14th century. Beyond the fountain is the **Capilla del Obispo** (Bishop's Chapel), which first belonged to the adjoining Palacio Vargas. The Baroque, cherub-covered dome of the **Iglesia de San Andrés** can be seen to the left. Nearby is a cluster of interlinked squares, ending in the Plaza Puerta de Moros, a reminder of the Muslim community which once occupied the area. From here, a right turn leads to the domed bulk of San Francisco el Grande, an impressive landmark.

La Latina 29

Map 4 D4. *La Latina.*

THE DISTRICT OF La Latina, together with the adjacent Lavapiés, is considered to be the heart of *castizo* Madrid *(see p105)*. This term describes the culture of the traditional working classes of Madrid – that of the true *Madrileño*.

La Latina runs along the city's southern hillside from the Plaza Puerta de Moros through the streets where El Rastro flea market is held. To the east it merges with Lavapiés.

La Latina's steep streets are lined with tall, narrow houses, renovated to form an attractive neighbourhood. There are a number of old-fashioned bars around the Plaza de la Cebada, which add to the charm of this part of Madrid. It is worth wandering through simply to savour its rich atmosphere and authenticity.

Shoppers taking a leisurely Sunday stroll around El Rastro flea market

El Rastro 30

Calle de la Ribera de Curtidores.
Map 4 E4. *La Latina, Embajadores.*
🕐 *10am–2pm Sun & public hols.*

MADRID'S CELEBRATED flea market *(see p165)*, established in the Middle Ages, has its hub in the Plaza de Cascorro and sprawls downhill towards the Río Manzanares. The main street is the Calle de la Ribera de Curtidores, or "Tanners' Riverbank", once the centre of the slaughterhouse and tanning industry.

Although some people claim that El Rastro has changed a great deal since its heyday during the 19th century, there are still plenty of *Madrileños*, as well as tourists, who shop here. They come in search of a bargain from the stalls which sell a huge range of wares – anything from new furniture to second-hand clothes. The wide range of goods and the lively crowds in El Rastro make it an ideal way to spend a Sunday morning.

The Calle de Embajadores is the market's other main street. It runs down past the dusty Baroque façade of the **Iglesia de San Cayetano**, designed by José Churriguera and Pedro de Ribera. Its interior has been restored since fire destroyed it in the Civil War *(see p18)*.

Further along is the former Real Fábrica de Tabacos (Royal Tobacco Factory), begun as a state enterprise in 1809 and now an art gallery. Its female workers had a reputation for taking an uncompromising stance in industrial disputes.

The atmospheric Plaza de la Paja, once the heart of medieval Madrid

BOURBON MADRID

To the east of Old Madrid, there once lay an idyllic district of market gardens known as the Prado – the "Meadow". In the 16th century a monastery was built here. The Habsburgs extended it to form a palace, of which only fragments now remain; the palace gardens are now the popular Parque del Retiro *(see p77)*. The Bourbon monarchs, especially Carlos III, expanded the area in the 18th century. Around the Paseo del Prado they built grand squares with fountains, a triumphal gateway, and what was to become the Museo del Prado, one of the world's greatest art galleries. More recent additions to the area are the Centro de Arte Reina Sofía, a collection of modern Spanish art, and the Museo Thyssen-Bornemisza.

SIGHTS AT A GLANCE

Historic Buildings and Monuments
Ateneo de Madrid **17**
Banco de España **5**
Bolsa de Comercio **7**
Casa de Lope de Vega **20**
Círculo de Bellas Artes **13**
Congreso de los Diputados **16**
Edificio Metrópolis **15**
Estación de Atocha **30**
Hotel Palace **11**
Hotel Ritz **9**
Ministerio de Agricultura **27**
Observatorio Astronómico **28**
Palacio de Comunicaciones **3**
Palacio de Fernán Núñez **31**
Palacio de Linares **2**
Puerta de Alcalá **1**
Real Academia de la Historia **19**
Real Academia Española **23**
Teatro Español **18**

Museums and Galleries
Centro de Arte Reina Sofía pp86–9 **32**
Museo del Ejército **24**
Museo del Prado pp80–83 **21**
Museo Nacional de Antropología **29**
Museo Nacional de Artes Decorativas **8**
Museo Naval **6**
Museo Thyssen-Bornemisza pp70–73 **12**

Churches
Iglesia de San Jerónimo el Real **22**
Iglesia de San José **14**

Streets, Squares and Parks
Parque del Retiro **25**
Plaza Cánovas del Castillo **10**
Plaza de Cibeles **4**
Real Jardín Botánico **26**

GETTING THERE
The metro is the fastest and easiest way to get to and around Bourbon Madrid. Lines 1, 2 and 4 serve all the main sights. Useful bus routes are 1, 2, 8, 14, 15, 27, 74 & 146 to the Plaza de Cibeles.

KEY

	Street-by-Street map *pp64–5*
Ⓜ	Metro station
🚉	Railway station
🚏	Main bus stop
⚑	Tourist information
P	Parking

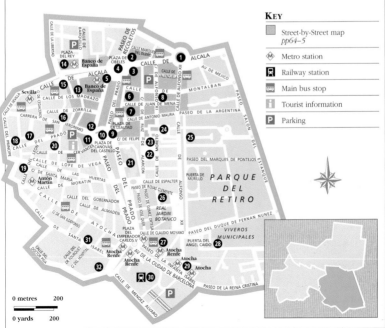

◁ **The Monument of Alfonxo XII in the Parque del Retiro** *(see p77)*

Street-by-Street: Paseo del Prado

IN THE LATE 18TH CENTURY, before the museums, sumptuous palaces and lavish hotels of Bourbon Madrid took shape, the Paseo del Prado was laid out and soon became a fashionable spot for strolling. Today the main attractions of the wide, tree-lined Paseo are its museums and galleries. Most notable are the Museo del Prado (just south of the Plaza Cánovas del Castillo) and the Museo Thyssen-Bornemisza, both displaying world-famous art collections. Among the grand monuments built under Carlos III are the Puerta de Alcalá, the Fuente de Neptuno and the Fuente de Cibeles, all at the centre of busy roundabouts.

★ Plaza de Cibeles
A fountain with a statue of the Greco-Roman goddess of nature, Cybele, stands in this square ❹

Banco de España Metro

Iglesia de San José
Designed by Pedro Ribera, this Baroque church was built from 1730 to 1742 ⓮

Banco de España
Spain's central reserve bank is housed in this massive building with three façades at the Plaza de Cibeles ❺

Círculo de Bellas Artes
This cultural foundation, established in 1880, offers a theatre, library, artists' studios and a café overlooking Calle de Alcalá ⓭

★ Museo Thyssen-Bornemisza
This excellent art collection occupies the Neo-Classical Villahermosa Palace, completed in 1806 ⓬

Hotel Palace
A host of international artists, politicians and film stars have stayed at this elegant, centrally located hotel ⓫

Plaza Cánovas del Castillo
In the middle of this large square stands a sculpted fountain of the god Neptune in his chariot ❿

Museo del Prado

STAR SIGHTS

★ Plaza de Cibeles

★ Museo Thyssen-Bornemisza

★ Puerta de Alcalá

CALLE DE ALCALÁ

BARQUILLO

CALLE DEL MARQUES

CALLE DE LOS MADRAZO

DE CUBAS

ZORRILLA

PASEO DEL PRADO

PLAZA CÁNOVAS DEL CASTILLO

0 metres   100
0 yards   100

★ **Puerta de Alcalá**
*Sculpted from granite,
this former gateway
into the city is espe-
cially beautiful when
floodlit at night* ❶

Palacio de Comunicaciones
*Spain's postal service is headquar-
tered in this ornate building, which is
often likened to a wedding cake* ❸

LOCATOR MAP
See Street Finder maps 7 & 8

Palacio de Linares
*This grandly decorated
late 19th-century palace
now houses the Casa de
América, an organization
that promotes Latin
American culture* ❷

**Museo Nacional
de Artes Decorativas**
*This museum, near the Retiro,
was founded in 1912 as a
showcase for Spanish interior
design and ceramics* ❽

Museo Naval
*Part of the Ministry of
Defence, this museum
contains a wealth of navi-
gational instruments, maps,
models of ships and
reconstructions of cabins* ❻

Hotel Ritz
*With its belle époque
interior, the Ritz is one
of the most elegant
hotels in all of Spain* ❾

Bolsa de Comercio
*Madrid's stock exchange is
housed in this attractive Neo-
Classical building. Visitors
can view events on the trading floor from a gallery* ❼

KEY

– – – – – Suggested route

View through the central arch of the Puerta de Alcalá

Puerta de Alcalá ❶

Map 8 D1. 🚇 *Retiro.*

THIS CEREMONIAL GATEWAY is the grandest of the monuments erected by Carlos III *(see p21)* in his efforts to improve eastern Madrid. Designed by Francesco Sabatini, it replaced a smaller Baroque gateway which had been built by Felipe III *(see p20)* for his wife's entry into Madrid.

Construction of the gate was started in 1769 and lasted a total of nine years. It was built from granite in Neo-Classical style, with a lofty pediment and sculpted angels. It has five arches – three central and two outer rectangular ones.

Until the mid-19th century, the gateway marked the city's easternmost boundary. It now stands in the busy Plaza de la Independencia, and is best seen when floodlit at night.

Palacio de Linares ❷

Paseo de Recoletos 2. **Map** 8 D1.
📞 *91 595 48 00.* 🚇 *Banco de España.* ⬤ *to the public.* **Exhibition Room** ⏰ *11am–2pm, 5-8pm Tue–Sat, 11am–2pm Sun & public hols.* ⓦ *www.casamerica.es*

IN 1873 Amadeo I *(see p21)* rewarded the Madrid banker, José de Murga, for his financial support by granting him the title of Marqués de Linares. The newly designated aristocrat quickly set about building himself the most luxurious, palatial residence Madrid had ever known. The rooms inside the palace are an extravaganza of ornate Rococo decor, resplendent with gold plate, inlaid wood and marble floors, glittering chandeliers, nubile nymphs and allegorical murals. The most striking rooms are on the first floor. They include the gala dining room, ballroom, the Salón China (Oriental Room), and Byzantine-style chapel. In the garden is the Pabellón Romántico, a wooden, fairy-tale-style pavilion which is also known as the Casa de Muñecas (Dolls' House).

After the Marqués died, the family fortunes declined. Many furnishings and decorations were sold, and the rest disappeared during the Spanish Civil War *(see p18)*. By 1977 the palace was almost derelict. However, it was saved by the Spanish government's decision to restore it for Madrid's year as European Capital of Culture in 1992. The main entrance to this French Baroque palace is on Plaza de Cibeles but it is used only for rare ceremonial occasions. General access is by a side entrance on Paseo de Recoletos. The building now houses the **Casa de América**, a cultural organization which promotes Latin American art, literature and cinema.

Palacio de Comunicaciones ❸

Plaza de Cibeles. **Map** 7 C2. 🚇 *Banco de España.* **Post Office** 📞 *90 219 71 97.* ⏰ *8:30am–9pm Mon–Fri, 8:30am–2pm Sat.* **Museum** 📞 *91 396 26 79.* ⏰ *9am–2pm, 5–7pm Mon–Fri, 9am–2pm Sat.* ⓦ *www.correos.es*

Mailbox at the Palacio de Comunicaciones

OCCUPYING ONE corner of the Plaza de Cibeles, this impressive building is the headquarters of Spain's postal service. Built between 1905 and 1917 by Antonio Palacios, its appearance – white with tall pinnacles – is often likened to a wedding cake. Its central hall is lined with counters providing services and, in the centre, are brass-and-wood lecterns where customers write their letters or fill out forms. A side door on Calle de Montalbán leads to the **Museo Postal y Telegráfico**, a little-known museum of postal and telephone communications. As well as collections of stamps, there are mailmen's uniforms, bicycles, mailboxes and old switchboards. More curious exhibits are a stuffed carrier pigeon, a cage for mailing bees and a letter written on bread by a soldier who ran out of paper. There are also 50 letters with cryptic addresses, which had to be deciphered before delivery. This odd practice was banned in the 1970s.

The height of Rococo extravagance in the Palacio de Linares ballroom

Plaza de Cibeles ❹

Map 7 C1. Ⓜ *Banco de España.*

I N ADDITION to being one of Madrid's best-known landmarks, the Plaza de Cibeles is also one of the most beautiful. The **Fuente de Cibeles** stands in the middle of the busy traffic island at the junction of the Paseo del Prado and the Calle de Alcalá. This fine, sculpted fountain is named after Cybele, the Greco-Roman goddess of nature, and shows her sitting in her chariot, drawn by a pair of lions. Designed in the late 18th century by José Hermosilla and Ventura Rodríguez, it is considered a symbol of Madrid.

Four important buildings rise around the square, the most impressive being the **Palacio de Comunicaciones**, mockingly known as "Our Lady of Communications". On the northeast side is the **Palacio de Linares**, built in 1873 about the time of the second Bourbon restoration. In the northwest corner, surrounded by attractive gardens, the **Cuartel General del Ejército de Tierra**, housed in the former Palacio de Buenavista. Commissioned by the Duchess of Alba in 1777, construction was twice delayed by fires.

Finally, occupying a whole block on the opposite corner, is the Venetian-Renaissance **Banco de España**, restored to its 19th-century magnificence.

Banco de España ❺

Paseo del Prado 2. **Map** 7 C2. 🔲 *91 338 53 65.* Ⓜ *Banco de España.* ◻ *by appointment only – write to Servicio de Protocolo.* ⌀

V IEWING THIS VAST building, with façades facing Paseo del Prado, Plaza de Cibeles and Calle de Alcalá, you might wonder which is the main entrance. In fact it is the one on the Paseo del Prado, used only for ceremonial occasions nowadays. The original bank dates from 1882–91 and occupied the corner of Cibeles, while new wings were added later. The Bank of Spain itself was founded in 1856.

The Fuente de Cibeles, with the Palacio de Linares in the background

The bank's vast main staircase, made of Carrara marble and overlooked by stained-glass windows with mythological and allegorical themes, leads to the Patio del Reloj, a glass-roofed central courtyard with the cashiers' windows. It is a striking example of Art Deco design. The library, which is open to researchers, is located in another large hall, the interior of which is made entirely of wrought-iron filigree, painted off-white. There is also an older, smaller library with glassed-in mahogany bookshelves.

The various meeting rooms and hallways are decorated with the bank's sizeable collection of tapestries, vases, antique furniture and paintings, including a first printing of Goya's series of etchings of bullfighting, the *Tauro-maquia*. In the circular Goya room are eight further paintings by the Spanish master *(see p26)*, including portraits of Carlos IV and various governors of the Bank of Spain. In *Conde de Floridablanca in the Artist's Studio,* rather than looking out at the viewer, Goya is seen gazing at his companion.

Beneath the Patio del Reloj, 30 m (98 ft) below street level and off limits to visitors, is a chamber with an island-like structure ringed by a moat. On it is the vault containing the

bank's gold. Prior to sophisticated security gadgetry, this chamber would immediately flood were there any threat of a bank robbery.

Museo Naval ❻

Paseo del Prado 5. **Map** 7 C2. 🔲 *91 379 52 99.* Ⓜ *Banco de España.* ◻ *10am–2pm Tue–Sun.* ◻ *Aug & some public hols.* ⌀ ☒ Ⓦ *www.museonavalmadrid.com*

A DDED TO THE Ministry of Defence building in 1977, the copper-tinted-glass Naval Museum has 18 display halls charting Spain's centuries-old history of seafaring. As well as a large collection of scale models of ships throughout the ages, often dating from the same period as the ships themselves, there are numerous figureheads, amphorae, globes, astrolabes, sextants, compasses and maps. Weapons used in Spain's conquest of the New World *(see p14)* also feature here. One unusual exhibit is a map of the world dated 1500. It was drawn for Isabel and Fernando *(see p20)*, and features the Americas for the first time. There is also a piece of the tree trunk upon which Hernán Cortés is said to have rested after *La Noche Triste* (The Sad Night) in 1520, when he and his men fled from Montezuma's Aztec capital, Tenochtitlán.

Astrolabe from the Museo Naval

View from the gallery – dealers at work in the grand Bolsa de Comercio

Bolsa de Comercio ●7

Plaza de la Lealtad 1. **Map** 7 C2.
[C] 91 589 22 64. Ⓜ Banco de España. ◯ by appointment. ◉ Sat, Sun & public hols. ∅ Ⓕ by appointment. Ⓦ www.bolsamadrid.es

T HE MADRID Stock Exchange was established in 1831. It operated in 11 different, generally inadequate venues – at one time, it was housed in a convent – before moving in 1893 to the purpose-built headquarters it currently occupies. Designed by Enrique María Repullés y Vargas, the building took more than six years to construct, at a cost of around three million pesetas. Nearly one third of this went on the concave, Neo-Classical façade and main entrance, with its six giant columns topped by Corinthian capitals.

Dealers occupy the **Sala de Contratación** (trading floor). This large, vaulted space of 970 sq m (10,400 sq ft) has an ornate Neo-Baroque clock on a marble plinth at its centre. Visitors can watch the proceedings from the **Salón de los Pasos Perdidos** (Hall of the Lost Steps). This gallery is often used for exhibitions on the history of the institution.

Museo Nacional de Artes Decorativas ●8

Calle de Montalbán 12. **Map** 8 D2.
[C] 91 532 64 99. Ⓜ Retiro, Banco de España. ◯ 9:30am–3pm Tue–Sat, 10am–3pm Sun & public hols. 🅼 (free Sun). ♿ Ⓕ by appointment. Ⓦ www.mcu.es/nmuseos/decora

H OUSED IN AN aristocratic residence built in the 19th century and overlooking the Parque del Retiro (see p77), the National Museum of Decorative Arts contains an interesting collection of furniture and *objets d'art*. The exhibits are mainly from Spain and date back to Phoenician times.

A star attraction is the 18th-century kitchen, moved here from a Valencian mansion. Its 1,500 painted tiles depict a domestic scene from the era. There are excellent ceramics from Talavera de la Reina, a town famous for the craft, and a collection of jewellery and ornaments from the Far East.

Hotel Ritz ●9

Plaza de la Lealtad 5. **Map** 7 C3.
[C] 91 521 28 57. Ⓜ Banco de España. ∅ ♿ Ⓦ www.ritz.es

A FEW MINUTES' WALK from the Prado (see pp80–83), this hotel is said to be Spain's most extravagant. It was commissioned in 1906, around the time that Alfonso XIII (see p21) was embarrassed by the lack of luxury accommodation in the city for his wedding guests.

At the start of the Civil War (see p18), the hotel became a hospital, and anarchist leader Buenaventura Durruti died here of his wounds in 1936.

The opulence of the Ritz is reflected in its prices (see p148). Each of the 158 rooms is beautifully decorated in a different style, with carpets made by hand at the Real Fábrica de Tapices (see p112).

Plaza Cánovas del Castillo ●10

Map 7 C3. Ⓜ Banco de España.

T HIS BUSY ROUNDABOUT takes its name from Antonio Cánovas del Castillo, one of the leading statesmen of 19th-century Spain, who was assassinated in 1897.

Dominating the plaza is the **Fuente de Neptuno**, a fountain with a statue of Neptune in his chariot, being pulled by two horses. The statue was designed in 1780 by Ventura Rodríguez as part of a grand scheme by Carlos III (see p20) to beautify eastern Madrid.

The Fuente de Neptuno

The relaxed elegance of the Palace's glass-domed Rotunda Hall lounge

Westin Palace

Plaza de las Cortes 7. **Map** 7 B3.
91 360 80 00.   Sevilla, Banco de España & Atocha.   www.palacemadrid.com

THE FORMER PALACE of the Duque de Medinaceli was torn down to build this hotel, which opened in 1912. Alfonso XIII wanted his capital to have elegant hotels to match those in other European cities, and actively encouraged the project. Its life as an elegant hostelry was interrupted only during the Civil War, when it housed a hospital and refuge for the homeless, as well as the Soviet Embassy.

For many years, the Westin Palace (formerly the Hotel Palace) and the Ritz were the only grand hotels in Madrid. However, while the Ritz was the exclusive reserve of its titled guests, none of whom would dare to venture from their rooms without a tie, the no less luxurious but more informal Palace was open to non-residents and was a lively meeting place for *Madrileños*. It was the first establishment in Madrid where ladies could take tea unaccompanied. It is still a favourite rendezvous and the wood-panelled **Palace Bar** and **Rotunda Hall** lounge, with its huge glass dome roof, are Madrid landmarks.

Statesmen, spies, literati and film stars have all stayed here. Past guests include Henry Kissinger, Mata Hari, Ernest Hemingway, Orson Welles, David Bowie, Richard Attenborough, Michael Jackson and Salvador Dalí, who once drew lewd pictures on the walls of his hotel room. Unfortunately, an over-zealous maid scrubbed the walls clean the next day.

The hotel underwent extensive renovation in 1997, adding a Royal Suite, solarium and fitness centre, as well as a wine cellar for tastings and sales.

Museo Thyssen-Bornemisza

See pp70–73.

La Pecera café in the Círculo de Bellas Artes

Círculo de Bellas Artes

Calle del Marqués de Casa Riera 2.
Map 7 B2.   91 360 54 00.
  Banco de España, Sevilla.
  10am–10pm (café closes 1am).
  Aug.   by appointment.
Exhibitions   90 242 24 42.
5–9pm Tue–Sat, 11am–2pm Sat–Sun.
  www.circulobellasartes.com

THE CÍRCULO DE Bellas Artes is a cultural foundation established in 1880. Since 1926, it has been housed in this building designed by Antonio Palacios, architect of the Palacio de Comunicaciones *(see p66)*. The building has a vast ballroom, exhibition halls, a theatre, library and studios for use by artists and sculptors. As well as exhibitions, workshops and lectures, it hosts cultural and social events, such as the Carnival Masquerade Ball held every February.

Although the foundation is for members only, the token admission fee gives visitors access to parts of the building, including the café. Known as **La Pecera** (Fishbowl) for its large windows, it is a great place to observe life on the Calle de Alcalá. There is also a cinema at a separate entrance.

Iglesia de San José

Calle de Alcalá 43. **Map** 7 B1.
91 522 67 84.   Banco de España.   7am–1:30pm, 6:30–8:30pm daily (Sun from 9am).

THIS CHURCH WAS once part of a Carmelite convent founded in 1605. The convent was demolished in 1863 to build a theatre, and the church itself was rebuilt during the reign of Felipe V *(see p20)*. When the Gran Vía *(see p48)* opened in 1908, the church was changed yet again. Adorning the façade, with its three arched entrances, is an attractive statue of the Virgen del Carmen. A number of the church's treasures are housed in the Prado *(see pp80–83)*, but a few interesting images remain on the Neo-Classical main altar and in the Baroque side chapels. Many are by French sculptor Robert Michel, who carved the Cibeles fountain's lions *(see p67)*. No. 41, next door, is still referred to as the **Casa del Párroco** (parish priest's house). On 10 March 1908, Alfonso XIII symbolically struck the church with a pickaxe to signal the start of demolition work which would make way for the Gran Vía.

Museo Thyssen-Bornemisza ⑫

THIS MAGNIFICENT MUSEUM is based on the collection assembled by Baron Heinrich Thyssen-Bornemisza and his son, Hans Heinrich, the preceding baron. In 1992 it was installed in Madrid's 18th-century Villahermosa Palace, and was sold to the nation the following year. From its beginnings in the 1920s, the collection sought to illustrate the history of Western art, from Italian and Flemish primitives through to Expressionism and Pop Art. It is regarded by many as the most important privately assembled art collection in the world and includes masterpieces by Titian, Goya, Van Gogh and Picasso. In spring 2004 a new extension opened, displaying the 17th-century Dutch paintings and Impressionist works acquired by Baroness Carmen Thyssen-Bornemisza.

★ **Our Lady of the Dry Tree** (*c.1450*)
This tiny painted panel is by Bruges master Petrus Christus. The letter A hanging from the tree stands for "Ave Maria".

★ **Harlequin with a Mirror**
The figure of the harlequin was a frequent subject of Picasso's. The careful composition on this 1923 canvas, which is thought by some to represent the artist himself, is typical of Picasso's "Classical" period.

GALLERY GUIDE

The galleries are arranged around a covered central courtyard, which rises the full height of the building. The top floor starts with early Italian art and goes through to the 17th century. The first floor continues the story with 17th-century Dutch works and ends with German Expressionism. The ground floor is dedicated to 20th-century paintings.

STAR PAINTINGS

- ★ **Our Lady of the Dry Tree by Christus**

- ★ **Harlequin with a Mirror by Picasso**

- ★ **The Toilet of Venus by Rubens**

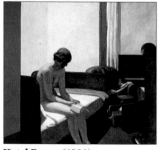

Hotel Room (*1931*)
Edward Hopper's painting is a study of urban isolation. The solitude is made less static by the suitcases and the train timetable on the woman's knee.

Portrait of Baron Thyssen-Bornemisza
This informal portrait of the previous baron, against the background of a Watteau painting, was painted by Lucian Freud.

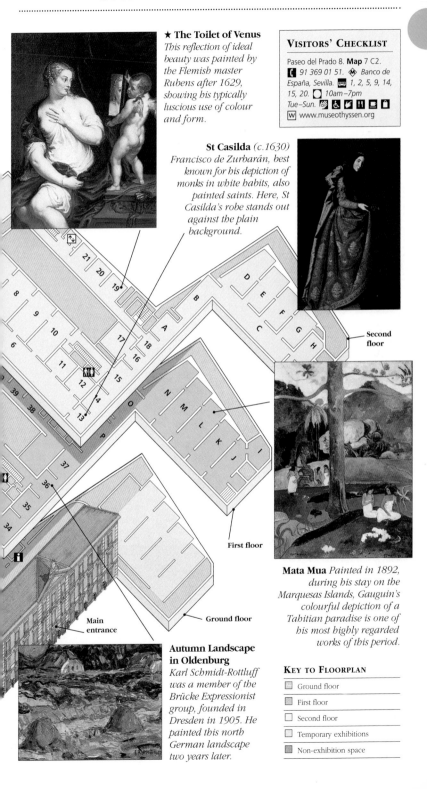

★ **The Toilet of Venus**
This reflection of ideal beauty was painted by the Flemish master Rubens after 1629, showing his typically luscious use of colour and form.

VISITORS' CHECKLIST

Paseo del Prado 8. **Map** 7 C2.
91 369 01 51. Banco de España, Sevilla. 1, 2, 5, 9, 14, 15, 20. 10am–7pm Tue–Sun.
W www.museothyssen.org

St Casilda (c.1630)
Francisco de Zurbarán, best known for his depiction of monks in white habits, also painted saints. Here, St Casilda's robe stands out against the plain background.

Second floor

First floor

Main entrance

Ground floor

Mata Mua Painted in 1892, during his stay on the Marquesas Islands, Gauguin's colourful depiction of a Tahitian paradise is one of his most highly regarded works of this period.

Autumn Landscape in Oldenburg
Karl Schmidt-Rottluff was a member of the Brücke Expressionist group, founded in Dresden in 1905. He painted this north German landscape two years later.

KEY TO FLOORPLAN

☐ Ground floor
☐ First floor
☐ Second floor
☐ Temporary exhibitions
☐ Non-exhibition space

Exploring the Museo Thyssen-Bornemisza

T HIS COLLECTION provides a sweeping overview of Western art between the 14th and 20th centuries, touching on every school and trend in European art over the last 500 years. It is strong in areas where the Prado is weak, such as in Italian and Dutch primitives, 19th-century American painting, Impressionism and Expressionism. Portraiture from different periods is also well represented. The addition of a new extension to hold the Carmen Thyssen-Bornemisza Collection means that many paintings will be moved to other rooms.

Christ and the Samaritan Woman (1311) by Duccio

THE BIRTH OF THE RENAISSANCE

E ARLY ITALIAN art (room 1), while still influenced by medieval aesthetics and often overwhelmingly religious in subject matter, shows a gradual return to naturalism. Paintings become more three-dimensional and strive to tell a story, as in Duccio's *Christ and the Samaritan Woman* (1311).

The section on medieval art (room 2) illustrates how Italian influences combined with the Gothic style popular in Europe, such as Koerbecke's *Assumption of the Virgin* (c.1457).

Room 3 shows early Dutch art, including two jewels of the collection, Jan van Eyck's *The Annunciation* (c.1435–41) and Petrus Christus's *Our Lady of the Dry Tree* (c.1450). The stage is set for the aesthetic revolution of the Renaissance and a return to Classical forms, which began in Italy in the 1400s. The best example is Bramantino's *Resurrected Christ* (room 4).

Later, religion ceases to be the dominant theme, as seen in the outstanding series of early Renaissance portraits (room 5), including Holbein's detailed *Henry VIII* (c.1534–6).

RENAISSANCE TO BAROQUE

T HIS SECTION encompasses the height of the Renaissance, ending with Baroque art and 18th-century Italian painting. Outstanding examples of high Renaissance in Italy (room 7) include Carpaccio's *Young Knight in a Landscape* (1510) and Raphael's *Portrait of a Young Man* (c.1515).

Rooms 8–10 are dedicated to German and Dutch painters of the same period, including Dürer, with his *Jesus among the Doctors* (1506). Room 11 has works by Titian (*St Jerome in the Wilderness* c.1575), Tintoretto and El Greco.

Room 12 begins with early Baroque, when artists started to break with the rigid Classical rules of the Renaissance and introduce elements of drama and pathos into their work. This new trend flourishes in the art in rooms 13–15, with examples from Italy, France and Spain, where the period corresponded with the *Siglo*

Young Knight in a Landscape (1510) by Vittore Carpaccio

de Oro (Golden Century) of the arts. Included here is Murillo's *Madonna with Child with St Rosalina of Palermo* (c.1670).

Italy's continuing influence on European art is recognized in rooms 16–18, devoted to 18th-century Italian art, in which landscapes make an appearance. This is illustrated by two views of the *Canal Grande in Venice*, one by Canaletto (before 1723) and a later one by Francesco Guardi.

DUTCH AND FLEMISH PAINTING

T HE REMARKABLE series of Dutch and Flemish art is a strong point of the collection. The first series (room 19) features 17th-century Flemish

Esau Selling His Birthright (c.1627) by Hendrick ter Brugghen

painting, with works by Jan Brueghel the Elder and Van Dyck, though the big attraction is *The Toilet of Venus* (c.1629), one of four Rubens on display.

The growing distinction between Flemish and Dutch works can be seen by comparing the preceding works with the Dutch art in rooms 20–21. The theme here is the Italian influence on Dutch portraiture and painting, for example in *Esau Selling His Birthright* (c.1627) by Brugghen.

Some of the most interesting works are in rooms 22–26, where everyday scenes, landscapes and informal portraits reveal the unique quality of Dutch art. Excellent examples are Frans Hals's *Family Group in a Landscape* (c.1645–8) and Nicholas Maes's *The Naughty Drummer* (c.1655). Dutch still lifes from the period are well represented in room 27.

Waverly Oaks (1864) by Winslow Homer

ROCOCO TO REALISM

Rococo to Neo-Classicism is the theme of this section, indicating a rapid shift in tastes over a relatively brief period. Rococo took Europe by storm at the beginning of the 18th century. It is best represented here in room 28 by Antoine Watteau's *The Rest* (c.1709) and *Pierrot Content* (c.1712), and by François Boucher's *La Toilette* (1742). However, the increasingly exaggerated forms of Rococo were eventually rejected in favour of more restrained and elegant lines.

Meanwhile, different developments were taking shape across the ocean. Rooms 29–30 display 19th-century American painting. Landscape art fulfilled a need to express America's romantic spirit and pride in the land, as seen in the paintings of Thomas Cole. American artists were increasingly interested in depicting everyday scenes, such as idyllic fishing trips and strolls through the woods.

The coming of age of American art at the end of the century is represented by the paintings of Winslow Homer, especially *Waverly Oaks* (1864), James Whistler and John Singer Sargent.

In Europe, the 19th century saw the dawn of Romanticism (room 31), a transition best illustrated here through three works by Goya. The series also demonstrates a growing trend towards Realism, a shift that is plainly depicted in Constable's *The Lock* (1824).

MODERN MASTERS

The year 1863 was pivotal in the evolution of modern art, because artists whose work was rejected by Paris's art salon were displayed in a parallel Salon des Refusés. This show of discarded art marked the birth of Impressionism, a revolution which broke ties with academic restraints. Some of the most highly regarded exponents of the movement are represented in rooms 32–33, including Manet, Degas with *Swaying Dancer* (1877–9), Renoir and Sisley. Impressionism freed the artist and led to further developments, such as Post-Impressionism and Symbolism, which centred on the artist as an individual. Such is the case with Vincent van Gogh, represented here by *Les Vessenots in Auvers* (1888), Toulouse-Lautrec with *Gaston*

Swaying Dancer (1877–9) by Degas

Bonnefoy (1891), Cézanne with his *Portrait of a Farmer* (c.1900) and Gauguin, whose *Mata Mua* (c.1892) is now part of the Carmen Thyssen-Bornemisza Collection. A series of works in room 34, belonging to the Fauve school, demonstrates this short-lived movement based on bright colours and simplified forms.

A name that did endure was Expressionism, which started in Germany. This school drew on the artist's emotions, and sought to precipitate an emotion in the viewer. Its earliest practitioners were centred around the Dresden group, "The Bridge," founded in 1905. Among its members was Karl Schmidt-Rottluf, whose *Autumn Landscape in Oldenburg* (1907) is shown here. The collection of Expressionist art in rooms 35–40 is one of the museum's highlights.

Eight ground-floor rooms (41–48) deal with modern and contemporary art, divided into three themes – "Experimental Avant-Garde", "The Synthesis of Modern" and "Surrealism, Figurative Tradition and Pop Art". Among the gems here are Picasso's *Harlequin with a Mirror* (1923) and Edward Hopper's *Hotel Room* (1931).

Parisian-inspired cupola of the Edificio Metrópolis

Edificio Metrópolis ⑮

Calle de Alcalá 39. **Map** 7 B1.
Ⓜ Sevilla. ◉ to the public.

O F UNMISTAKABLE French inspiration, this building, jutting out like a ship's prow at the corner of Calle Alcalá and the Gran Vía (see p48), is a Madrid landmark. Inaugurated in 1911, it was designed by Jules and Raymond Février for the Unión y el Fenix Español insurance company.

The restrained ground level is topped by ornate colonnaded upper floors, each pair of columns serving as a pedestal for allegorical statues representing Commerce, Agriculture, Industry and Mining. The rounded corner tower is crowned by a double-layered dome of dark slate with gilded ornaments. It used to hold the symbol of the Unión y el Fenix company – a bronze statue representing the mythological Phoenix and, astride it, a human figure with upraised arm representing Ganymede. In the early 1970s, the company sold the building to its present owners, the Metrópolis insurers. In a controversial move, they decided to take the statue – by then a familiar element of the Madrid skyline – to their ostentatious new headquarters on the Paseo de la Castellana. Eventually the statue was replaced by a new one, representing Winged Victory; the original Phoenix is in the garden of the Unión y el Fenix's modern building.

Almost unnoticed on the ground just in front of the circular tower of the Edificio Metrópolis is "La Violetera", a small statue of a young woman selling violets. It recalls a character from a popular *zarzuela* (Spanish light opera), which later inspired the film, *La Violetera*, starring Sara Montiel. The violet-sellers – Madrid's answer to Eliza Doolittle of *Pygmalion* – would sell their flowers to theatre-goers on the Gran Vía after each performance. An inscription at the base of the statue bears the following simple message: "*Como ave precursora de primavera, en Madrid aparece la violetera*" ("The violet-seller appears in Madrid like a bird announcing spring").

LA TERTULIA – LITERARY GROUPS IN MADRID

Interior of the Café Comercial

The Ateneo de Madrid was one of many homes for the unique Madrid institution of *la tertulia*. Groups of people with common interests gathered to discuss everything from politics or the arts to the finer points of bullfighting. Not a formal club, yet more than a casual conversation among friends, *tertulias* were a major source of news, ideas and gossip in the 19th century, and more than one political plot was hatched over cups of coffee. They were usually held at Madrid's historic 19th-century cafés. Those which occupied choice bits of real estate, such as the Pombo, El Oriental and the Paix, have since disappeared, but there are a few survivors. The best known are the Café Comercial on Glorieta de Bilbao and the Café Gijón (see p94) on Paseo de Recoletos.

Congreso de los Diputados ⑯

Plaza de las Cortes. **Map** 7 B2.
Ⓒ 91 390 60 00. Ⓜ Sevilla.
◐ by appointment (fax 91 390 64 35)
Mon–Fri, 10:30am–12:30pm Sat.
◉ Aug. ⊘ ♿ Ⓦ www.congreso.es

T HIS IMPOSING yet attractive building is home to the Spanish parliament, the Cortes. Built in the mid-19th century, it is characterized by Classical columns, heavy pediments and bronze lions. It was here, in 1981, that Colonel Tejero of the Civil Guard held the deputies at gunpoint, as he tried to spark off a military coup (see p19). His failure was seen as an indication that democracy was firmly established in Spain.

Bronze lion guarding the Cortes

Ateneo de Madrid ⑰

Calle del Prado 21. **Map** 7 B2 Ⓒ 91 429 17 50. Ⓜ Antón Martín, Sevilla.
◐ by appointment (Secretario Primero, C/ del Prado 21, Madrid 28014).

F ORMALLY FOUNDED IN 1835, this learned association has strongly liberal political leanings. It is similar to a gentlemen's club in atmosphere, with a grand stairway and panelled hall hung with the portraits of famous fellows. Often closed down during past periods of repression and dictatorship, it is still a mainstay of liberal thought in Spain. Many leading Socialists are members, along with writers and other Spanish intellectuals.

La Zarzuela – Spanish Light Opera

THE ZARZUELA, a direct descendant of Italian light opera, started out as an amusement for kings, but was soon appropriated by the common people as Madrid's most characteristic performing art genre. The name is derived from the Palacio de La Zarzuela, current home of the Spanish royal family, outside Madrid. *Zarzuelas* were initially performed during the reign of Felipe IV, in the 17th century. With the ascendancy of the Bourbon kings *(see p15)*, who preferred traditional Italian opera, the *zarzuela* left the royal palaces and was taken up in the *corrales de comedias*,

Statue of "La Violetera"

the popular theatres of Madrid. It was here that it evolved into the light-hearted spectacle we know today, halfway between opera and musical comedy. Although no new *zarzuelas* have been written in decades, the genre has a tremendous following in Madrid, where there are regular performances and where record shops always have a section devoted to it. The best known title is *La Revoltosa*, a portrayal of the chemistry between the residents in a typical Madrid *corral de vecinos*, which were humble dwellings grouped around a central courtyard.

Calderón de La Barca, the famous 17th-century Spanish playwright, was one of the first great exponents of this type of opera. Others followed, most notably Tomás Breton (born 1850), who composed nearly 40 zarzuelas. His most famous is La Verbena de la Paloma.

The central theme of zarzuelas is life in castizo *Madrid* (see p105), with its streetwise majas (women) and cocky chulos (men) dressed in traditional costumes. It combines singing, spoken dialogue and a variety of dances, such as the Madrid jig, the chotis.

By the middle of the 19th century, zarzuela was so popular that a theatre was specially built for performances. Today, the 1,200-seat Teatro de la Zarzuela (see p174) continues to stage zarzuelas, as do several others. In summer, there are also outdoor shows at La Corrala (see p113).

A colourful *zarzuela* performance by the Compañía de Zarzuela J Tamayo

Sunlit balconies of the magnificent Teatro Español

Teatro Español ⑱

Calle del Príncipe 25. **Map** 7 A3.
📞 *91 360 14 80.* Ⓜ *Sol, Antón Martín & Sevilla.* ⏰ *for performances from 7pm Tue–Sun.* 🅿️ ♿
🅦 *www.telentrada.com*

D OMINATING the Plaza de Santa Ana *(see p47)* is the Teatro Español, one of the oldest and most beautiful theatres in Madrid. In the late 16th century many of Spain's finest plays were performed in the Corral del Príncipe which originally stood here. Replaced by the Teatro del Príncipe in 1745, it underwent extensive restoration in the mid-19th century and was renamed Teatro Español. Engraved on the Neo-Classical façade are names of great Spanish dramatists, including that of Federico García Lorca *(see p26)*.

Real Academia de la Historia ⑲

Calle del León 21. **Map** 7 A3. 📞 *91 429 06 11.* Ⓜ *Antón Martín.* ⏺ *for renovation until mid-2005.* 🅦 *www.rah.insde.es*

T HIS AUSTERE BRICK building, housing the Royal Academy of History, was built by Juan de Villanueva in 1788 and is aptly located in the Barrio de los Literatos (Writers' Quarter).
From 1898 to 1912, the great intellectual and bibliophile, Marcelino Menéndez Pelayo, was director of the academy. The library holds over 200,000

books and several important manuscripts. The antiquities owned by the academy will be displayed in a new museum scheduled to open mid-2005.

Casa de Lope de Vega ⑳

Calle de Cervantes 11. **Map** 7 B3.
📞 *91 429 92 16.* Ⓜ *Antón Martín.* ⏰ *9:30am–2pm Tue–Fri, 10am–2pm Sat.* ⏺ *Aug, public hols.* 🅿️ *(free Sat).* 📷 🚫

F ÉLIX LOPE DE VEGA, a leading Golden Age writer *(see p26)*, moved into this sombre house in 1610. Here he wrote over two-thirds of his plays, thought to total almost 2,000. Meticulously restored in 1935, using some of Lope de Vega's own furniture, the house gives a great feeling of Castilian life in the early 17th century. A dark chapel with no external windows occupies the centre, separated from the writer's

Félix Lope de Vega

bedroom by only a barred window. The small garden at the rear, complete with the original well, is planted with the flowers and fruit trees mentioned by the writer in his works. He died here in 1635.

Museo del Prado ㉑

See pp80–83.

Iglesia de San Jerónimo el Real ㉒

Calle de Moreto 4. **Map** 8 D3. 📞 *91 420 35 78.* Ⓜ *Banco de España, Atocha.* ⏰ *Oct–Jun: 10am–1pm, 5:30–8:30pm daily (6–8:30pm Jul–Sep).* ⏺ *Easter Sat.* ♿

B UILT IN THE 16th century for Isabel I *(see p20)*, but since remodelled, San Jerónimo is Madrid's royal church. From the 17th century it was virtually a part of the Buen Retiro palace which once stood here.
Originally attached to the Hieronymite monastery, which today stands beside it in ruins, the church was the location for the marriage of Alfonso XIII *(see p21)* and Victoria Eugenia von Battenberg in 1906. The church is still a popular venue for society weddings. The cloisters and part of the atrium form an annex of the Prado's new extension.

Real Academia Española ㉓

Calle de Ruiz de Alarcón 17. **Map** 8 D3.
📞 *91 420 14 78.* Ⓜ *Banco de España, Retiro.* ⏺ *to the public.* 🅦 *www.rae.es*

S PAIN'S ROYAL ACADEMY motto is *"Limpia, brilla y da esplendor"* ("Cleans, polishes and shines"). It describes the function of the organization, which is to preserve the purity of the Spanish language. Founded in 1713, the academy only moved to this Neo-Classical building in 1891. The elegant façade boasts a majestic entrance with Doric columns and a carved pediment. The 46 members include scholars, writers and journalists – the post, which is for life, is unpaid

– who occupy seats identified by a letter of the alphabet. They meet regularly to assess the acceptability of any new trends in the language.

Museo del Ejército ②

Calle de Méndez Núñez 1. **Map** 8 D2.
📞 91 522 89 77. Ⓜ Retiro, Banco de España. ⏰ 10am–2pm Tue–Sun.
🔴 public hols. 🎫 (free Sat). 📷 by appointment. ♿
🌐 www.ejercito.mde.es/ihycm

Spain's army museum occupies one of the few remaining parts of a 17th-century palace, the Real Sitio del Buen Retiro. It still has most of the original decoration, some by Velázquez (see p26). Individual rooms are dedicated to military history and house a vast array of weapons, from Moorish times to the present day. The grandest room, the Salón de Reinos, is named after the kingdoms which once made up Spain, depicted on the ceiling.

One of the highlights of the army museum is the sword of El Cid – La Tizona – on display in the Sala de Armas. The tunic and sword of Boabdil, the last Moorish ruler of Granada, are exhibited in the Sala Árabe.

In the Sala Colonial is a fragment of the cross that Columbus planted in the ground upon reaching the New World (see p14). More recent events are illustrated by busts and flags from Spain's War of

The sword of El Cid, *La Tizona*, in the Museo del Ejército

Independence (see p16) in the Sala del Dos de Mayo.

As well as rooms devoted to the Spanish Civil War and the Nationalist Campaign (see p18), which contain portraits of General Franco, there is also an entire room filled with tin soldiers.

Parque del Retiro ②

Map 8 E3. 📞 91 409 23 36.
Ⓜ Ibiza, Retiro, Atocha. **Park** ⏰ May–Sep: 6am–midnight; Oct: 6am–11pm; Nov–Apr: 6am–10pm. ♿
Casa de Vacas ⏰ 11am–8pm daily.

Retiro park, in Madrid's smart Jerónimos district, was once the setting for Felipe IV's palace (see p20), the Real Sitio del Buen Retiro. All that remains is the Casón del Buen

Retiro (see p83) and the Museo del Ejército. In the 17th century the park was the private playground of the royal family, and only became fully open to the public in 1869. Today, it is a popular place for relaxing in the open air.

A short stroll from the park's northern entrance is the lake, where rowing boats can be hired. On one side, in front of a half-moon colonnade, a statue of Alfonso XII (see p21) rides high on a column. On the other, portrait painters and fortune-tellers ply their trade.

To the south of the lake are the Palacio de Velázquez and the Palacio de Cristal, both built by Ricardo Velázquez Bosco. His other work includes the grandiose Ministerio de Agricultura building (see p84).

The Palacio de Velázquez was intended as a pavilion to stage the National Exhibition of Mining, Metal, Ceramics, Glass and Mineral Water industries in 1884. Today it is simply used for temporary exhibitions.

Nearby, the iron-and-glass Palacio de Cristal was modelled on the Crystal Palace built for London's Great Exhibition in 1851. Designed to stage an exhibition of tropical plants in the Philippines Exposition of 1887, the palace has become a forum for receptions and art displays. Its reflection in the lake remains one of the best known images of Madrid.

In the Paseo de Colombia, the Casa de Vacas puts on free exhibitions of Madrid art.

Monument of Alfonso XII (1901) facing the boating lake in the Parque del Retiro

Museo del Prado ㉔

THE PRADO MUSEUM contains the world's greatest assembly of Spanish painting – especially works by Velázquez and Goya – ranging from the 12th to 19th centuries. It also houses impressive foreign collections, particularly of Italian and Flemish works. The Neo-Classical building was designed in 1785 by Juan de Villanueva on the orders of Carlos III, and it opened as a museum in 1819. The Prado has undergone major renovations in several phases over the last few years. The Casón del Buen Retiro, the Prado's annexe, is currently being refurbished and is due to open to the public by 2005.

★ Velázquez Collection
The Triumph of Bacchus *(1629), Velázquez's first portrayal of a mythological subject, shows the god of wine (Bacchus) with a group of drunkards.*

The Three Graces *(c.1635)*
This was one of the last paintings by the Flemish master Rubens, and was part of the artist's personal collection. The three women dancing in a ring – the Graces – are the daughters of Zeus, and represent Love, Joy and Revelry.

The Martyrdom of St Philip
(c.1639) José de Ribera moved from his native Valencia to Naples as a young man. There he was influenced by Caravaggio's dramatic use of light and shadow, known as chiaroscuro, as seen in this work.

> **STAR EXHIBITS**
>
> ★ **Velázquez Collection**
>
> ★ **Goya Collection**

The Garden of Delights *(c.1505)*
Hieronymus Bosch (El Bosco in Spanish), one of Felipe II's favourite artists, is especially well represented in the Prado. This enigmatic painting depicts paradise and hell.

◁ The expansive Parque del Retiro which once formed the gardens of a Habsburg palace

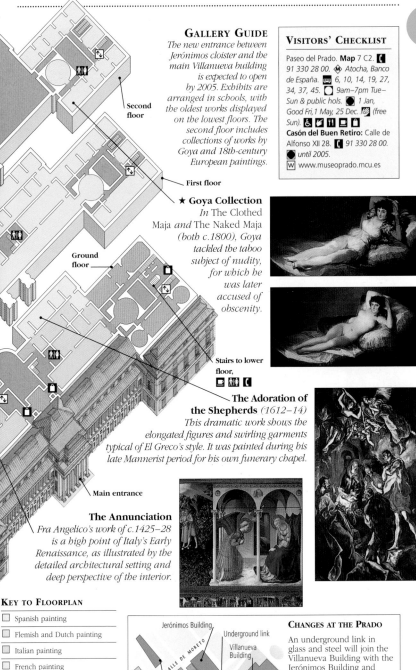

GALLERY GUIDE
The new entrance between Jerónimos cloister and the main Villanueva building is expected to open by 2005. Exhibits are arranged in schools, with the oldest works displayed on the lowest floors. The second floor includes collections of works by Goya and 18th-century European paintings.

Second floor

First floor

Ground floor

VISITORS' CHECKLIST

Paseo del Prado. **Map** 7 C2. 91 330 28 00. Atocha, Banco de España. 6, 10, 14, 19, 27, 34, 37, 45. 9am–7pm Tue–Sun & public hols. 1 Jan, Good Fri,1 May, 25 Dec. (free Sun).

Casón del Buen Retiro: Calle de Alfonso XII 28. 91 330 28 00. until 2005.

www.museoprado.mcu.es

★ Goya Collection
In The Clothed Maja *and* The Naked Maja *(both c.1800), Goya tackled the taboo subject of nudity, for which he was later accused of obscenity.*

Stairs to lower floor,

The Adoration of the Shepherds *(1612–14)*
This dramatic work shows the elongated figures and swirling garments typical of El Greco's style. It was painted during his late Mannerist period for his own funerary chapel.

Main entrance

The Annunciation
Fra Angelico's work of c.1425–28 is a high point of Italy's Early Renaissance, as illustrated by the detailed architectural setting and deep perspective of the interior.

KEY TO FLOORPLAN

- Spanish painting
- Flemish and Dutch painting
- Italian painting
- French painting
- German painting
- British painting
- Sculpture
- Temporary Exhibitions
- Non-exhibition space

Jerónimos Building

CALLE DE MORETO

Underground link

Villanueva Building

Casón del Buen Retiro

CALLE DE FELIPE IV

Museo del Ejército

PASEO DEL PRADO

CHANGES AT THE PRADO

An underground link in glass and steel will join the Villanueva Building with the Jerónimos Building and house a shop, café, restaurant and cloakroom. In the final phase the Museo del Ejército (*see p275*) will become part of the Prado.

- Museum Buildings
- Due to open in 2007

Exploring the Prado's Collection

THE IMPORTANCE OF THE PRADO is founded on its royal collections. The wealth of foreign art, including many of Europe's finest works, reflects the historical power of the Spanish crown. The Low Countries and parts of Italy were under Spanish domination for centuries. The 18th century was an era of French influence, following the Bourbon accession to the Spanish throne. The Prado is worthy of repeated visits, but if you go only once, see the Spanish works of the 17th century.

St Dominic of Silos Enthroned as Abbot (1474–7) by Bermejo

SPANISH PAINTING

RIGHT UP TO THE 19th century, Spanish painting focused on religious and royal themes. Although the limited subject matter was in some ways a restriction, it also offered a sharp focus that seems to have suited Spanish painters.

Spain's early medieval art is represented somewhat sketchily in the Prado, but there are some examples, such as the

anonymous mural paintings from the Holy Cross hermitage in Maderuelo, which show a Romanesque heaviness of line and forceful characterization.

Spanish Gothic art can be seen in the Prado in the works of Bartolomé Bermejo and Fernando Gallego. The sense of realism in their paintings was borrowed from Flemish masters of the time.

Renaissance features began to emerge in the works of painters such as Pedro de Berruguete, whose *Auto-de-fé* is both chilling and lively. *St Catherine*, by Fernando Yáñez de la Almedina, shows the influence of Leonardo da Vinci, for whom Yáñez probably worked while training in Italy.

What is often considered as a truly Spanish style – with its highly-wrought emotion and deepening sombreness – first started to emerge in the 16th century in the paintings of the Mannerists. This is evident in Pedro Machuca's fierce *Descent from the Cross* and in the Madonnas of Luis de Morales, "the Divine". The elongation of the human figure in Morales' work is carried to a greater extreme by Domenikos Theotocopoulos, who is better known as El Greco *(see p139)*. Although many of his masterpieces remain in his adopted

Saturn Devouring One of his Sons (1820–23) by Francisco de Goya

town of Toledo, the Prado has an impressive collection, including *The Nobleman with his Hand on his Chest*.

The Golden Age of the 17th century was a productive time for Spanish art. José de Ribera, who lived in (Spanish) Naples, followed Caravaggio in combining realism of character with the techniques of *chiaroscuro* (use of light and dark) and tenebrism (large areas of dark colours, with a shaft of light). Another master who used this method was Francisco Ribalta, whose *Christ Embracing St Bernard* is here. Zurbarán, known for still lifes and portraits of saints and monks, is also represented in the Prado.

This period, however, is best represented by the work of Diego de Velázquez. As Spain's leading court painter from his late twenties until his death, he produced scenes of heightened realism, royal portraits, and religious and mythological paintings. Examples of all of these are displayed in the Prado. Perhaps his greatest work is *Las Meninas (see p27)*.

Another great Spanish painter, Goya, revived Spanish art in the 18th century. He first specialized in cartoons for tapestries, then became a court painter. His work went on to embrace the horrors of war, as seen in *The 3rd of May in Madrid (see p16)*, and culminated in a sombre series known as *The Black Paintings*.

Still Life with Four Vessels (c.1658–64) by Francisco de Zurbarán

CASÓN DEL BUEN RETIRO

On the hill behind the Prado is its annexe, the Casón del Buen Retiro, once part of the Palacio del Buen Retiro *(see p77)*. Its exhibits have included late 19th-century and early 20th-century works, as well as Neo-Classical and Romantic art, and paintings on historical themes. The Casón del Buen Retiro is expected to be fully open to the public by 2005, following refurbishment and the addition of two floors.

Children at the Beach (1910) by Joaquín Sorolla

FLEMISH AND DUTCH PAINTING

SPAIN'S LONG CONNECTION with the Low Countries led naturally to an intense admiration for the so-called Flemish primitives. Many exceptional works of art now hang in the Prado. *St Barbara*, by Robert Campin, has a quirky intimacy, and Rogier van der Weyden's *The Deposition* is an unquestioned masterpiece. Most notable of all, however, are Hieronymus Bosch's weird and eloquent inventions, which were collected by Felipe II. The Prado has some of his major paintings, including the *Temptation of St Anthony* and *The Haywain*. Works from the 16th century include the magnificent *Triumph of Death* by Brueghel the Elder. There are nearly 100 canvases by the 17th-century Flemish painter Peter Paul Rubens, of which the greatest is *The Adoration of the Magi*. The two most notable Dutch paintings on display are by Rembrandt: *Artemisia*, and a fine self-portrait.

David Victorious over Goliath (c.1600) by Caravaggio

ITALIAN PAINTING

THE PRADO IS THE ENVY of many museums, not least for its vast collection of Italian paintings. Botticelli's dramatic wooden panels telling *The Story of Nastagio degli Onesti*, a vision of a knight forever condemned to hunt down and kill his own beloved, are a sinister high point. Raphael contributes the superb *Christ Falls on the Way to Calvary* and the sentimental *The Holy Family of the Lamb*.

Christ Washing the Disciples' Feet, by Tintoretto, is a profound masterpiece. Venetian masters Veronese and Titian are also very well represented. Titian served as court painter to Charles V, and few works express the drama of Habsburg rule so deeply as his sombre painting *The Emperor Charles V at Mühlberg*. Also on display are works by Giordano, Caravaggio and Tiepolo, the master of Italian Rococo.

FRENCH PAINTING

MARRIAGES BETWEEN French and Spanish royalty in the 17th century, culminating in the Bourbon accession to the throne in the 18th century, brought French art to Spain. The Prado has eight works attributed to Poussin, among them his serene *Parnassus* and *Landscape with St Jerome*. The magnificent *Landscape with the Embarkation of St Paula Romana at Ostia* is the best work here by Claude Lorrain. Among the 18th-century artists featured are Antoine Watteau and Jean Ranc. *Felipe V* is the work of the royal portraitist Louis-Michel van Loo.

GERMAN PAINTING

ALTHOUGH GERMAN ART is not especially well represented in the Prado, there are several paintings by Albrecht Dürer, such as his lively *Self-Portrait*, painted at the age of 26. Lucas Cranach also figures. Works by the late 18th-century painter Anton Raffael Mengs include portraits of Carlos III.

The Deposition (c.1430) by Rogier van der Weyden

Real Jardín Botánico

Plaza de Murillo 2. **Map** 8 D4. **C** *91 420 30 17.* **M** *Atocha.* **O** *10am–dusk daily.* **W** *www.rjb.csic*

SOUTH OF THE PRADO *(see pp80–3)*, and a suitable place to rest after visiting the gallery, are the Royal Botanic Gardens. The inspiration of Carlos III *(see p21)*, they were designed in 1781 by Gómez Ortega and Juan de Villanueva, architect of the Prado.

Interest in the plants of the Philippines and South America was taking hold in Spain around this time, and the neatly laid out beds offer an enormous variety of flora, ranging from trees and shrubs to medicinal plants and herbs.

Statue of Bourbon King, Carlos III, in the Real Jardín Botánico

Ministerio de Agricultura

Paseo de la Infanta Isabel 1. **Map** 8 D5. **C** *91 347 53 48.* **M** *Atocha.* **O** *by appointment.* **W** *www.mapya.es*

THIS MAGNIFICENT, imposing building was originally the home of the Ministry of Development, whose remit was to promote economic, industrial and scientific growth in Spain in the late 19th century. Today the enormous edifice houses the Ministry of Agriculture, and as such is frequently the target of protests by Spanish farmers and olive oil producers.

The elaborate but daunting face of Spain's Ministerio de Agricultura

The building itself is adorned with sculptures, friezes and painted tiles and brings together elements of both Neo-Classical and Romantic styles. It was constructed between 1884 and 1886 by Ricardo Velázquez Bosco, architect of the Palacio de Velázquez in the Parque del Retiro *(see p77)*. The artist Ignacio Zuloaga was later involved in its design.

Gigantic Corinthian columns line the exterior walls, with areas of coloured bricks and decorative glazed tiles enhancing the spaces between them. The pediment above the columns is decorated with the Spanish coat of arms. Crowning the building are allegorical sculptures created by Agustín Querol. The three central figures represent Glory personified bestowing laurels on Science and Art. On either side are statues of Pegasus. These were originally made of marble, but were replaced by bronze replicas when the stone deteriorated.

Observatorio Astronómico

Calle de Alfonso XII 3. **Map** 8 E5. **C** *91 527 01 07.* **M** *Atocha.* **O** *10am–2pm Mon–Fri.* **O** *public hols & some areas closed for renovation until mid-2006.* **C** *by appointment (fax 91 527 19 35).* **W** *www.oan.es*

WHEN THIS BUILDING opened in 1790, it was one of only four observatories in Europe. It was designed by Juan de Villanueva along Neo-Classical lines. The vertical slit window was used for telescopes, and the colonnaded roof cupola for weather observation.

There is one room open to the public where 18th- and 19th-century telescopes, as well as a Foucault pendulum, are on display. Apply in writing to view the larger telescopes, a collection of English clocks and to peer through a telescope made in 1790 by Sir Frederick William Herschel, the astronomer who discovered Uranus. These visits only take place once a month at night, weather permitting.

Colonnaded roof cupola of the Observatorio Astronómico

Museo Nacional de Antropología

Calle de Alfonso XII 68. **Map** 8 D5. **C** *91 539 59 95.* **M** *Atocha.* **O** *10am–7:30pm Tue–Sat, 10am–2pm Sun.* **O** *public hols.* **W** *(free Sat pm & Sun).* **W** *book 15 days in advance.* **W** *www.mcu.es/nmuseos/antropologia*

PREVIOUSLY KNOWN AS the Museo Nacional de Etnología, this three-floor museum, which is built around a grand open hall, was inaugurated by Alfonso XII *(see p21)* in 1875.

Through the displays, the anthropology and ethnology of geographical groups of people are studied. The ground floor houses an important collection from the Philippines. Originally shown in 1887 in the Palacio de Velázquez *(see p77)*, the centrepiece is a 10 m- (33 ft-) long dug-out canoe made from a single tree trunk. There are also some gruesome exhibits, such as deformed skulls from Peru and the Philippines, the mummy of a Guanche from Tenerife and the skeleton of Don Agustín Luengo y Capilla, a late 19th-century giant from Extremadura. He was 2.35 m (7 ft 4 in) tall and died aged 26.

The first floor is dedicated to Africa. As well as clothing, weapons, ceramics and utensils, there is a reproduction of a Bubi ritual hut from Equatorial Guinea, in which tribal members met the *boeloelo* (witch doctor). On the second floor is the American section, with exhibits on the lifestyles of indigenous groups.

Estación de Atocha ③⓪

Plaza del Emperador Carlos V. **Map** 8 D5. 90 224 02 02. Atocha RENFE. 5:30am–midnight daily.

MADRID'S FIRST rail service, from Atocha to Aranjuez, was inaugurated in 1851 by Isabel II (*see p21*). Forty years later, the original station at Atocha was replaced by the present one. The older part of the station was one of the first large-scale constructions in Madrid to be built from glass and wrought iron. Now, it houses an extraordinary indoor palm garden for travellers to

Entrance of Madrid's **Estación de Atocha, busy with travellers**

enjoy. Adjoining it is the modern AVE terminus, providing high-speed train links to Seville, Córdoba, Zaragoza and Lleida, extending to Barcelona and France by 2006 (*see p196*).

Palacio de Fernán Núñez ③①

Calle de Santa Isabel 44. **Map** 7 B4. 91 527 18 12. Atocha. to the public.

ALSO KNOWN AS the Palacio de Cervellón, this building has a plain façade that gives scant indication of the riches within. Built for the Duke and Duchess of Fernán Núñez in 1847, the palace served as the

family home until 1936. It was requisitioned by the Republican militia at the start of the Civil War (*see p18*); the lower part served as a bomb shelter while the upper floor was occupied by a Socialist Youth organization. Amazingly, when the palace was returned to the duke's family, they found that none of its treasures had been damaged or stolen.

In 1941, the palace was sold and became the headquarters of the Spanish State Railway. It now houses the Foundation of Spanish Railways, which organizes exhibitions here.

That the palace was built in two phases is clear. The large, restrained rooms in the first section contrast sharply with the Rococo flourishes of the second. The older section has some interesting carpets from the Real Fábrica de Tapices (*see p112*), as well as antique furniture, clocks and copies of paintings by Goya (*see p26*). Attention, however, is inevitably drawn to the lavish gold-plated ornamentation of the later section, especially the ballroom with its mirrors, chandeliers and cherubs playing musical instruments. Rooms in this part are often used for official receptions.

Near the palace is the cloistered Convento Santa Isabel with its octagonal dome. It was founded in 1595 by Felipe II.

The sumptuously decorated ballroom of the Palacio de Fernán Núñez

Centro de Arte Reina Sofía ㉜

THE HIGHLIGHT of this museum of 20th-century art is Picasso's *Guernica*. However, there are also other major works by influential artists, including Miró. The collection is housed in Madrid's former General Hospital, built in the late 18th century. Major extensions to the museum, designed by Jean Nouvel, are due to be completed in 2004, allowing the permanent collection to extend to the first and third floors. The new glass buildings include 2 temporary exhibition rooms, a library, café and art shops.

Portrait II *(1938)*
Joan Miró's huge work shows element of Surrealism, but was painted more than ten years after his true Surrealist period ended.

New extension

★ Woman in Blue *(1901)*
Picasso disowned this work after it won only an honourable mention in a national competition. Decades later it was located and acquired by the Spanish state.

Landscape at Cadaqués
Salvador Dalí was born in Figueres in Catalonia. He became a frequent visitor to the town of Cadaqués, on the Costa Brava, where he painted this landscape in the summer of 1923.

Accident
Alfonso Ponce de León's disturbing work, painted in 1936, prefigured his death in a car crash later that same year.

STAR EXHIBITS

- **★ Woman in Blue by Picasso**

- **★ La Tertulia del Café de Pombo by Solana**

- **★ Guernica by Picasso**

★ **La Tertulia del Café de Pombo** *(1920)*
José Gutiérrez Solana depicts a gathering of intellectuals (tertulia) *in a famous café in Madrid, which no longer exists.*

**Toki-Egin
(Homenaje a San Juan de la Cruz)** *(1952)*
In his abstract sculptures, Eduardo Chillida used a variety of materials, such as wood, iron and steel, to convey strength.

Glass elevator

Entrance

VISITORS' CHECKLIST

Calle Santa Isabel 52. **Map** 7 C5.
📞 91 467 50 62. Ⓜ *Atocha.*
🚌 *6, 14, 18, 19, 27, 45, 55, 68.*
🕙 *10am–9pm Mon & Wed–Sat, 10am–2:30pm Sun.* ⚫ *1 Jan, 24, 25, 31 Dec & some public hols.* 💰 *(free Sat pm & Sun).* 🚫 ♿ 🎁 ⛔ 🍴
W *www.museoreinasofia.mcu.es*

GALLERY GUIDE

The permanent collection is on the second, third and fourth floors, arranged around an open courtyard. It traces art chronologically through the 20th century, starting on the second floor. The third floor displays works from mid-1930s to 1960s and the fourth floor continues through to present day works. Individual rooms are allocated to significant artists such as Dalí, Miró and Picasso. Two temporary exhibition rooms are located in a new, adjoining building.

KEY TO FLOORPLAN

☐ Exhibition space
▨ Non-exhibition space

Visitors admiring *Guernica*

★ GUERNICA BY PICASSO

The most famous single work of the 20th century, this Civil War protest painting was commissioned by the Spanish Republican government in 1937 for a Paris exhibition. The artist found his inspiration in the mass air attack of the same year on the Basque town of Gernika-Lumo, by German pilots flying for the Nationalist air force. The painting hung in a New York gallery until 1981, reflecting the artist's wish that it should not return to Spain until democracy was re-established. It was moved here from the Museo del Prado in 1992.

Exploring the Centro de Arte Reina Sofía

THE 20TH CENTURY has undoubtedly been the most brilliant period in the history of Spanish art since the Golden Age of the 17th century. Many facets of the Spanish artistic genius are on show in the Centro de Arte Reina Sofía. Sculpture, paintings and even work by the Surrealist filmaker Luis Buñuel provide a skilfully arranged tour through an eventful century. Please note that the location of the artworks referred to below is changing as a result of the extensive refurbishment that has made it possible to extend the permanent collection.

Guitar in Front of the Sea by Juan Gris (1925)

THE BEGINNINGS OF MODERN SPANISH ART

FOLLOWING THE STORM of creativity that culminated with Goya in the 19th century, Spanish painting went through an unremarkable period. A few artists, such as Sorolla, managed to break the mould, hinting at the dawn of a new era of artistic brilliance. An emerging middle class, particularly in places like the Basque country and Barcelona, gave rise to a generation of innovative artists who constitute the introduction to this collection, including Zuloaga, Anglada-Camarasa and Nonell. Here also are paintings by María Blanchard, one of the few women represented in the collection and a close friend of the Cubist artist, Juan Gris. Continuing round, you'll find the brooding, dark-coloured works of Gutiérrez Solana, whose favourite subjects are the *fiestas* and the people of his native Madrid. Influenced by the Spanish masters, especially Goya, his paintings include *La Tertulia del Café de Pombo* (1920) and the menacing *La Procesión de la Muerte* (1930).

There are also works by Blanchard, Delaunay and Lipchitz. Hinting at Cubism, they make a good introduction to the work of Juan Gris. Trained as a graphic designer, Gris moved to Paris in 1906 where, under the influence of Picasso, he produced *Portrait*

The Great Prophet by Pablo Gargallo (1933)

of *Josette* (1916) and *Guitar in Front of the Sea* (1925). Also displayed are works in forged iron by Zaragoza-born sculptor Pablo Gargallo. His *Masque de Greta Garbo à la Meche* (1930), inspired by the actress, consists of delicate curves of iron hanging in space. Look out too for his slightly later work, *The Great Prophet* (1933).

PABLO PICASSO

THE WORKS on display span five decades in the life of Pablo Picasso. Born in the Andalusian city of Málaga, Picasso embraced a wide variety of styles in the course of his long career, including Realism, Cubism and Surrealism. He defied classification, creating some of the most important works of art of the 20th century. The first image the visitor notices is the haunting *Woman in Blue* (1901), one of Picasso's earliest

works dating from his so-called "blue" period. Dominating the area is the most-visited piece in the collection – the vast *Guernica* (1937). Aside from its unquestionable artistic merits, the canvas has a deep historical significance for Spaniards, recalling one of the most harrowing episodes of the Spanish Civil War *(see p18)*. The painting is complemented by a series of sketches and preliminary studies completed in the week following the bombing of the Basque town of Gernika-Lumo.

It is interesting to see many of the symbols Picasso chose for *Guernica* appearing in his earlier work, the *Minotauromaquia* (1935). This painting is of the fearsome Minotaur of Greek legend – a bull-headed devourer of human flesh.

JULIO GONZÁLEZ

A FRIEND and contemporary of Gargallo and Picasso, Julio González is known as the father of modern Spanish sculpture, chiefly because of

Minotauromaquia by Pablo Picasso (1935)

his pioneering use of iron as a raw material. Born in Barcelona, González began his career as a welder, learning to forge, cut, solder and bend the iron which had hitherto been considered an entirely industrial material. In the 1920s and 1930s he worked alongside Picasso and Gargallo in Paris, producing many three-dimensional pieces in the Cubist style. Look out for González' humorous self-portrait entitled *Tête dite "Lapin"* or *Head called "Rabbit"* (1930). In his work, you can also see many sketches that relate to the sculptures.

Girl at the Window by Salvador Dalí (1925)

MIRÓ, DALÍ AND THE SURREALISTS

JUAN MIRÓ turned his hand to many styles. His Surrealist experiments of the 1920s provide evidence of his love of the vivid colours and bold shapes of Catalan folk art. Similar elements remain in later pieces, such as *Portrait II* (1938).

His fellow Catalan, Salvador Dalí, is especially well known as a member of the Surrealist movement – the style of art inspired by the work of Sigmund Freud, which depended on access to subconscious images without censorship by the rational mind. Other prominent Surrealists whose work is displayed here are Benjamín Palencia (*Bulls*, 1933), Oscar Domínguez and Luis Buñuel.

Dalí's Surrealist masterpiece, *The Great Masturbator* (1929) hangs in contrast to the realistic portrait, *Girl at the Window* (1925). Like many of his contemporaries, Dalí embraced widely differing styles of working in the course of his career. *The Great Masturbator* was painted after he visited Paris, and came into contact with the French Surrealists. His work starts to reflect all the unfettered obses-

sions and fetishes that haunted this eccentric artist. Another product of this period are the films of Luis Buñuel whose 17 minute *Un Chien Andalou* (1929), in collaboration with Dalí, made a deep impression on the Surrealist movement.

Bulls by Benjamín Palencia (1933)

THE PARIS SCHOOL

THE TURBULENT HISTORY of Spain in the 20th century *(see pp18–19)* has resulted in a steady stream of talented Spanish artists leaving their native land. Many of them, including Picasso, Dalí, Juan Gris and Miró, passed through Paris, some staying for a few months, others staying for years. Artists of other nationalities also congregated in the French capital, mainly from Eastern Europe, Germany and the United States, including the German abstract painter Hans Hartung and the Russian Nicholas de Staël. All of these artists were part of the Paris

School and it is possible to see the mutual influence of this closely-knit, yet constantly evolving group of young artists. On display are works by a wide range of less well-known Paris School painters, including Daniel Vázquez Díaz and Francisco Bores

FRANCO AND BEYOND

THE CIVIL WAR (1936–9) had an enormous effect on the development of Spanish art. Under Franco, the state enforced rigid censorship; artists worked in an environment where communication with the outside world was sporadic, and where their work did not benefit from official approval. They sought mutual support in groups such as El Paso and Grupo 57, whose members included Antonio Saura, Manuel Millares and Eduardo Chillida. Painting mainly in black and white, Saura used religious imagery, such as the twisted crucifix in *Scream No.7* (1959). Chillida's work includes the use of forged iron.

The best-known member was Antoni Tàpies. Concerned with texture, he used a variety of materials, including oil paint mixed with crushed marble, to explore the magical qualities of everyday objects.

Later works by the Equipo Crónica, Luis Gordillo and Eduardo Arroyo – such as *It's The Talk of the Town* (1982) – illustrate the transitional period that started even before the dictator's death in 1975 and culminated with the restoration of democracy in Spain.

It's The Talk of The Town by Eduardo Arroyo (1982)

AROUND LA CASTELLANA

THE AXIS of modern Madrid is the tree-lined Paseo de la Castellana, a long, grand boulevard. A journey along it gives a glimpse of Madrid as Spain's commercial and administrative capital. The main north-south artery, it was first developed in the 19th century by the city's aristocracy with a string of summer palaces from Plaza de Colón northwards. The Museo Lázaro Galdiano, one of Madrid's best art museums, is housed in the former mansion of the financier José Lázaro Galdiano. To the east, La Castellana skirts the Barrio de Salamanca, an up-market district of stylish boutiques and apartment blocks named after the 19th-century aristocrat who built it. To the southwest are Chueca and Malasaña, neighbourhoods offering a more authentic *Madrileño* atmosphere. The southern section of the boulevard is called Paseo de Recoletos. Nearby are the Museo Arqueológico Nacional, founded by Isabel II in 1867, and Café Gijón, an intellectuals' café founded in the early 20th century.

Façade detail, Iglesia de Santa Bárbara

SIGHTS AT A GLANCE

Museums and Galleries
Fundación Juan March 11
Museo Arqueológico Nacional pp96–7 8
Museo de Cera 6
Museo de Escultura al Aire Libre 14
Museo Lázaro Galdiano pp100–101 12
Museo Municipal 16
Museo Romántico 15
Museo Sorolla 13

Churches
Iglesia de Santa Bárbara 4

Streets, Squares, Parks and Districts
Calle de Serrano 9
Calle del Almirante 2
Malasaña 17
Plaza de Chueca 3
Plaza de Colón 7
Salamanca 10

Historic Buildings
Café Gijón 1
Cuartel del Conde Duque 18
Palacio de Liria 19
Tribunal Supremo 5

GETTING THERE

The metro is the easiest way to get to and around this area. Lines 1, 4, 5, 6, 8, 9 and 10 serve the main sights. Useful buses include routes 27, which runs the length of La Castellana, and 5, 7, 12, 13, 40, 45 and 150. The Airport bus terminal lies beneath Plaza de Colón.

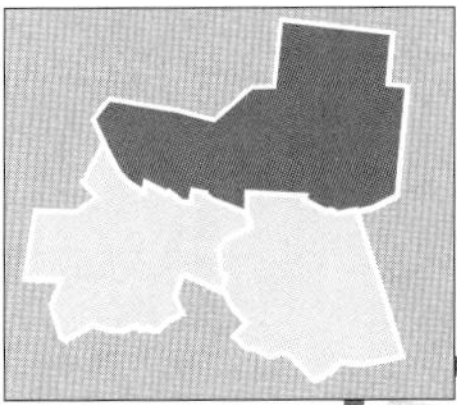

KEY

Street-by-Street map *pp92–3*

Metro station

Main bus stop

Parking

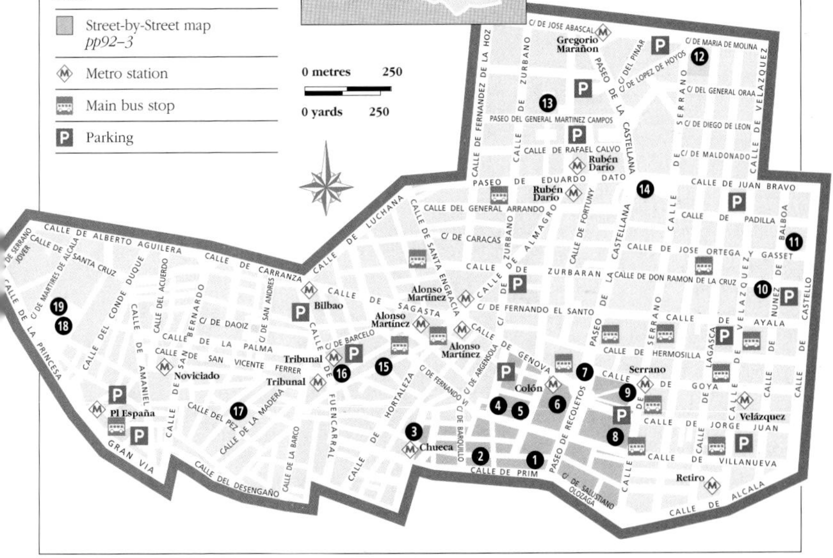

◁ **One of four enormous concrete sculptures at the Plaza de Colón**

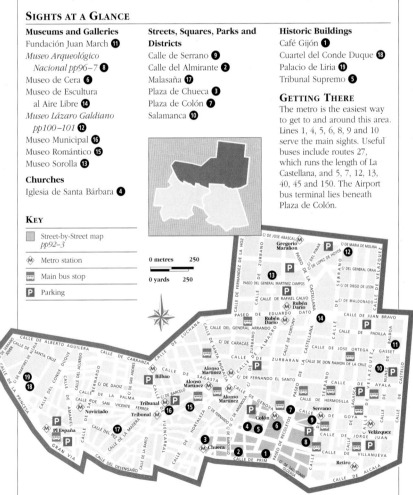

Street by Street: Paseo de Recoletos

Plaza de Colón is bordered by the fashionable designer shopping streets Calle de Serrano and Calle de Goya, the Museo Arqueológico Nacional, the Biblioteca Nacional (National Library) and Paseo de Recoletos, which is home to the classic Café Gijón. Between Calle del Almirante, another popular fashion street, and Calle de Génova is the Tribunal Supremo and the Iglesia de Santa Bárbara. Towards the Gran Vía are the narrow streets of Chueca with some interesting old taverns and eclectic bistros.

Iglesia de Santa Bárbara
Both Bárbara de Braganza and her husband, Fernando VI (see p21), are entombed in this fine Baroque church ❹

Tribunal Supremo
Spain's supreme court of law is located in the former convent and school of the adjoining Iglesia de Santa Bárbara ❺

Calle de Barquillo
contains the best shops in the city for stereo equipment, mobile phones and other electronic goods.

| 0 metres | 100 |
| 0 yards | 100 |

CALLE SAN LUCAS

CALLE BARBARA DE

CALLE LUIS DE GONGORA

CALLE CONDE DE XIQUENA

PLAZA DE CHUECA

CALLE DE LA LIBERTAD

CALLE DEL BARQUILLO

CALLE DEL ALMIRANTE

CALLE DE PRIM

CALLE AUGUSTO FIGUEROA

Star Sights

★ **Museo Arqueológico Nacional**

★ **Plaza de Colón**

Plaza de Chueca
The immaculate, exquisitely decorated Bodega de Angel Sierra bar in the Plaza de Chueca has hardly changed since it was built in 1897 ❸

Calle del Almirante
Originally a street of basket shops, Calle del Almirante now boasts several of the city's own-label fashion shops ❷

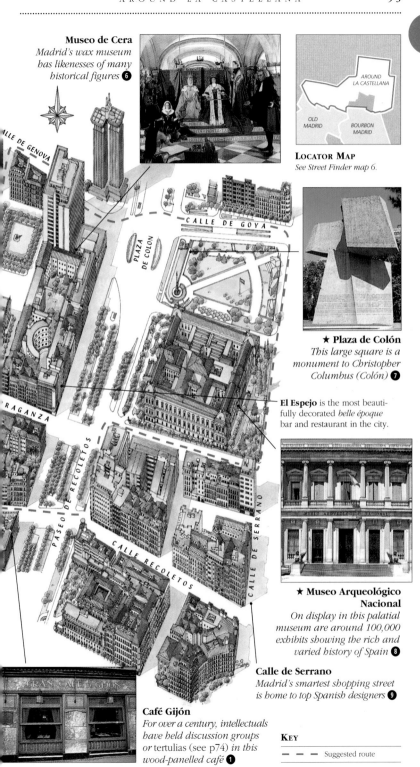

Museo de Cera
Madrid's wax museum has likenesses of many historical figures 6

LOCATOR MAP
See Street Finder map 6.

★ **Plaza de Colón**
This large square is a monument to Christopher Columbus (Colón) 7

El Espejo is the most beautifully decorated *belle époque* bar and restaurant in the city.

★ **Museo Arqueológico Nacional**
On display in this palatial museum are around 100,000 exhibits showing the rich and varied history of Spain 8

Calle de Serrano
Madrid's smartest shopping street is home to top Spanish designers 9

Café Gijón
For over a century, intellectuals have held discussion groups or tertulias *(see p74) in this wood-panelled café* 1

KEY
– – – Suggested route

Café Gijón ❶

Paseo de Recoletos 21. **Map** 5 C5.
📞 91 521 54 25. 🚇 *Banco de España.* ⏰ *7:30 am–1:30am Sun–Fri, 8am–2am Sat & public hols.* ♿

MADRID'S CAFÉ LIFE was one of the most attractive features of the city from the turn of the 20th century, right up to the outbreak of the Civil War. Many intellectuals' cafés once thrived (*see p74*), but the Gijón is one of the few that survives. It still attracts a lively crowd of *literati*. Although it is better known for its atmosphere than its appearance, the café has a striking interior with cream-painted wrought-iron columns and black and white table tops.

Interior of the literary Café Gijón

Calle del Almirante ❷

Map 5 C5. 🚇 *Banco de España, Colón & Chueca.*

RUNNING BETWEEN the Paseo de Recoletos and Calle Barquillo, this street is famous for its dozen own-label fashion shops. For most of the 20th century it was known as "Calle de Cesterías" (basketwork street). Now the only cane shop left is that of Antonio del Pozo, founded in 1891.

In earlier days there were five cane shops, where baskets, chairs and other woven wares were sold. There were also several taverns where neighbours gathered to pass the time. Such was the fame of the street that the wives of both Winston Churchill and the Shah of Persia visited the del Pozo cane shop.

During the transition to democracy following Franco's death in 1975, Calle del Almirante gained a certain notoriety. Fewer police patrolled the area, and street crime rose. Two gay bars opened in the street and male prostitutes touted openly for business.

During this time Jesús del Pozo – Antonio's brother and a fashion designer – opened the first boutique selling clothes of his own design next to the family cane shop. However, it was not until the 1980s, with the cultural movement of *La Movida* (*see p104*), that the area became fashionable and other clothes shops opened, along with a number of chic furnishings and decor outlets. Now the street is referred to as "Calle de la Moda" (fashion street), and is a favourite haunt of the wealthy and business people from neighbouring offices.

Jesús del Pozo has become famous, and his showrooms on the first floor at No. 9 Calle del Almirante sell outfits for society weddings and events. However, the street also retains other original shops and cafés. Manolo Huerta's family have run the *panadería* (bakery) since 1910 and the Cafetería Almirante, which serves *bocatas* (sandwiches) for those in a hurry, has been run by Juan Encinas since 1972.

At No. 23 is the fascinating Regalos Originales, a must-see for browsers of antiques and old curiosity shops.

View along the fashionable Calle del Almirante

Newsstand in the Plaza de Chueca

Plaza de Chueca ❸

Map 5 B5. 🚇 *Chueca.*

THE PLAZA DE CHUECA is situated between Calle Augusto Figueroa and Calle Gravina. The square was originally called Plaza de San Gregorio after a statue of the saint that stood in Calle San Gregorio, at the main gate to the manor house of the Marqueses of Minaya. In 1943 the square was renamed after Federico Chueca (1846–1908), a composer of *zarzuelas* (*see p75*). His works include *Agua, Azucarillos and Aguardiente* and *La Gran Vía*.

Lining the plaza are small shops, bars and apartment buildings. On one side of the square is the Bodega de Angel Sierra (*see p92*), a *taberna* full of character that was founded in 1897. On the outside there are Andalusian-style tiles advertising vermouth, beers and wines, while inside there is a bar adorned with finely polished faucets (taps).

The neighbourhood around the plaza is an intricate maze of little streets. Also called Chueca, by night it is the main focus of Madrid's gay community, with a good selection of modish bars and chic restaurants.

Iglesia de Santa Bárbara

Calle General Castaños 2. **Map** 5 C5.
C 91 319 48 11. **M** *Alonso Martínez,
Colón.* ☐ *9am–1pm, 5–9pm
Mon–Sat, 10am–12:30pm, 5–8:30pm
Sun & public hols.*

No EXPENSE WAS SPARED on
this fine Baroque church,
which was built, along with an
adjoining convent (now the
Tribunal Supremo), for Bárbara
de Braganza, wife of Fernando
VI. To run the convent, which
was to include a school for
daughters of the nobility,
Bárbara chose Las Salesas
Reales – an order of nuns
founded in 1610 by St Francis
de Sales and St Jane Frances
de Chantal in Annecy, France.
The church is sometimes referred to as Las Salesas Reales.

François Carlier (1707–60),
whose father worked on the
gardens of La Granja de San
Ildefonso *(see p127)*, was
appointed architect. The first
stone was laid in 1750 and, in
1757, the huge edifice was finished by builder Francisco de
Moradillo. He added towers
on the roof to Carlier's plans.

The main door is reached
through pleasant gardens,
added in 1930. The central
medallion on the façade, by
Doménico Olivieri, shows
The Visitation of the pregnant
Virgin to her cousin Elizabeth.
The angels on either side hold
the Cross and the two tablets
of the Ten Commandments.

The extravagant interior
decoration was assigned to
Doménico Olivieri. To the
right of the entrance is a
painting of St Francis de Sales
and St Jane de Chantal by
Corrado Giaquinto. Opposite
is *La Sagrada Familia* (The
Holy Family), painted by
Francesco Cignaroni.

To the right of the central
aisle is the tomb of Fernando
VI, adorned with tiers of angels
crafted by Francisco Gutiérrez
to a Neo-Classical design by
Francesco Sabatini. Above the
nearby altar is a painting of
Francisco Javier and Santa
Bárbara. It is by Francesca de
Mora, as is *La Visitación* above
the high altar. The high altar
is decorated with sculptures
of San Fernando and Santa

Elaborately decorated interior of the Iglesia de Santa Bárbara

Bárbara. To the left is the
19th-century tomb of General
O'Donnell by sculptor Jerónimo Suñol. Alongside it is the
Surrender of Seville by the
French artist Charles Joseph
Flipart. The tomb of Bárbara
de Braganza is to the right of
the altar in a separate chapel.

Tribunal Supremo ❺

Plaza de la Villa de Paris. **Map** 5 C5.
C 91 397 12 00. **M** *Alonso
Martínez, Colón.* ☐ *by appointment
in writing (Gabinete Técnico, Plaza de
la Villa de Paris, Madrid 28071; fax 91
319 47 20).*

Built BY FRANÇOIS CARLIER in
the 1750s as a convent and
school for the adjoining Iglesia
de Santa Bárbara, this stately
Baroque building was run by
the Las Salesas Reales nuns. It
was built on the orders of
Bárbara de Braganza, wife of
Fernando VI. After her death,
the nuns were allowed to
remain in the convent until
1870, when the building was
expropriated by the secular
government to become the
Palace of Justice. The building
fell into disrepair, which was
made worse by fires in 1907

and 1915. Fortunately, the
Iglesia de Santa Bárbara was
unaffected. Later restoration
work was undertaken by
Joaquin Rojí in 1991–5. In the
1990s, the building became
the country's supreme court.

In front of the palace is the
Plaza de la Villa de Paris, a
large French-style square. In
the middle of it are statues of
Fernando VI and Bárbara de
Braganza. Across the square
is the Audiencía Nacional
(National Court). The surrounding roads are often lined with
official cars and reporters.

**Statue of Bárbara de Braganza in
the Plaza de la Villa de Paris**

Museo Arqueológico Nacional ⑧

A bison, one of the wall paintings in the replica of the Altamira cave

WITH HUNDREDS OF EXHIBITS, ranging from prehistoric times to the 19th century, this palatial museum is one of Madrid's best. It was founded by Isabel II in 1867 and contains many items uncovered during excavations all over Spain, as well as pieces from Egypt, ancient Greece and the Etruscan civilization. Highlights include items from the ancient civilization of El Argar in Andalusia, 7th-century gold votive crowns from Toledo province, Roman mosaics and Islamic pottery. Steps outside the entrance lead underground to an exact replica of the Altamira cave in Cantabria, northern Spain. The walls are covered with copies of superb superior Paleolithic paintings.

Basement

★ Visigothic Crown

This 7th-century gold crown with pearls, sapphires and garnets was found at Guarrazar, Toledo. Letters spelling "RECCESVINTHVS REX OFFERET" hang from it, indicating it was a church offering from Visigoth King Recesvinto.

Moorish Arch

Constructed from plaster, this 11th-century arch was more decorative than functional. It formed part of the Palacio de Aljafería in Zaragoza (north central Spain).

STAR SIGHTS

★ **Visigothic Crown**

★ **Roman Mosaic**

★ **Dama de Baza**

Medieval religious paintings and icons

Carved Ivory Crucifix

Belonging to King Fernando I and Queen Sancha, this small Latin crucifix was made in 1063 and donated to the church of San Isidoro in León on its dedication. At the back is a recess for a relic of the True Cross.

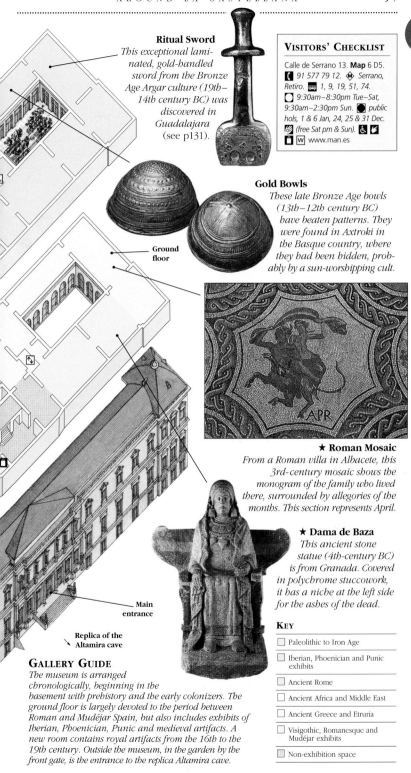

Ritual Sword
This exceptional laminated, gold-handled sword from the Bronze Age Argar culture (19th–14th century BC) was discovered in Guadalajara (see p131).

VISITORS' CHECKLIST

Calle de Serrano 13. **Map** 6 D5.
91 577 79 12. Serrano, Retiro. 1, 9, 19, 51, 74.
9:30am–8:30pm Tue–Sat, 9:30am–2:30pm Sun. public hols, 1 & 6 Jan, 24, 25 & 31 Dec. (free Sat pm & Sun).
W www.man.es

Gold Bowls
These late Bronze Age bowls (13th–12th century BC) have beaten patterns. They were found in Axtroki in the Basque country, where they had been hidden, probably by a sun-worshipping cult.

Ground floor

★ Roman Mosaic
From a Roman villa in Albacete, this 3rd-century mosaic shows the monogram of the family who lived there, surrounded by allegories of the months. This section represents April.

★ Dama de Baza
This ancient stone statue (4th-century BC) is from Granada. Covered in polychrome stuccowork, it has a niche at the left side for the ashes of the dead.

Main entrance

Replica of the Altamira cave

KEY

- ☐ Paleolithic to Iron Age
- ☐ Iberian, Phoenician and Punic exhibits
- ☐ Ancient Rome
- ☐ Ancient Africa and Middle East
- ☐ Ancient Greece and Etruria
- ☐ Visigothic, Romanesque and Mudéjar exhibits
- ☐ Non-exhibition space

GALLERY GUIDE
The museum is arranged chronologically, beginning in the basement with prehistory and the early colonizers. The ground floor is largely devoted to the period between Roman and Mudéjar Spain, but also includes exhibits of Iberian, Phoenician, Punic and medieval artifacts. A new room contains royal artifacts from the 16th to the 19th century. Outside the museum, in the garden by the front gate, is the entrance to the replica Altamira cave.

Museo de Cera ❻

Paseo de Recoletos 41. **Map** 6 D5.
☎ 91 319 26 49. Ⓜ *Colón.*
🕐 *10am–2pm, 4–8pm Mon– Fri,
10am–8pm Sat–Sun & public hols.*
Ⓦ www.museoceramadrid.com

Madrid's wax museum, off Plaza de Colón, houses some 450 wax dummies of well known Spanish and inter-national figures, mostly set in scenes. A wax likeness of Miguel de Cervantes, author of *Don Quixote*, sits at his desk writing, with windmills behind him. Another scene imitates Goya's famous paint-ing, *The 3rd of May*, depicting French reprisals for the rebel-lions of 2 May 1808 in Madrid *(see p16)*. Also shown is Chris-topher Columbus' return from the New World. Other scenes show navigators and scientists, the Last Supper and the history of the Spanish colonies.

More recent figures include cowboys from the Wild West, pop stars, Hollywood actors, athletes and the Pope. There is also a café scene where visitors to the museum are encouraged to try to identify Spanish intellectuals, past and present. Those with children should bear in mind that some of the scenes are quite ghoulish. Particularly gruesome is a bullfighting scene with a horn piercing a matador's eye.

Upstairs is *Multivision*, a cin-ema where 27 projectors are used simultaneously to show a 60-minute history of Spain.

Wax figure of Miguel de Cervantes in the Museo de Cera

Modern monument to Christopher Columbus, Plaza de Colón

Plaza de Colón ❼

Map 6 D5. Ⓜ *Serrano, Colón.*

This large square, one of Madrid's focal points, is dedicated to Christopher Columbus (Colón in Spanish). It is overlooked by 1970s' high-rise buildings, which replaced the 19th-century mansions that once stood here. On the south side is a palace housing the National Library and Archeological Museum *(see pp96–7)*. On the north side, on the corner of La Castellana, the Post-Modernist skyscraper of the Heron Corporation towers over the square.

The real feature of the square, however, is the pair of monuments dedi-cated to the discoverer of the Americas. The oldest, and prettiest, is a Neo-Gothic spire built in 1885, with Columbus at its top, pointing west. Carved reliefs on the plinth give highlights of his discoveries. Across the square is the second, more modern monument – a cluster of four large concrete shapes inscribed with quotations relating to Columbus' historic journey to America.

Constantly busy with the flow of traffic, the plaza may seem an unlikely venue for cultural events. Beneath it,

**Statue of
Columbus, Plaza
de Colón**

however, is an extensive com-plex, the Centro Cultural de la Villa de Madrid, which includes the city's municipal art centre, exhibition halls, lecture rooms, a theatre and a café. The terminal for the bus which runs to and from the airport *(see p192)* is also located underground.

Museo Arqueológico Nacional ❽

See pages 96–7.

Calle de Serrano ❾

Map 8 D1. Ⓜ *Serrano.*

Named after a 19th-century politician, Madrid's smart-est shopping street runs north from the triumphal Plaza de la Independencia to the Plaza del Ecuador, in the well-heeled district of Salamanca. The street is lined with shops *(see p164)* – many specializing in luxury items – housed in old-fashioned mansion-blocks. Several of Spain's top designers, including Adolfo Domínguez and Roberto Verino, have boutiques in the middle of the street. Towards the northern end are the ABC Serrano mall *(see p165)* and the Museo Lázaro Galdiano *(see pp100–101)*. A wide selection of luxury goods shops can be found on Calle de José Ortega y Gasset, including branches of the Italian shops Versace, Armani and Gucci, as well as Chanel, Calvin Klein and Escada. Lower down Calle de Serrano, towards Serrano metro station, are two branches of El Corte Inglés and the stylish clothes and leather goods shop Loewe. On the Calle de Claudio Coello, which runs parallel with Serrano, there are several lavish antique shops, in keeping with the area's up-market atmosphere.

Statue of Salamanca's founder, the Marqués de Salamanca

Salamanca ⑩

Map 6 E3. Velázquez, Serrano, Núñez de Balboa, Lista, Príncipe de Vergara, Goya, Diego de León.

MADRID'S SALAMANCA district (Barrio de Salamanca) was developed in 1862–3 as an area for the bourgeoisie, and takes its name from its founder, José "Pepito" Salamanca, Marqués de Salamanca (1811–83). He was a lawyer who, by the age of 23, had already been elected as a deputy to the Cortes (Spanish parliament). The Marqués had a great flair for politics and business, and made his vast fortune from salt, railways and the building of Salamanca. He was also the founder of Banco de Isabel II, which was the forerunner of Banco de España *(see p67)*.

The Marqués inaugurated his magnificent palace at Paseo de Recoletos 10, (now the Banco Hipotecario) in 1858, and by 1862 began developing his land behind it. The streets were planned to run north-south or east-west, and the area was to comprise apartment blocks, churches, schools, hospitals and theatres. He also built the first tramways in Madrid, connecting the Barrio de Salamanca with the centre of Madrid. A statue of the Marqués stands at the confluence of Ortega y Gasset and Príncipe de Vergara.

To this day the *barrio* consists mainly of six- to eight-floor apartment blocks, and is home to many well-to-do families. This is an area where just a hint of cool weather brings out the mink coats. Some of Madrid's best shops and markets can be found here, as well as a number of discreet restaurants. The *pijos* (rich spoilt children) gather at the *cervecerías* and bars around Calle de Goya and Calle de Alcalá.

The oldest church of the *barrio*, San Andrés de los Flamencos (Calle de Claudio Coello 99), built in 1884, now houses the Fundación Carlos de Amberes, a cultural centre maintaining links between Spain, Holland and Belgium. Behind the altar is a painting of St Andrew by Rubens. The unofficial parish church of Salamanca is the Iglesia de la Concepción (Calle de Goya 26), built between 1902 and 1914, with a notable white iron spire topped by a statue of the Virgin. At Calle de Hermosilla 45 is the charming Protestant Church of St George (1926).

The best preserved of the area's Neo-Classical palaces is Palacio de Amboage (1918) by Joaquín Roji on the corner of Velázquez and Juan Bravo. It is now the Italian Embassy, and features a lovely garden.

Modern and fascinating is the architecture inside Teatriz, an avant-garde restaurant at Calle de Hermosilla 15, designed by Philippe Starck. Diners sit in the auditorium of a former theatre and cinema, while on the stage is a back-lit onyx bar and steel stools, all reflected in a gigantic mirror.

Sculpture by Chillida, Fundación Juan March

Fundación Juan March ⑪

Calle de Castelló 77. **91 435 42 40.** Núñez de Balboa. 11am–8pm, Mon–Sat, 10am–2pm Sun & public hols. W www.march.es

ESTABLISHED IN 1955 with an endowment from financier Juan March, this cultural and scientific foundation is best known for its art exhibitions and concerts. The marble-and-glass headquarters, in Madrid's Barrio de Salamanca, opened in 1975. The foundation has published over 380 books and collections. It also owns the Museo de Arte Abstracto in Cuenca and a gallery of modern Spanish art in Palma de Mallorca. The ground floor houses a shop, as well as the main exhibition area. Works by Kandinsky, Picasso and Matisse have been shown here, alongside a permanent collection made up of over 1,300 contemporary Spanish artworks. There is a 400-seat auditorium in the basement where free concerts are held. The second-floor library has a collection of contemporary Spanish music, with listening desks. There is also a library on contemporary Spanish theatre and entertainment.

Hidden away from the public are the Juan March Institute for Study and Investigation – one of the world's top forums in the field of biology – and the Centre for Advanced Study in the Social Sciences.

Sculpture by Barrocol, by the main entrance to the Fundación Juan March

Museo Lázaro Galdiano ⓬

Second floor

THIS NEO-RENAISSANCE MANSION houses nearly 5,000 items from the private collection of financier and editor José Lázaro Galdiano (1862–1947). The exhibits, ranging from the 7th century BC to the 20th century, include archeological finds, religious artifacts, Limoges enamels, Old Masters, medieval ivory, armour, jewellery and silver. In 1903 Galdiano married Argentine heiress Paula Florido and they built the mansion to celebrate – and to show off the growing collection. By the time Galdiano died, some 15,000 items were brought together in Madrid.

Portrait of a Lady
Joshua Reynolds painted this portrait in the late 18th century. Other British artists represented in the museum include Constable, Romney and Hopper.

Marquetry Writing Desk
This elaborate, 16th-century German desk was among many exported to Spain by cabinet-makers in Augsburg and Nuremberg. Felipe II is known to have bought desks similar to this.

First floor

★ The Witches' Sabbath *(1798)*
This painting by Francisco de Goya is based on a legend from Aragón, the artist's birthplace. It shows two sisters who poisoned their children in order to attract the devil, represented here by a huge billy goat.

STAR EXHIBITS

★ **The Witches' Sabbath**

★ **Jarra Púnica**

★ **Crosier Head**

GALLERY GUIDE

The ground floor houses archeological artifacts, Limoges enamels, 15th- and 16th-century religious items, jewellery and Italian Renaissance art. The first floor contains Spanish paintings, silverware and furniture. Highlights on the second floor include works by Goya, Hieronymus Bosch and El Greco.

Main entrance

St John the Baptist

Surrounded by the lamb of spiritual life and other allegorical animals and birds, Hieronymus Bosch's contemplative St John the Baptist (c.1485–1510) reclines in an almost pastoral landscape punctuated by grotesque plants.

VISITORS' CHECKLIST

Calle Serrano 122. **Map** 6 E1.
📞 91 561 60 84. ⊕ *Rubén Darío, Gregorio Marañón.*
🚌 *9, 12, 16, 19, 51.* ⏱ *10am–4:30pm Wed–Mon.*
🔴 *Tue & public hols.* 💳 *(free Wed).* 🚫 ♿ 🛗 📷
Ⓦ www.flg.es

Doña Inés de Zúñiga

This painting of the Countess of Monterrey was executed by Juan Carreño de Miranda in the late 17th century. She is dressed in a wide Spanish farthingale.

Ground floor

★ Crosier Head

This beautiful gilded and enamelled object was made in Limoges in the 13th century for the top of a bishop's staff (crosier). It is decorated with stylized plants to evoke the tree of life and a figure, believed to be St Matthew, holding a book.

★ Jarra Púnica

One of the oldest and most interesting archeological items displayed in the museum is this Phoenician bronze jug, which has a fine feline head as its spout. It was made in the mid-7th century BC, in the Punic era.

KEY TO FLOORPLAN

☐	Ground floor
☐	First floor
☐	Second floor
☐	Non-exhibition space

Former studio of Impressionist Joaquín Sorolla in the Museo Sorolla

Museo Sorolla ⑬

Paseo del General Martínez Campos 37.
Map 5 C1. 🚇 *91 310 15 84.*
Ⓜ *Rubén Darío, Iglesia, Gregorio
Marañón.* ◯ *9:30am–3pm Tue–
Sat, 10am–3pm Sun.* 🌐 *(free Sun).*
Ⓦ *www.mcu.es/nmuseos/sorolla*

THE STUDIO-MANSION of
Valencian Impres-
sionist painter Joaquín
Sorolla is now a
museum displaying his
art, left virtually as it was
when he died in 1923.

Although Sorolla is
perhaps best known
for his brilliantly lit
Mediterranean beach
scenes, the changing
styles of his paintings are well
represented here, with examples of his gentle portraiture
and works depicting people
from different parts of Spain.
Also on display are various
objects amassed during the
artist's lifetime, including tiles
and ceramics. The house,
built in 1910, is surrounded
by an Andalusian-style garden,
designed by Sorolla himself.

Museo de Escultura al Aire Libre ⑭

Paseo de la Castellana. **Map** 6 E2.
Ⓜ *Rubén Darío.*

IN THE EARLY 1970s J Antonio
Fernández Ordóñez and
Julio Martínez Calzón, the
architects of the Calle Juan
Bravo bridge, filled the space
underneath it with abstract
sculptures by 20th-century
Spanish artists. The space on
the east side of Paseo de la

Castellana is dominated by
Sirena Varada, or *Stranded
Mermaid* (1972–3), a concrete
sculpture hanging from four
rods by Eduardo Chillida,
the noted Basque sculptor.
Alberto Sánchez's *Toros
Ibéricos* is another dramatic
installation, and there is a
penguin by Joan Miró.
Other sculptors repre-
sented here are Andrés
Alfaro, Julio González,
Rafael Leoz, Mariel
Martí, José María
Subirachs, Francisco
Sobrino, Martín Chirino
and Eusebio Sempere.
On the west side are
two bronzes by Pablo
Serrano. Visitors should
take care when crossing the
busy Paseo de la Castellana.

**Toros Ibéricos,
Alberto Sánchez**

Museo Romántico ⑮

Calle de San Mateo 13. **Map** 5 A4.
🚇 *91 701 7000.* Ⓜ *Tribunal,
Alonso Martínez.* ⬤ *for refurbishment until 2005/2006.*
Ⓦ *www.mcu.es/nmuseos/romantico*

THIS SMALL Neo-Classical
mansion was designed
by Manuel Martín in 1776
for the Marqués de Matallana.
By 1924 it had been turned
into a museum by the
Marqués de la Vega-Inclán,
the founder of Spain's fine
network of state-owned
parador hotels *(see p145),*
who was an avid art lover
and collector. The Marqués
donated his hoard of 19th-
century paintings, books and
some furniture to form the
nucleus of a museum. Three

years later the museum was
acquired by the state, and
reorganized to look like the
home of a wealthy mid-19th-
century family, evoking the
epoch of the Romantic period.

The exhibits are housed in
20 rooms on the first floor of
the building. As well as a vast
array of 19th-century objects,
such as musical instruments,
photographs, dolls and ornaments, there are many portraits
by leading artists. They include
General Prim by Esquivel,
José de Madrazo's *Fernando
VII* and *María Cristina* by
Salvador Gutiérrez. Several
works by Leonardo Alenza
include the disturbing *Satire
of a Romantic Suicide*.

In the ballroom is a Pleyel
piano that belonged to Isabel
II *(see p21)*. The ceiling is by
González, and the carpet
comes from the Real Fábrica
de Tapices *(see p112)*.

The Museo Romántico
contains a fine collection of
works by the *costumbristas* –
artists who painted scenes
of everyday life in Andalusia
and Madrid. Many of their
works depict local festivals
and traditions.

Earlier works on display in
the museum include a painting of *St Gregory the Great* by
Goya *(see p26)*, which can be
seen above the altar in the
intimate chapel.

The Mariano José de Larra
Room is dedicated to this
great satirical journalist and
writer. Among his personal
effects is the duelling pistol he
used to kill himself, after
being rejected by his lover.

Goya's *St Gregory the Great* in the
chapel of the Museo Romántico

Baroque façade of the Museo Municipal, by Pedro de Ribera

Museo Municipal ⑯

Calle de Fuencarral 78. **Map** 5 A4.
📞 91 588 86 72. 🚇 Tribunal.
🕐 9:30am–8pm Tue–Fri (9:30am–
2pm Aug), 10am–2pm Sat & Sun. ⬤
public hols & some areas closed for
renovation until 2007. ♿ 🎫 by
arrangement. 🌐 www.munimadrid.es

THE MUNICIPAL MUSEUM is worth visiting just for its majestic Baroque doorway by Pedro de Ribera, arguably the finest in Madrid. Housed in the former hospice of St Ferdinand, the museum was inaugurated in 1929. The basement is devoted to the city's archeology, while upstairs is a series of maps showing how radically Madrid has been transformed. Among them is Pedro Texeiro's 1656 map, thought to be the oldest of the city. There is also a meticulous model of Madrid, made in 1830 by León Gil de Palacio.

Modern exhibits include the reconstructed study of Ramón Gómez de la Serna, a key figure of the literary gatherings in the Café de Pombo (see p87). In the garden is the *Fuente de la Fama* (Fountain of Fame), also by Ribera.

Malasaña ⑰

Map 2 E4. 🚇 Tribunal, Bilbao, San Bernardo.

OFFICIALLY CALLED *Barrio de Maravillas*, or District of Miracles, after a 17th-century church that once stood here, this area is more widely known as Malasaña. Thin streets slope down from Carranza and Fuencarral to its bohemian hub, the **Plaza del Dos de Mayo**.

In 1808, *Madrileños* made an heroic last stand here against Napoleon's occupying troops at the gate of Monteleón barracks. The arch in the square is all that is left of the barracks. In front of it is a memorial by Antonio Solá to artillery officers Daoiz and Velarde, who defended the barracks.

In the 1940s and '50s the area deteriorated, but residents fiercely fended off demolition threats. It acquired its bohemian atmosphere in the 1960s, when hippies were lured into the district by cheap rents. Later it became the centre of *La Movida (see p104)*, the frenzied nightlife that began after the death of Franco.

Today Malasaña's streets combine the best of both worlds. Artists and writers have once again moved into the area, along with antiques sellers and yuppies. The charming streets have been cobbled, and boast pretty fountains and plenty of trees. At night, however, the streets are still thronged with people looking for a wild time.

Malasaña is rich in sites of historical and cultural interest. **Plaza de San Ildefonso**, one of many squares remodelled by José I (Joseph Bonaparte) *(see p17)*, has an attractive central fountain with serpents entwined around conch shells. Near the Neo-Classical **Iglesia de San Ildefonso**, built in 1827, is the **Vaquería**, a

dairy shop opened in 1911 and hardly changed since. Outside decorative cows frame the door, while inside there are ageing oil paintings of the seasons in Art Deco style.

In Calle de la Puebla, the 17th-century **Iglesia de San Antonio de los Alemanes** is remarkable for its elliptical interior, swathed in frescoes by Juan Carreño, Francisco de Ricci and Luca Giordano.

Close by is the 17th-century **Iglesia de San Placido** with a cupola painted by Francisco Rizi and the work of Claudio Coello adorning the altars.

The **Iglesia de San Martín**, in Calle de San Roque, was built in 1648. The painting above the altar depicts St Martin of Tours giving half his cloak to a naked beggar.

The main altar of Iglesia de San Placido in Malasaña painted by Claudio Coello

MANUELA MALASAÑA

The daughter of Juan Manuel Malasaña, a craftsman and hero of the 1808 uprising *(see p16)*, Manuela Malasaña died at the age of 16 in the struggle against Napoleon. She was a seamstress who, according to local legend, was caught carrying a pair of scissors by the French and was subsequently shot for possession of a concealed weapon. In 1961 Calle de Manuela Malasaña, which lies between Fuencarral and San Bernardo where the Monteleón artillery park had been, was named after this local heroine.

Ribera's sculptured door at the Cuartel del Conde Duque

Cuartel del Conde Duque ⑱

Calle del Conde Duque 9–11. **Map** 2 D4. **C** *91 588 58 61*. **M** *Noviciado, San Bernardo.* ○ *10am–2pm, 5–9pm Tue–Sat, 10:30am–2:30pm Sun & public hols.* **&** **W** *www.munimadrid.es*

THIS ENORMOUS rectangular complex is named after Gaspar de Guzmán (1587–1645), Conde Duque de Olivares. As a minister of Felipe IV (*see p20*), the count had a palace on this site. After his death, the palace was neglected and fell into ruin. Subsequently, the plot was divided into two distinct sections. On one section, the Palacio de Liria was built for the Duke of Alba. On the other, the barracks for Los Guardias de Corps were constructed between 1717 and 1730 by Pedro de Ribera, who adorned them with a Baroque façade. The three-floor barracks were in use for over a century but, in 1869, they suffered a major fire and eventually fell into a state of total dilapidation. A hundred years later, in 1969, Madrid's city hall made the decision to restore the old army barracks.

The building now houses a police station, council offices, a municipal library, a cultural centre with five exhibition halls and the **Museo Municipal de Arte Contemporáneo**. This new museum of modern art exhibits the work of young Spanish artists alongside that of better

established names. The cultural centre is a venue for major concerts, and jazz and flamenco festivals are often staged in the main patio. The entrance to the cultural centre is the uppermost door, opposite Calle de Montserrat.

Palacio de Liria ⑲

Calle de la Princesa 20. **Map** 1 C4. **C** *91 547 53 02*. **M** *Ventura Rodríguez.* ○ *by appointment a year before (fax 91 541 03 77).*

THE LAVISH BUT much restored Palacio de Liria was completed by Ventura Rodríguez in 1780. It was once the

---

---

residence of the Alba family, and is still owned by the Duchess. The sumptuous palace rooms are home to the Albas' outstanding collection of art and Flemish tapestries. The walls are adorned with paintings by many famous masters, among them Titian, Rubens and Rembrandt.

Spanish art itself is particularly well represented, and the Albas' collection includes a number of major works by Goya (*see p26*). One such significant canvas is his 1795 portrait of the Duchess of Alba. Also featured are several interesting works by El Greco (*see p139*), Zurbarán and Velázquez (*see p26*).

Room adorned with paintings by Goya in the Palacio de Liria

Castizos of Madrid

T HE TRUE WORKING-CLASS *Madrileños*, whose families have lived in the neighbourhoods of Old Madrid, Chamberí and Cuatro Caminos for many generations, are known as *castizos*. Around 1850, in their revolt against the bourgeoisie, who were basking in the Romantic and patriotic cultural revolution that followed the defeat of the French earlier in the 19th century, the *castizos* decided to reclaim their proud heritage. The Madrid equivalent of

Religious celebration – festivities on vehicle floats

London's Cockneys, *los castizos Madrileños* not only revived their district fiestas, one of the world's best neighbourhood-bonding traditions, but also reinvented costumes to go with them and formed numerous associations that still thrive today. At any of the traditional Madrid fiestas or *romerías* (processions) you will see the *castizos,* or *majos* (dandies) as they are known, with their *manolas*, or partners, attired in what is now their smart, traditional uniform.

Typical **manola** *costume* consists of a flowery headscarf with at least one carnation in the front, an alfombra (literally translated as carpet), which is actually a huge embroidered shawl, or mantón de Manila, worn over the shoulders, and a falda vestida (long dress), sometimes with an apron.

Carnation on the headscarf

Alfombra – shawl with a long fringe

Colourful dress (falda vestida)

Black-and-white parpusa (hat)

White barbosa (shirt)

Black alares (trousers)

Men's clothes are referred to in castizo argot: black or black-and-white check parpusa (cap), a white barbosa (shirt), a black chupín (waistcoat), a black or black-and-white check chupa (jacket), a safo (white handkerchief), a peluco (pocket watch), a red carnation in the buttonhole, black or black-and-white check alares (trousers), picantes (socks) and shining calcos (shoes).

In May, the castizos are out in force during the Dos de Mayo fiesta. On 15 May is the Fiesta de San Isidro, with a romería from the Puerta de Toledo down to the Río Manzanares. The next major fiestas are on 13 June at San Antonio de la Florida; and 15 August, with the Fiesta de la Virgen de Paloma, a castizo favourite. Castizo processions include the Romería de San Blas on 3 February, and the Romería de San Eugenio on 14 November.

FURTHER AFIELD

S EVERAL OF MADRID's best sights, including interesting but little-known museums, lie outside the city centre. The Museo de la Ciudad gives an overview of the development of the city, with models of buildings and districts, while the Museo de América displays artifacts from Spain's former colonies. There is a wealth of historic buildings outside the city centre, ranging from the Egyptian Templo de Debod to the Puerta de Toledo, a triumphal arch

Mosaic by Miró on the Palacio de Congresos y Exposiciones in Azca

begun in 1813 on the orders of José I (Joseph Bonaparte), to the old-style apartment building of La Corrala. There are a number of other attractions surrounding the centre of Madrid. To the north lies the modern commercial district of Azca, with skyscrapers, office blocks and upmarket shops. If you need to escape from the bustle of the city for a while, west of Old Madrid, across the Río Manzanares, is Madrid's vast, green recreation ground, the Casa de Campo.

SIGHTS AT A GLANCE

Historic Buildings
Arco de la Victoria ❷
Estación de Príncipe Pío ❼
La Corrala ⓫
Puente de Segovia and
   Río Manzanares ⓭
Puerta de Toledo ⓬
Real Fábrica de Tapices ❾
Sala del Canal de Isabel II ❸
Templo de Debod ⓰

Churches and Convents
Ermita de San Antonio de la
   Florida ⓯

Museums and Galleries
Museo Casa de la Moneda ❽
Museo de América ❶
Museo de Ciencias Naturales ❺
Museo de la Ciudad ❻
Museo Nacional Ferroviario ❿

Squares, Parks & Districts
Azca ❹
Casa de Campo ⓮
Plaza de Toros de Las
   Ventas ❼

0 kilometres 1

0 miles   1

KEY

	Main sightseeing area
	Parks and open spaces
🚉	Railway station
═	Highway/Motorway
▬	Major road
═	Minor road

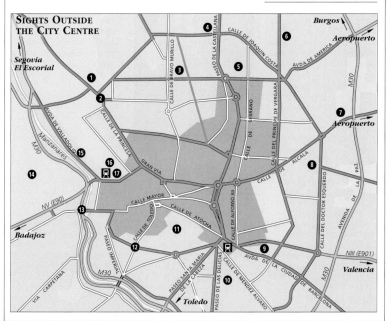

SIGHTS OUTSIDE THE CITY CENTRE

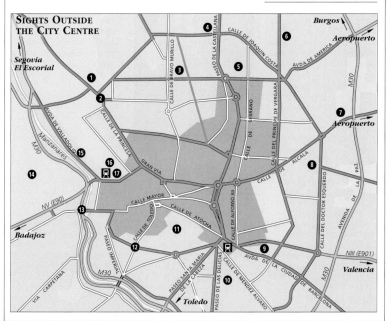

◁ Mudéjar arches and tilework on the exterior of the Plaza de Toros de Las Ventas

Old and new – the Mirador del Faro alongside the Museo de América

Museo de América ❶

Avenida de los Reyes Católicos 6.
📞 91 549 26 41. Ⓜ Moncloa.
🕐 9:30am–3pm Tue–Sat, 10am–3pm Sun & public hols. 🎫 some public hols. 📷 (free on Sun). ♿
🌐 www.mcu.es/nmuseos/america

A UNIQUE COLLECTION of arti-facts relating to Spain's colonization of the Americas is housed in this fine museum. Many of the exhibits, which range from prehistoric to more recent times, were brought to Europe by the early explorers of the New World (see p14).

The collection is arranged on the first and second floors, and individual rooms are given cultural themes such as society, religion and communication. Documentation is given about the Atlantic voyages made by the first explorers.

For many visitors, the high-light of the museum is the rare Mayan *Códice Tro-cortesiano* (AD 1250–1500) from Mexico. This is a type of parchment illustrated with hieroglyphics of scenes from everyday life.

Also worth seeing are the Treasure of the Quimbayas, a collection of pre-Columbian gold and silver objects from around AD 500–1000, and the collection of contemporary folk art from some of Spain's former American colonies.

Arco de la Victoria ❷

Avenida de la Victoria. **Map** 1 A1.
Ⓜ Moncloa.

E RECTED IN 1956, this white arch was designed to cele-brate the Nationalist victory in the 1936–9 Spanish Civil War (see p18). General Franco would have passed by it each time he came to Madrid from his home in the Palacio de El Pardo (see p134). Topped by a green sculpture of a chariot with horses, the arch stands 39 m (128 ft) tall – one of the city's highest commemorative *puertas* (gateways). The archi-tects, Pascual Bravo and Modesto López Otero, built a room high up inside the arch. It contains a 25-sq m (270-sq ft) model of the neighbouring university and the plans for the arch itself. However, it is not open to the public.

Nearby is the **Faro de Moncloa** observation tower. Opened in 1992, it measures 92 m (300 ft). The tower offers excellent views of Madrid and the Guadarrama mountains.

The imposing Arco de la Victoria

Sala del Canal de Isabel II ❸

Calle de Santa Engracia 125.
📞 91 545 10 00. Ⓜ Ríos Rosas.
🕐 11am–2pm, 5–8:30pm Tue–Sat, 11am–2pm Sun & public hols.
⬤ 1 Jan & 25 Dec. ♿

T HIS RENOVATED WATER tower is used to great effect as a venue for photographic exhi-bitions but, on the whole, most visitors come to marvel at its

Sala del Canal de Isabel II, a water tower turned exhibition centre

complex construction. In the late 19th century the water supply for Madrid was based on a project patronized by Isabel II (see p21) in 1851 and known as Canal de Isabel II, the name given to Madrid's water company. The first dam was built in the Lozoya Valley, about 80 km (50 miles) north of Madrid in the Guadarrama mountains, and a duct carried the water south to a reservoir.

More reservoirs were built to cope with the capital's ever-increasing needs but, in 1903, the development of the high-lying suburbs of Chamberí and Cuatro Caminos dictated the need for a water tower to supply new pipes by gravity. Martín y Montalvo was the engineer enlisted to carry out the task. He designed a polygonal tower of brick and iron, 36 m (118 ft) high, sur-mounted by a 1,500-sq m (16,145-sq ft) tank resting on an iron ring. Work started in 1908, and by 1911 the water tower was finished at a cost of nearly 350,000 pesetas. It was in service until 1952.

The regional government of Madrid decided to restore the tower in 1985, taking out the water works but retaining the huge tank. Access to the exhi-bition floors within the tower has been made possible by hydraulically driven elevators (lifts) and steel staircases.

Bordering the tower are the busy Calle de Santa Engracia and the gardens and turf that form a roof over one of the major underground reservoirs of the Canal de Isabel II.

Azca ❹

🚇 Nuevos Ministerios, Santiago Bernabeú.

IN 1969, WORK BEGAN on the development of this "mini-Manhattan" along the west side of the Paseo de la Castellana. It stretches from the **Nuevos Ministerios** complex in the south to the **Palacio de Congresos y Exposiciones** in the north. The idea was to create a modern commercial area away from the congested city centre. Today, some 30,000 people work here.

By day Azca is a mecca for shoppers. A branch of the department store El Corte Inglés (*see p164*) runs alongside Nuevos Ministerios metro and railway station, and there is a Moda shopping mall served by Santiago Bernabeú metro. Across from the Plaza de Lima is the **Estadio Santiago Bernabeú**, home of Real Madrid Football Club. It was built in 1950, but has had a few facelifts since, especially for the 1982 World Cup Finals.

Major companies operate in the tower blocks, alongside hotels, apartments, cinemas, restaurants and bars. The elderly are drawn by bingo halls, while the young throng the discos at the weekends.

In the centre of Azca is the multi-level pedestrian **Plaza Pablo Ruíz Picasso** with trees, benches, fountains and walkways. If driving, do not try to negotiate the maze of roads underneath the complex unless you are very sure about where you intend to park or emerge.

Azca is dominated by the aluminium-clad **Torre Picasso**, Madrid's tallest office building. Completed in 1989, it has 46 floors, bronzed windows and a heliport. It was designed by Minoru Yamasaki, architect of the twin towers of New York's World Trade Centre, which were destroyed in the terrorist attack of 2001.

The **Torre Europa** on Plaza de Lima is another notable building. Designed by Miguel Oriol e Ybarra and completed in 1982, its exterior concrete supports incorporate a clock. As well as 28 floors of offices, it has three commercial floors below street level.

The rust-coloured **Banco Bilbao Vizcaya** on Azca's south corner was designed by Francisco Javier Sáenz de Oíza. Built in 1980, it stands over the underground rail line between Chamartín and Atocha.

Museo de Ciencias Naturales ❺

Paseo de la Castellana 80. ☎ 91 411 13 28. 🚇 Gregorio Marañón, Nuevos Ministerios, Republica Argentina. ⏰ 10am–6pm Tue–Fri, 10am–8pm Sat, 10am–2:30pm Sun & public hols. ⏰ 1 Jan, 1 May, 25 Dec. 🎫 🎥 by arrangement. ♿ 🌐 www.mncn.csic.es

THIS MUSEUM, built in 1887, contains 16,400 minerals, 220 meteorites, 30,000 birds and mammals and many more items in its archives. The

Inside the modern Origins of Life section of Madrid's Museo de Ciencias Naturales

entrance on the left leads to the Rhythm of Nature section. This is an ecological display of numerous examples of wildlife, from exotic birds to rare animals, insects and butterflies. Lions, tigers and deer stare out from the walls, while the shelves are heavy with bottled lizards, fish and snakes. An interactive computer display room provides valuable insight into the sounds and habitats of animals and birds.

A recent addition to this part of the museum is a cross-section of the Atapuerca site near Burgos, north of Madrid, where Europe's earliest human remains (some 780,000 years old) were discovered in 1997. There is also a huge African elephant. Shot by the Duke of Alba in the Sudan in 1916, the elephant's skin was sent back to Spain and reassembled.

The right entrance to the museum, by the gift shop, leads to a modern two-floor section, with displays on the origins of the earth and of life. The star of the show is the 1.8-million-year-old skeleton of *Megatherium americanum*, a bear-like creature from the late Cenozoic period found in Argentina in 1788. Nearby is a Glyptodon (giant armadillo), also from Argentina, and a life-size reproduction of a Diplodocus dinosaur skeleton found in the United States.

The Industrial Engineers' School is also housed in the museum building and behind are the headquarters of Spain's state scientific institute, CSIC. Opposite the entrances is a pleasant terrace bar which looks out over a small park with a fountain and a statue of Isabel I (*see p20*).

The Torre Europa rising above the commercial centre of Azca

Interior of the Museo de la Ciudad arranged around a central atrium

Museo de la Ciudad ❻

Calle del Príncipe de Vergara 140.
📞 *91 588 65 99.* Ⓜ *Cruz del Rayo.*
🕐 *10am–2pm, 4–7pm Tue–Fri, 10am–2pm Sat & Sun.*
⬤ *public hols.* ♿
Ⓦ *www.munimadrid.es*

T HIS MODERN MUSEUM in the northeast of Madrid shows how the city has evolved since the earliest settlement, using detailed panoramic models.

The museum consists of five floors built around an octagonal atrium. Here stands a copy of the Mariblanca statue in the Puerta del Sol (see p44). Right of the entrance is a bookshop. The ground and first floors house temporary exhibitions.

The displays on the second floor concern Madrid's utility companies. A subject that fascinates visiting schoolchildren is how Madrid gets its water from the mountains. Also on this floor is a huge model of the city, from Barajas Airport to Cuatro Ventas airfield.

The third floor deals with the history of Madrid from prehistory to Bourbon times. As well as books, charts and maps, there are models of Old Madrid, some monuments and the Palacio Real (see pp54–7).

The fourth floor is devoted to the 19th and 20th centuries, and has a superb model of the new part of the city from Plaza de Colón (see p98) to Torre Europa (see p109). Nearby there is also an impressive model of Plaza de Toros de Las Ventas, Madrid's bullring.

Plaza de Toros de Las Ventas ❼

Calle de Alcalá 237. 📞 *91 356 22 00.*
Ⓜ *Ventas.* 🗐 *for bullfights and concerts only.* **Museo Taurino** 📞 *91 725 18 57.* 🕐 *Mar–Oct: 9:30am–2:30pm Tue–Fri, 10am–1pm Sun; Nov–Feb: 9:30am– 2:30pm Mon–Fri.* ♿

W HATEVER YOUR opinion of bullfighting, Las Ventas is undoubtedly one of the most beautiful bullrings in Spain. Built in 1929 in Neo-Mudéjar style, it replaced the city's original bullring, which stood near the Puerta de Alcalá (see p66). Its horseshoe arches around the outer galleries and elaborate tilework decoration make it an attractive venue for the *corridas* (bullfights), held from May to October. The statues outside the bullring are monuments to two renowned Spanish bullfighters, Antonio Bienvenida and José Cubero.

Adjoining the bullring is the **Museo Taurino**. This contains a varied collection of bullfighting memorabilia, including portraits and sculptures of famous matadors, as well as the heads of several bulls killed during fights at Las Ventas. Visitors can examine bullfighters' capes and *banderillas* – sharp darts used to wound the bull. The gory highlight of the exhibition, for some people, is the blood-drenched *traje de luces* worn by Manolete during his fateful bullfight at Linares in Andalusia in 1947. Also on display is a costume which belonged to Juanita Cruz, a

female bullfighter of the 1930s who was forced, in the face of prejudice, to leave Spain. In September and October the bullring is used as a venue for a season of rock concerts.

Museo Casa de la Moneda ❽

Calle del Doctor Esquerdo 36. 📞 *91 566 65 44.* Ⓜ *O'Donell.* 🕐 *10am– 7:30pm Tue–Fri, 10am–2pm Sat & Sun.* ⬤ *public hols.*
Ⓦ *www.fnmt.es/museo*

T HE SPANISH MINT and stamp factory is located in a vast granite building. The recently renovated museum, in the north side of the building, traces the history of currency, from early trading in salt, shells and bracelets up to the Euro – the monetary unit of the European Union.

Coins feature prominently, with maps and photographs complementing displays of Greek and Roman coins. The earliest coins have images of mythical gods; the picture of Cybele, mother of the gods, on a Roman coin from 78 BC is similar to the sculpture in the Plaza de Cibeles (see p67).

As well as later Roman coins endowed with more symbolic images, there are Visigothic and Moorish coins. Early Moorish coins are inscribed in Latin and later ones in Arabic.

There are also engravings for currency notes, stamps, medals and official documents.

Plaza de Toros de Las Ventas, Madrid's beautiful Neo-Mudéjar bullring

The Art of Bullfighting

Poster for a bullfight

BULLFIGHTING IS A sacrificial ritual in which men (and a few women) pit themselves against an animal bred for the ring. In this "authentic religious drama", as poet Federico García Lorca *(see p26)* described it, the spectator experiences the same intensity of fear and exaltation as the matador. There are three stages, or *tercios*, in the *corrida* (bullfight). The first two are aimed at progressively weakening the bull. In

the third, the matador moves in for the kill. Despite opposition on the grounds of cruelty, bullfighting is still very popular. For many Spaniards, talk of banning bullfighting is an assault on the essence of their being. For them, the *toreo*, the art of bullfighting, is a noble part of their heritage. However, fights today are often debased by practices designed to disadvantage the bull, in particular shaving its horns to make them blunt.

The **toro bravo** *(fighting bull), bred for courage and aggression, enjoys a full life prior to its time in the ring. Bulls must be at least four years old before they can fight.*

Manolete *is regarded by most followers of bullfighting as one of Spain's greatest ever matadors. He was finally gored to death by the bull Islero at Linares, Jaén, in 1947.*

The matador wears a *traje de luces* (suit of lights), a colourful silk outfit embroidered with gold sequins.

Banderillas (barbed darts) are thrust into the bull's back muscles to weaken them.

Joselito *was a leading matador, famous for his purist style and his superb skill with the* capa *(red cape) and the* muleta *(matador's stick). He has recently returned to the* ruedos *(bullring) from retirement.*

THE BULLRING

The *corrida* audience is seated in the *tendidos* (stalls) or in the *palcos* (balcony), where the *presidencia* (president's box) is situated. Opposite are the *puerta de cuadrillas*, through which the matador and team arrive, and the *arrastre de toros* (exit for bulls). Before entering the ring, the matadors wait in a *callejón* (corridor) behind *barreras* and *burladeros* (barriers). Horses are kept in the *patio de caballos* and the bulls in the *corrales*.

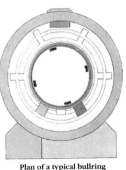

Plan of a typical bullring

KEY

☐	Tendidos
▨	Palcos
▨	Presidencia
▨	Puerta de cuadrillas
■	Arrastre de toros
▨	Callejón
▨	Barreras
■	Burladeros
☐	Patio de caballos
☐	Corrales

Real Fábrica de Tapices 9

Calle de Fuenterrabia 2. **Map** 8 F5.
91 434 05 51. Menéndez Pelayo.
10am–2pm Mon–Fri. *public hols, Aug.*
www.realfatapices.com

FOUNDED BY Felipe V in 1721, the Royal Tapestry Factory alone survives from the factories opened by the Bourbons in the 18th century. In 1889 the factory was moved to this building, just south of the Parque del Retiro *(see p77)*.

Visitors can see the making by hand of the carpets and tapestries, a process which has changed little since the factory was built. Goya *(see p26)* and his brother-in-law Francisco Bayeu drew cartoons on which the tapestries for the royal family were based. Some of the cartoons are on display here, in the newly opened museum; others are in the Prado *(see pp80–83)*. Several tapestries can be seen at the Palacio de El Pardo *(see p134)* and at El Escorial *(see pp122–5)*. Today the factory makes and repairs the beautiful carpets decorating the Hotel Ritz *(see p68)*.

Museo del Ferrocarril 10

Paseo de las Delicias 61. *91 506 83 33.* Delicias. 10am–3pm Tue–Sun. *1 Jan, Aug, 25 Dec.*
(free on Sat). book ahead.
www.museodelferrocarril.org

ALTHOUGH RAILWAYS had existed in the country since 1848, it was only in 1880 that Madrid's first proper railway terminus opened – the station of Delicias. This was the main station for Portugal, and it remained in use until 1971.

In 1984 the station re-opened as a railway museum. The majority of exhibits, in the form of trains, are located in the main terminus on tracks next to the original platforms. There are

Cafeteria of the Museo del Ferrocarril, set in a 1930s dining car

1950s Talgo locomotive at the railway museum

more than 30 locomotives – steam, diesel and electric – as well as rolling stock. Explanatory plaques give details and describe the routes of the locomotives. You can explore some of the carriages, including a 1930s dining car that now serves as the site's cafeteria.

One of the most interesting engines is "La Pucheta", a steam locomotive built in 1884 by Sharp Stewart in Britain. Its water supply was on top of the boiler, in a container that resembles a bowler hat.

A 1931 electric locomotive, built in Spain, earned itself the nickname "The Lioness" because of its weight – more than 150 tonnes. This was the heaviest engine ever used by the Spanish state railways (RENFE), and the longest, measuring approximately 25 m (82 ft).

Also of special interest is a 1950s Talgo. These Spanish-designed express trains revolutionized railway transport in the country, and this model was in service until 1971. The train was light, with a very low centre of gravity, reduced height, and an articulated system, all of which enabled it to travel much faster than conventional carriages.

The 1928 wooden-sided carriage, the ZZ-307 Coche Salon, was the most luxurious the West Railway Company had to offer. Peering through the windows, you can still see an elegantly laid table in the dining room, the sleeping compartments and a tiny galley.

One of the popular sights on show is the Mikado, a steam locomotive built in 1960, which has been cut away to reveal the mysteries of steam propulsion. This engine was in service until 1975, when the use of regular steam-hauled services came to an end in Spain.

To one side of the station are four large halls that house detailed model train layouts, scale models of train stations and railway memorabilia, including signals, lights, telegraphs and photographs.

La Corrala ⓫

Calle de Mesón de Paredes, between Calle Tribulete & Calle del Sombrerete. **Map** 4 F5. Ⓜ *Lavapiés.* ◯ *to the public.*

CORRALAS ARE timber-framed apartment blocks, or tenements, built during the 19th century mainly in poorer parts of the city, especially in the neighbourhood of Lavapiés.

A *zarzuela* performance, using La Corrala as a backdrop

The buildings were arranged around an interior courtyard; balconies overlooked the courtyard and provided access to individual apartments.

La Corrala exemplifies this type of housing. Construction began in 1872, but some of the building permits were not in order, which may explain why only half of the building seems to exist. The courtyard, rather than being completely surrounded by the building, opens out on to a plaza. Its exposure means that there are good views of the building, and of the ubiquitous laundry hanging from the balconies.

In 1977, La Corrala was declared a monument of historic interest, and two years later it underwent complete restoration. On summer nights,

La Corrala is now used as a backdrop to outdoor *zarzuela,* or light opera *(see p75),* which is staged in the plaza.

In the near vicinity are several other corralas. One can be seen on the corner of Calle de Miguel Servet with Calle del Espino, one at Calle de Provisiones 12 and another at Calle de la Esperanza 11.

Puerta de Toledo ⓬

Glorieta de Puerta de Toledo. **Map** 4 D5. Ⓜ *Puerta de Toledo.*

THE CONSTRUCTION of this triumphal arch began in 1813 on the orders of French-born Joseph Bonaparte, José I *(see p17).* It was intended to commemorate his accession

to the Spanish throne after the 1808 rout of Madrid. But in 1814, after a short-lived reign, José I fled Spain and was replaced by Fernando VII *(see p17).* By the time the arch was completed in 1827, by the architect Antonio López Aguado, it had to be dedicated to Fernando VII.

The Puerta de Toledo is one of Madrid's two remaining city gates, and is topped by a group of sculptures that represent a personification of Spain. On either side of these are the allegorical figures of Genius and the Arts. All were carved in their entirety from Colmenar stone by Ramón Barba and Valeriano Salvatierra, and are flanked on each side by sculptures based on military themes.

The majestic form of the Puerta de Toledo, one of Madrid's two remaining triumphal arches

Puente de Segovia and Río Manzanares ⑬

Calle de Segovia. *Puerta del Angel.*

PUENTE DE SEGOVIA, a grand granite bridge over the Río Manzanares, was commissioned by Felipe II *(see p20)* not long after he had decided to establish his court in Madrid. The bridge was to be a main entry point to Madrid and he chose Juan de Herrera, his favourite architect, to build it. Construction began in 1582. The bridge, with its nine arches topped with decorative bosses, was rebuilt in 1682.

Further downstream is the magnificent pedestrian bridge, **Puente de Toledo**, built between 1718 and 1732 for Felipe V *(see p21)*. The architect was Pedro de Ribera. The Manzanares, which is more of a stream than a river, never deserved such splendid bridges. It was the butt of many jokes; a German ambassador by the name of Rhebiner once said the river was the best in Europe because it had the advantage of being "navigable by horse and carriage". Alexandre Dumas (1802–70), author of *The Three Musketeers*, wrote of the Manzanares during his visit to Madrid that "however hard I looked for it, I could not find it".

The river now has several dams, and the introduced fish and ducks have been able to survive, proving that the water is fairly clean. Rising in the Sierra de Guadarrama and eventually joining the River Tagus, the river forms a link between Spain's capital and Lisbon, the capital of Portugal.

Tiger from the zoo at Casa de Campo

Casa de Campo ⑭

Avenida de Portugal. **◻** *91 463 63 34.* *Batán, Casa de Campo, Lago, Príncipe Pío.*

THIS FORMER ROYAL hunting ground of pine forests and scrubland extends over 17.5 sq km (6.7 sq miles) of western Madrid. Its range of amenities and proximity to the centre make it a popular recreation area for *Madrileños*. Among its attractions are tennis courts, swimming pools, a boating lake, funfair – the **Parque de Atracciones** with over 50 rides – and the **Zoo-Aquarium**. In summer the park also stages concerts. One way to visit the park and take in the city's sights is to ride the **Teleférico** (cable car), which connects the Parque del Oeste with the Casa de Campo.

✕ Zoo-Aquarium
◻ *91 512 37 70.* *Batán.*
◻ *10:30am–dusk daily.* 🎫 ♿
W www.zoomadrid.com
✕ Parque de Atracciones
◻ *91 463 29 00.* *Batán.* **◻** *Sep–Apr: from noon Sat & Sun; Apr–Sep: from noon daily. Closing times vary from month to month, check locally.* 🎫
W www.parquedeatracciones.es
◻ Teleférico
Paseo del Pintor Rosales. **◻** *91 541 74 50.* *Argüelles.* **◻** *Oct–Mar: noon–dusk Sat, Sun & public hols; Apr–Sep: 11am–dusk daily.* 🎫 ♿

Ermita de San Antonio de la Florida ⑮

Glorieta San Antonio de la Florida 5.
◻ *91 542 07 22.* *Príncipe Pío.*
◻ *10am–2pm, 4–8pm Tue–Fri, 10am–2pm Sat & Sun.*
◻ *public hols.* 🚫 ♿
W www.munimadrid.es

GOYA ENTHUSIASTS should not miss this remarkable Neo-Classical church, built during the reign of Carlos IV *(see p21)*. Standing on the site of two previous churches, the present building is dedicated to St Anthony and is named after the pastureland of La Florida, on which the original churches were built.

It took Goya *(see p26)* just four months in 1798 to paint the cupola's immense fresco. It depicts St Anthony raising a murdered man from the dead so that he can prove innocent the saint's falsely accused

The buttressed arches of Puente de Segovia over the Río Manzanares

Egyptian temple of Debod, with two of its original gateways

park is the site of the former Montaña barracks. In 1936, they were stormed by the people of Madrid in their hunger for weaponry. It was a desperate bid on their part to arm themselves against General Franco's encroaching army at the start of the Spanish Civil War *(see p18)*. It is also a place where many lost their lives to Napoleon in 1808.

Nearby is the **Paseo del Pintor Rosales**, popular for its pavement (sidewalk) cafés.

Estación de Príncipe Pío ⓱

Paseo de la Florida 2. **Map** 3 A1.
📞 90 224 02 02. Ⓜ *Príncipe Pío.*

ＡLSO KNOWN AS Estación del Norte, this railway station was opened in 1880 to supply train services between Madrid and the north of Spain. Built by French engineers Biarez, Grasset and Mercier, iron from French and Belgian foundries was its main component. In 1915, the station's look was enhanced by Mudéjar-style pavilions designed by Demetrio Ribes. The entrance façade was added by architect Luis Martínez Ribes in 1926.

In the main building of the former station, the largest concert hall in Madrid, as well as cinemas and a shopping centre, are under construction until 2006. Another part of the station is a major transport interchange. Above the platforms is a splendid latticework canopy. Looking out along the tracks, it is possible to see the Sierra de Guadarrama.

father. Ordinary characters from late 18th-century Madrid are also featured in the painting. They include low-life types and lively *majas* – shrewd but elegant women. The fresco is considered one of Goya's finest works. The artist lies buried under the dome of this church.

Templo de Debod ⓰

Paseo del Pintor Rosales. **Map** 1 B5.
📞 91 366 74 15. Ⓜ *Plaza de España, Ventura Rodríguez.* ⌚ 10am–2pm Sat & Sun; Apr–Sep: 10am–2pm, 6–8pm Tue–Fri; Oct–Mar: 10am–2pm, 4–6pm Tue–Fri.
⬤ *public hols.*
📷 *Sat, by arrangement.*
ⓦ www.munimadrid.es/templodebod

ＴHE AUTHENTIC Egyptian temple of Debod was built in the 2nd century BC. It was given to Spain in 1968 by the Egyptian government as a tribute to Spanish engineers involved in rescuing ancient monuments from the floodwaters of the Aswan Dam on

the River Nile. The temple's carvings depict Amen, a Theban god with a ram's head, symbolizing life and fertility, to whom the temple is dedicated.

Situated on high ground above the Río Manzanares, and surrounded by the landscaped gardens of the **Parque del Oeste**, the temple stands in a line with two of its original three gateways. From here there are sweeping views stretching as far as the Guadarrama mountains. The

The elegant main entrance to the Estación de Príncipe Pío

BEYOND MADRID

BEYOND MADRID

S PAIN'S VAST CENTRAL PLATEAU *consists mainly of wheat fields and awesome expanses of sienna and ochre plains which exude an empty beauty. Yet it also has mountains, gorges, forests and lakes filled with wildlife, while the towns and cities are permeated with history, reflected in some stunning architecture – Toledo's Gothic cathedral, Segovia's alcázar and the 15th-century castle at Manzanares el Real.*

It is surprising how quickly one can escape past Madrid's dormitory towns and industrial estates to the real countryside. There is plenty of superb scenery and good walking country in the sierras to the north – a refuge for city dwellers who go there to ski in winter or sail and windsurf during the torrid summers. The Sierra Norte offers a paradise for birdwatchers, especially around the Moorish town of Buitrago del Lozoya.

In the western foothills of these mountains stands El Escorial, the royal monastery-palace built by Felipe II, from which he ruled his empire. Close by is the Valle de los Caídos, the war monument erected by Franco. The smaller royal palace of El Pardo is on the outskirts of Madrid, and south of the city is the 18th-century Aranjuez summer palace, set in lush parkland.

Historic towns include Alcalá de Henares – the birthplace of Cervantes, Sigüenza, with its impressive castle-parador, and Chinchón, where local garlic, wine and anis are sold beneath the creaking wooden balconies of its medieval plaza. Segovia, from where Felipe II's predecessors ruled Castile, is packed at weekends as visitors sample the famous roast lamb and suckling-pig and stop to admire its aqueduct – the largest Roman structure in Spain.

Toledo, which was the capital of Visigothic Spain, is an outstanding museum city. Its rich architectural and artistic heritage derives from a coalescence of Muslim, Christian and Jewish cultures with medieval and Renaissance ideas.

The picturesque Monasterio de El Parral in Segovia

◁ **Celebration of Mass in the church of the Monasterio de Santa María de El Paular**

Exploring Beyond Madrid

STRETCHING ALONG THE northern horizon of the province of Madrid are the peaks of the Sierra de Guadarrama. Reaching to 2,430 m (7,972 ft), they are often capped with snow until June. There are many hiking and even skiing opportunities in these mountains. Below, in the pine-scented southern folds of the Guadarrama, basks the monolithic monastery of El Escorial.

To the south lies the *meseta*, Spain's vast central plateau. Thanks to the mountains, rivers flow towards the arid plains, creating fertile valleys where olives grow. The historic towns of Castile nestle amid the rocky promontories. The River Jarama joins the Tagus *(Tajo)* near the 18th-century Royal Summer Palace and gardens in Aranjuez. Downstream it curls around ancient Toledo.

The 15th-century Casa de los Picos *(see p128)* in Segovia

Vast, fertile plain of the Spanish *meseta*

SIGHTS AT A GLANCE

SEGOVIA ⑦

LA GRANJA DE SAN ⑥
ILDEFONSO
REVENGA ●   MONAST.
                             DE SANTA M
N603   DE EL PA
SIERRA CENTRO DE
GUADARRAMA   ④
                             MANZA
NAVACERRADA   E

GUADARRAMA
SANTA CRUZ ②   NVI
DEL VALLE DE
LOS CAÍDOS ①   A6
                EL ESCORIAL

MAJADAHO

MÓSTOLE

NV (E90)   R5

Rio Guadarrama

ILL

Exterior of Casa-Museo de El Greco *(see p139)* in Toledo

N403

TOLEDO ⑱

GETTING AROUND

The best way to explore sites beyond Madrid is with a car and a good map reader. Six toll-free divided highways (dual carriageways), the NI to NVI (or A6), and one toll highway (motorway), the N401 to Toledo, fan out from the city, linked by the M30 and M40 ring roads. Be aware that as Spain is in the process of changing its road numbering system some of the roads featured here may differ from new road signs. Scheduled bus services can be slow. Railways serve the historic cities.

SIERRA NORTE **9**

NI (E5)

MAJAELRAYO

PRÁDENA DEL RINCÓN

Embalse de Alcorlo

10 SIGÜENZA

8 BUITRAGO DEL LOZOYA

TAMAJÓN

Embalse de Belena

ZOYA

EL CUADRÓN

Embalse de El Atazar

Río Jarama

PUEBLA DE BELENA

Río Henares

JADRAQUE

UCEDA

NII (E90)

SOTO DEL REAL

TORRELAGUNA

TORRE DEL BURGO

alse de illana

NII (E90)

COLMENAR VIEJO

N320

NI (E5)

KEY

mbalse de Pardo

13 PALACIO DE EL PARDO

GUADALAJARA

11

	Highway (motorway)
	Major road
	Minor road
	Scenic route
	River
☼	Viewpoint

AZUQUECA DE HENARES

MADRID

NII (E90)

NIII (E90)

USEO DEL AIRE

12

ALCALÁ DE HENARES

SEE ALSO

- *Where to Stay* pp150–51

- *Restaurants, Cafés and Bars* p163

M30

NIV (E5)

CIEMPOZUELOS

15 CHINCHÓN

16

PALACIO REAL DE ARANJUEZ

Tajo   N400

0 km   10

0 miles   10

The tranquil Montes de Toledo

El Escorial ❶

Fresco by Luca Giordano

FELIPE II'S IMPOSING GREY PALACE of San Lorenzo de El Escorial stands out against the foothills of the Sierra de Guadarrama to the northwest of Madrid. It was built between 1563 and 1584 in honour of St Lawrence, and its unornamented severity set a new architectural style which became one of the most influential in Spain. The interior was conceived as a mausoleum and contemplative retreat rather than a splendid residence. Its artistic wealth, which includes some of the most important works of art of the royal Habsburg collections, is concentrated in the museums, chapterhouses, church, royal pantheon and library. In contrast, the Royal Apartments are remarkably austere.

★ Royal Pantheon
The funerary urns of Spanish monarchs line the marble mausoleum.

Tourist entrance

Bourbon Palace

Architectural Museum

Sala de Batallas

Basílica
The highlight of this huge, decorated church is the lavish altarpiece. The chapel houses statues of Felipe II and Carlos I (Holy Roman Emperor Charles V) at prayer.

The Alfonso XII College was founded by monks in 1875 as a boarding school.

Patio de los Reyes

Main entrance

★ Library
This impressive library held Felipe II's personal collection. At its peak it boasted 40,000 volumes and an exceptional number of precious manuscripts. The long Print Room has beautiful 16th-century ceiling frescoes by Tibaldi.

STAR FEATURES

★ Royal Pantheon

★ Library

★ Museum of Art

The Royal Apartments,
on the second floor of the
palace, consist of Felipe II's
modestly decorated living
quarters. His bedroom
opens directly on to the
high altar of the basílica.

★ Museum of Art
*Flemish, Italian and
Spanish paintings are on
display in this ground
floor museum. One
highlight is The Calvary,
by 15th-century
Flemish artist Rogier
van der Weyden.*

The Patio de los Evangelistas
is a temple by Herrera.

Chapterhouses
*On display here
is Carlos I's
portable altar.
The allegorical
ceiling frescoes
are grotesque
in style.*

Felipe II commissioned the
monastery in 1558. Since
1885, it has been run by
Augustinian monks.

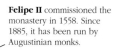

***The Glory of the Spanish
Monarchy* by Luca Giordano**
*This fresco above the main
staircase depicts Carlos I,
Felipe II, and the building of
the monastery.*

The Building of
El Escorial
*When chief architect Juan
Bautista de Toledo died
in 1567 he was replaced
by Juan de Herrera, royal
inspector of monuments.
The plain architectural
style of El Escorial is
called* desornamentado,
literally, "unadorned".

Exploring El Escorial

Felipe II built this palace as the final resting place of his revered father, Carlos I of Spain – Holy Roman Emperor Charles V – whom he succeeded in 1556. The gigantic building, with around 2,600 windows, was sited on the slopes of the Guadarrama and offered a stunning view that stretched away to the Spanish Empire. Felipe II, as King of Naples, Sicily, Milan, The Netherlands, Spain and the New World, used the finest talent available in the realm to decorate the austere monastery. The official tour goes through the Royal Apartments and Royal Pantheon in 45 minutes, leaving you to explore the rest by yourself.

Infanta Isabel Clara by Bartolomé González in the Royal Apartments

Royal Apartments

The palacio de los Austrias, or Royal Apartments, are built around and adjoining the basilica. From her bed, the Infanta Isabel Clara (Felipe II's daughter) could see the high altar and the officiating priest. On the right wall are paintings of her and her sister Catalina by Bartolomé González (1564–1627); between them is a portrait of Felipe II by Sánchez Coello (1531–88).

The **Sala de Retratos** is full of portraits, beginning above the fireplace with *Carlos I* by Juan Pantoja de la Cruz (1553–1608) – a copy of the original painting by Titian lost in a fire in 1604. Moving anti-clockwise, the next portrait is of *Felipe II* by Antonio Moro (1519–76), then *Felipe III* by Pantoja de la Cruz, young *Felipe IV* by Bartolomé González and young *Carlos II* by Juan Carreño de

Miranda (1614–85). In a corner of the room, in a glass case, is the folding chair that Felipe II, afflicted by gout, used during the last years of his life.

At both ends of the **Salas de los Paseos** are magnificent German marquetry doors. Blue Talavera tiles cover the lower part of the walls, while the upper parts are decorated with 16th-century maps and paintings of famous Spanish military victories. Inlaid in the floor of this room and the next-door dining room are solar adjusters made in 1755 for setting clocks.

In the king's chamber, the bed stands where Felipe II died in September 1598, with a view of the basilica's high altar. In his study is the last portrait of the king from Pantoja's studio.

Pantheons

Directly beneath the high altar of the basilica is the **Royal Pantheon**, where almost all Spanish monarchs since Carlos I are laid to rest. This pantheon, with Spanish

Altar in the Royal Pantheon, where most of the Spanish monarchs are laid to rest

black marble, red jasper and Italian gilt bronze decorations, was finished in 1654. Kings lie on the left of the altar and queens on the right. The most recent addition to the pantheon is the mother of Juan Carlos I.

Of the eight other pantheons, one of the most notable is that of **Juan de Austria**, Felipe II's half-brother, who became a hero after defeating the Turks at the Battle of Lepanto. Also worth seeing is **La Tarta**, a white marble polygonal tomb that resembles a cake, where royal children are buried.

Chapterhouses

The salas capitulares, or Chapterhouses, in the monastery's southeast corner, contain wooden benches for the monastery's 100 monks. These four light and spacious rooms with their fine vaulted ceilings are decorated with numerous paintings.

Among the highlights are some by Titian (1490–1576), who painted many scenes for El Escorial. Here can be seen his *St Jerome at Prayer* and *The Last Supper*, the latter unfortunately trimmed to fit its place. Diego de Velázquez (1599–1660) is also represented, with *Joseph's Tunic* (1630), painted

Enamelled and gold-plated retable in the Chapterhouses

while the artist was in Italy.

A collection of paintings by Hieronymus Bosch (1450–1516), known as "El Bosco", is found here. A version of *The Haywain* – the original hangs in the Prado *(see p80)* – was executed by the Bosch school. This painting is said to originate from the Flemish proverb, "The world is like a hay-cart and everybody takes what he can". Felipe II kept it in his bedroom, along with Bosch's *The Garden of Earthly Delights*, also in the Prado. A copy of one panel is displayed here.

Nearby is the beautiful enamelled and gold-plated wooden retable of Carlos I, Holy Emperor Charles V. The king took this portable altar with him on military campaigns.

The Martyrdom of St Maurice and the Theban Legion by El Greco

THE MUSEUMS

WITHIN EL ESCORIAL are several small museums. The north façade entrance leads to St Maurice's Hall, home of *The Martyrdom of St Maurice and the Theban Legion* by El Greco (1541–1614). Nearby stairs lead down to the small **Architectural Museum**, which contains plans, models and engravings of the palace.

Upstairs, the **Museum of Art** covers mostly 16th- and 17th-century works. The first room is dedicated to Italian masters, while the next two contain Flemish art. Michel Coxcie (1499–1592), known as the "Flemish Rafael", is featured here. Most notable is *The Martyrdom of St Philip* triptych.

The long fourth room is dominated by the superb *Calvary* by Rogier van der Weyden (c.1400–64), and copies of the Flemish master's *Virgin* and *St John* by Juan Fernández Navarrate (c.1538–79), on either side.

In the fifth room is *St Jerome Doing Penance* by José de Ribera (1591–1652). In the last room are 16th- and 17th-century Spanish and Italian paintings.

THE LIBRARY

ESTABLISHED BY Felipe II, this was the first public library in Spain, and boasts a vaulted ceiling and a marble floor. In 1619 the king issued a decree that a copy of each new publication in his empire should be sent to him. At its zenith, it contained some 40,000 books and manuscripts, mainly from the 15th and 16th centuries.

The long **Print Room** has a marble floor and glorious vaulted ceiling. The ceiling frescoes by Pellegrino Tibaldi (1527–96) depict Philosophy, Grammar, Rhetoric, Dialectics, Music, Geometry, Astrology and Theology. The Doric wooden shelving was designed by Juan de Herrera (1530–97).

On each of the four main pillars hang portraits of the members of the royal House of Austria – Carlos I, Felipe II, Felipe III and Carlos II. On display are coins and Felipe II's pine Ptolemaic sphere (1582), which placed the earth in the centre of the universe.

THE BASÍLICA

HISTORICALLY, ONLY the aristocracy were permitted to enter the basílica, while the townspeople were confined to the vestibule at the entrance. The Monks's Choir above is still closed to the public.

The basílica contains 45 altars. Among its highlights are the exquisite statue of *Christ Crucified* (1562) in Carrara marble by Benvenuto Cellini. It is found in the chapel to the left of the entrance, with steps leading up to it. Either side of the altar, above the doors leading to the royal bedrooms in the Palacio de los Austrias, are fine gilded bronze cenotaphs of Carlos I and Felipe II worshipping with their families.

The enormous altarpiece was designed by Juan de Herrera with coloured marble, jasper, gilt-bronze sculptures and paintings. The central tabernacle, backlit by a window, took Italian silversmith Jacoppo da Trezzo (1515–89) seven years to craft. The paintings are by Federico Zuccaro (1542–1609) and Pellegrino Tibaldi, who also executed the fresco above. The wood for the cross (also used for Felipe II's coffin) came from a Spanish ship, the *Cinco Llagas* (Five Wounds).

PALACE OF THE BOURBONS

IN CONTRAST TO the simple rooms of the Palacio de los Austrias (Felipe II's royal apartments), the Bourbon apartments are sumptuously furnished. They were created by Carlos IV (reigned 1788–1808), and are hung with framed tapestries, some by Goya, from the Real Fábrica de Tapices (*see p112*).

A china cabinet displays the dinner service which was part of the trousseau of Victoria Eugenia (Queen Victoria's grand-daughter), when she married Alfonso XIII in 1906.

Dining room in the sumptuous Palacio de los Borbones (Palace of the Bourbons)

Gigantic cross at Valle de los Caídos, a symbol of Franco's dictatorship

Santa Cruz del Valle de los Caídos ❷

Madrid. North of El Escorial on M600.
📞 91 890 56 11. 🚌 from El Escorial.
🕐 Oct–Mar: 10am–5pm Tue–Sun;
Apr–Sep: 10am–6pm Tue–Sun.
⬤ 1 & 6 Jan, 1 May, 17 Jul, 10 Aug,
24, 25 & 31 Dec. 🎟 (free Wed to EU
residents). 🗷
ⓦ www.patrimonionacional.es

GENERAL FRANCO had the
Holy Cross of the Valley
of the Fallen built as a memorial to those who died in the
Spanish Civil War *(see p18)*.
The vast cross is located some
13 km (8 miles) north of El
Escorial *(see pp122–5)*, and
can be seen for miles in every
direction. Some Spaniards
find it too chilling a symbol of
the dictatorship to be enjoy-
able, while for others its sheer
size is rewarding.

The cross is 150 m (490 ft)
high and rises above a basilica
carved 250 m (820 ft) deep

into the rock by prisoners of
war. A number of them are
said to have died during the
20-year project.

Next to the basilica's high
altar is the plain white tomb-
stone of Franco and, opposite,
that of José Antonio Primo de
Rivera, founder of the Falange
Española party. Another 40,000
coffins of soldiers from both
sides in the Civil War lie here
out of sight, including those
of two unidentified victims.

Manzanares el Real ❸

Madrid. 🏠 4,500. 🚌 ❶ Plaza del
Pueblo 1 (91 853 00 09). 🛒 Tue &
Fri. 🎉 Fiesta de Verano (early Aug),
Cristo de la Nave (14 Sep).

FROM A DISTANCE, the skyline
of Manzanares el Real is
dominated by its restored 15th-
century castle. Although the
castle is equipped with some
traditional military features,
such as double machicolations
and turrets, it was used mainly
as a residential palace by the
Dukes of Infantado. Below the
castle is a 16th-century church,
a Renaissance portico and fine
capitals. Behind the town, bordering the foothills of the Sierra
de Guadarrama, is **La Pedriza**,
a mass of granite screes and
ravines, very popular with
climbers. It now forms part of
an attractive nature reserve.

ENVIRONS: Colmenar Viejo,
12 km (7.5 miles) to the southeast of Manzanares, has a
superb Gothic-Mudéjar church.

Sierra Centro de Guadarrama ❹

Madrid. 🚉 Puerto de Navacerrada,
Cercedilla. 🚌 Navacerrada, Cercedilla.
❶ Navacerrada (91 856 03 08).

THE CENTRAL SECTION of the
Sierra de Guadarrama was
linked to Madrid by train in
the 1920s. The pine-covered
granite slopes are now dotted
with holiday chalets. Villages
such as **Navacerrada** and
Cercedilla have grown into
popular resorts for skiing,
mountain biking, rock climbing, horse riding and walking.

Breathtaking Navacerrada pass in the Sierra de Guadarrama

The **Valle de Fuenfría**, a nature reserve of wild forests, is best reached via Cercedilla. It has a well-preserved stretch of Roman road, as well as picnic spots and marked walks.

Altarpiece in the Monasterio de Santa María de El Paular

Monasterio de Santa María de El Paular ➎

Southwest of Rascafría on M604.
📞 91 869 14 25. 🚌 Rascafría. ⏰ noon–5pm Mon–Sat, 1–6pm Sun. ✉

CASTILE'S FIRST Carthusian monastery was founded in 1390 on the site of a medieval royal hunting lodge. Although Santa María de El Paular was built in the Gothic style, many Plateresque and Renaissance features were added later.

In 1836, when government minister Mendizábal ordered all church property to be given over to the state, the monastery was abandoned and fell into disrepair. It was not until the 1950s that the state decided to restore it. Today the complex, in a beautiful, tranquil setting, comprises a private hotel (*see p151*), a working Benedictine monastery and a church.

The church's delicate alabaster altarpiece dates from the 15th century and is thought to be the work of Flemish craftsmen. Its panels are decorated with scenes from the life of Jesus Christ. The sumptuous Baroque *camarín* (chamber), behind the altar, dates from 1718 and was designed by Francisco de Hurtado.

Every Sunday, the monks sing an hour-long Gregorian chant in the church. It is worth asking them to show you the cloister's Mudéjar brick vaulting and double sundial. They will normally be happy to do this if they are not busy.

The monastery constitutes an excellent starting point from which to explore the attractive country towns of **Rascafría** and **Lozoya** in the surrounding Lozoya valley. To the southwest lies the **Lagunas de Peñalara** nature reserve.

La Granja de San Ildefonso ➏

Segovia. 🗺 921 47 00 19.
🚌 from Madrid or Segovia. ⏰ mid-Oct–Mar: 10am–1:30pm, 3–5pm Tue–Sat, 10am–2pm Sun & public hols; Apr–mid-Oct: 10am–6pm Tue–Sun. **Gardens** ⏰ mid-Oct–Mar: 10am–6pm; Apr–mid-Oct: 10am–9pm. ⬤ 1, 6, & 23 Jan, 1 May, 25 Aug, 24, 25 & 31 Dec. 🎫 (free Wed to EU residents). ✉ 🖥 www.patrimonionacional.es

THIS ROYAL PLEASURE palace stands on the site of a hunting lodge built by Enrique IV in the 15th century.

In 1720, Felipe V embarked on a project to build the palace and numerous artists and architects contributed to the rich furnishings and the splendid gardens. Some rooms were damaged by fire in 1918, but nearly 8 million euros have been spent restoring them.

There are countless salons decorated with *objets d'art* and Classical frescoes. From the ceilings hang huge chandeliers. The church is adorned in high Baroque style, and the Royal Mausoleum contains the tomb of Felipe V and his queen, Isabel de Farnesio.

The spectacular garden fountains portray Felipe V and his queen as Apollo and Diana. They run on Saturdays and Sundays at 5:30pm.

Serenely beautiful royal gardens at La Granja de San Ildefonso

Segovia ⑦

Tower of San Esteban

SEGOVIA IS THE MOST spectacularly sited city in Spain. The old town is set high on a rocky spur and is surrounded by the Río Eresma and Río Clamores. From afar it looks like a ship, the medieval alcázar on its sharp crag forming the prow, the pinnacles of the Gothic cathedral rising up like masts, and the aqueduct trailing behind like a rudder. The view of the old town from the valley below at sunset is magical.

A relatively short journey from Madrid by car, bus or train, Segovia is readily accessible to visitors to the capital and well worth a look. Easy to negotiate on foot, there is plenty to see and do for a day trip or an overnight stay. Weekends, particularly in summer, are the busiest time in Segovia.

The imposing Gothic cathedral of Segovia

Exploring Segovia

Segovia is dotted with many notable churches, including the 11th-century Romanesque **San Juan de los Caballeros**, with a fine sculptured portico; 13th-century **San Esteban** with a five-storey tower; and 11th-century **San Martín** with its arcades, capitals and gilded altarpiece. The **Iglesia de San Millán**, a Romanesque jewel in the newer part of town, has a Mozarabic tower and a 14th-century Gothic crucifix. The **Iglesia de la Vera Cruz**, outside the old town, is a 12-sided crusader's church (1208).

🔒 Cathedral

Plaza Mayor. ☎ 921 46 22 05.
○ 9:30am–2pm, 4–6pm Mon–Sat (7pm Apr–Oct); 9:30am–6pm Sun (7pm Apr–Oct). ▨ (free Sun am). ♿
Dating from 1525, this massive Gothic structure replaced the old cathedral, which was destroyed in 1511. The old

cloister, however, survived and was rebuilt on the new site. Architect Juan Gil de Hontañón devised the austere but elegant design. The pinnacles, flying buttresses, tower and dome form an impressive silhouette.

The interior is light and elegantly vaulted, with stained-glass windows. It has a high altar designed by Sabatini in 1768. More than 20 beautiful chapels, most enclosed by graceful iron-work grilles, line the nave and apse. The most interesting is the Chapel of the Pietà, which took its name from the beautiful sculpture by Juan de Juni. The cloister, whose pointed arches are divided by

slender mullions and perforated tracery, is accessed through an outstanding Gothic arch by Juan Guas in the Chapel of Christ's Solace. The cloister leads to the chapterhouse museum, which houses 17th-century Brussels tapestries, paintings, sculptures, silver, furniture, books and coins.

🏛 Museo de Segovia

Casa del Sol, Calle Socorro 11. ☎ 921 46 06 13. ● till 2005 for renovation.
This archaeological museum contains 15,000-year-old Stone Age engravings as well as tools, arms, pottery and metalwork through the centuries. There are Roman coins and inscriptions, wall fragments from Arab houses and, in the centre, an interesting collection of belt buckles.

Also worth seeing are two huge Celtic stone bulls which were excavated in the Calle Mayor. It is thought they may have been divine protectors of people or livestock. In the nearby province of Avila, such icons are linked with burials.

▦ Casa de los Picos

Just inside the city walls is the Casa de los Picos, a mansion whose 15th-century façade is adorned with diamond-shaped stones. The building houses an art gallery and school.

⋔ Aqueduct

In use until the late 19th century, this aqueduct was built at the end of the 1st century AD by the Romans, who turned ancient Segovia into an important military base. With this feat of engineering, water from the Río Frío flowed into the city, filtered through a series of tanks along the way.

The Roman aqueduct running through the old town

The Alcázar, like a fairy-tale castle rising above the cliff

VISITORS' CHECKLIST

Segovia. 🏛 *54,300.* 🚉 🚌
🛈 *Plaza Mayor 10 (921 46 03 34).*
🗓 *Tue, Thu, Sat.* 🎉 *San Juan (24
Jun), San Pedro (29 Jun), San Frutos
(25 Oct).* 🌐 *www.infosegovia.com*

the Plateresque tombs of its benefactor, the Marqués de Villena, and his wife, María.

♠ Alcázar

Plaza de la Reina Victoria Eugenia.
🎫 *921 46 07 59.* ⏱ *Oct–Mar:
10am–6pm; Apr–Sep: 10am–7pm.*
🚫 *1 Jan, 6 Jan, 25 Dec.* 🎟 *(free Tue).*
📷 🚭 🌐 *www.alcazardesegovia.com*
Although there has been a fortress on this site since the Middle Ages, the present castle is mostly a reconstruction following a fire in 1862. Its rooms are decorated with armour, paintings and furniture for a medieval atmosphere. There is also a weaponry museum.

The virtually impregnable castle had its heyday in the Middle Ages. The rectangular Juan II tower was completed during the reign of Enrique IV in the 15th century and named after his father. It is worth climbing to the top for breathtaking views of Segovia and the Guadarrama mountains.

In 1764 Carlos III founded the Royal School of Artillery here. Two of its pupils, Doaiz and Velarde, became heroes in the 1808 uprising of *Madrileños* against the French *(see p16)*.

🏛 Palacio Episcopal

Plaza de San Esteban. 🎫 *921 46 09 63.*
⏱ *Jul–Sep: Tue–Sat; Oct–Jun: Sat.* 🎟
Built for the Salcedos family, this 16th-century building was later acquired by Bishop Murillo. Its museum contains paintings, sculptures and gold and silver objects.

🏠 Monasterio de El Parral

Subida al Parral 2. 🎫 *921 43 12 98.* ⏱
*10am–12:30pm, 4:30–6:30pm Mon–Sat;
10–11:30am, 4:30–6:30pm Sun.*
Just north of the city walls, Segovia's largest monastery has four cloisters and a Plateresque altarpiece. It contains

🏠 Convento de los Carmelitas

Alameda de la Fuencisla. 🎫 *921 43
13 49.* ⏱ *10am–1:30pm, 4–7pm
Tue–Sun (till 8pm Jun–Sep).*
In a secluded Eresma valley, St John of the Cross founded this convent in the 16th century and was Prior from 1588–91. The mystical poet was also co-founder, with Santa Teresa, of a barefooted *(descalzos)* order of Carmelites which ran to the strictest of disciplines.

The tree-lined Plaza Mayor

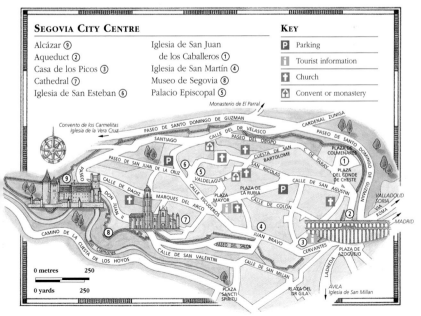

SEGOVIA CITY CENTRE

Alcázar ⑨
Aqueduct ②
Casa de los Picos ③
Cathedral ⑦
Iglesia de San Esteban ⑥

Iglesia de San Juan
  de los Caballeros ①
Iglesia de San Martín ④
Museo de Segovia ⑧
Palacio Episcopal ⑤

KEY

🅿   Parking

🛈   Tourist information

✝   Church

⛪   Convent or monastery

0 metres   250

0 yards   250

Buitrago del Lozoya, standing next to the river

Buitrago del Lozoya ❽

Madrid. 🏘 *1,600.* 🚌 🛈 *Calle Tahona 11 (91 868 00 56).* 🛒 *Sat.* 🎪 *La Asunción y San Roque (15 Aug), Cristo de los Esclavos (15 Sep).*

P ICTURESQUELY SITED above a meander in the Río Lozoya is the walled town of Buitrago del Lozoya. Founded by the Romans, it was fortified by the Arabs, and became a bustling market town in medieval times. The 14th-century Gothic-Mudéjar castle is in ruins, although the gatehouse, arches and stretches of the original wall survive. Today, the castle is used as a venue for bullfights and a festival of theatre and music in the summer.

The old quarter, within the town's walls, retains its charming atmosphere. The church of **Santa María del Castillo**, dating from the 15th century, has a Mudéjar tower and ceilings moved here from the old hospital. The **town hall**, or *ayuntamiento*, in the newer part of the town preserves a 16th-century processional cross. In the basement is the small **Museo Picasso**. The prints, drawings and ceramics on display were collected by the artist's friend and barber, Eugenio Arias, an inhabitant of the town.

🏛 **Museo Picasso**
Plaza de Picasso 1. 📞 *91 868 00 56.* ⬤ *Mon.*

Sierra Norte ❾

Madrid. 🚌 *Montejo.* 🛈 *Calle Real 64, Montejo (91 869 70 58).* 🌐 *www.sierranorte.com*

T HE BLACK SLATE HAMLETS of the Sierra Norte, which was once known as the Sierra Pobre (Poor Sierra), are located in the most rural part of the Comunidad de Madrid (Madrid province). At **Montejo de la Sierra**, the largest village in the area, an information centre organizes riding, rental of traditional houses and visits to the nature reserve of the **Hayedo de Montejo de la Sierra**. This is one of the southernmost beech woods in Europe and a relic of an era when climatic conditions were more suitable for the beech. From Montejo, you can drive on to picturesque hamlets such as **La Hiruela** or **Puebla de la Sierra**, both of which are set in lovely walking country.

The drier southern hills slope down to the **Embalse de Puentes Viejas**, a reservoir where summer chalets cluster around artificial beaches. On the eastern edge of the Sierra Norte lies **Patones**, which supposedly escaped invasion by the Moors and Napoleon due to its isolated location.

Sigüenza ❿

Guadalajara. 🏘 *4,700.* 🚌 🛈 *Ermita del Humilladero (949 34 70 07).* 🛒 *Sat.* 🎪 *San Juan (24 Jun), San Roque (15 Aug).* 🌐 *www.siguenza.com*

D OMINATING the hillside town of Sigüenza is its impressive castle-parador *(see p151).* The **cathedral**, in the old town, was begun in the 12th century. It is Romanesque

Semi-recumbent figure of El Doncel on his tomb in Sigüenza cathedral

in style, with later additions, such as the Gothic-Plateresque cloisters. In one of the chapels is the Tomb of *El Doncel* (the young nobleman). It was built for Martín Vázquez de Arce, Isabel of Castile's pageboy *(see p20)*, who was killed in a battle against the Moors in Granada in 1486. The sacristy has a beautiful ceiling carved with flowers and cherubs, by Alonso de Covarrubias.

It was founded as the Roman settlement of Arriaca, and then replaced by the Moorish settlement of Wad-al-Hajarah. In 1085 it was taken by Alfonso VI in the Christian Reconquest *(see p13)*, and rose to prominence in the 14th century.

The **Palacio de los Duques del Infantado**, built from the 14th to the 17th century by the powerful Mendoza dynasty, is an outstanding example of Gothic-Mudéjar architecture. The main façade and the two-storey patio are adorned with delicate carvings. Following Civil War bombing, the palace was restored. It now houses the Museo Provincial – the local art museum.

Among the town's churches is the **Iglesia de Santiago**, which has a Gothic-Plateresque chapel designed by Alonso de Covarrubias. In the 15th-century **Iglesia de San Francisco** was the family mausoleum of the Mendoza family, while the cathedral is built on the site of a mosque. The **Iglesia de Santa María**, which was built in the 13th century, has typical Mudéjar horseshoe arches and a bell tower.

Intricate diamond stonework on the façade of the Palacio de los Duques del Infantado

Guadalajara ⑪

Guadalajara. 🏛 68,200. 🚉 🚌 🅸
Plaza de los Caídos 6 (949 21 16 26).
🔺 Tue, Sat. 🎪 Virgen de la Antigua
(Sep). 🆆 www.jccm.es/turismo

ALTHOUGH GUADALAJARA'S history is largely lost in the modern industrial city, traces of its past splendour survive.

🚩 Palacio de los Duques del Infantado
Avenida del Infantado del Ejército.
📞 949 21 33 01. **Museum** 🕐
Tue–Sun. **Palace** 🕐 Open daily. 📷

Façade of Colegio de San Ildefonso in Alcalá de Henares

Alcalá de Henares ⑫

Madrid. 🏛 176,400. 🚉 🚌
🅸 Callejón Santa María (91 889 26 94). 🔺 Mon & Wed. 🎪 Feria de Alcalá (late Aug).
🆆 www.alcaladehenares-turismo.com

AT THE HEART of a modern industrial town is one of Spain's most renowned university quarters. Founded in 1499 by Cardinal Cisneros, Alcalá's **university** became one of the foremost places of learning in 16th-century Europe, famous for its language teaching. The university was transferred to Madrid in 1836. Although most of the original 40 colleges have since been destroyed and re-placed with new buildings, the most historic one, the much-restored Renaissance **Colegio de San Ildefonso**, survives. It has a Plateresque façade (1543) by Rodrigo Gil de Hontañón. Former students include Lope de Vega *(see p26)*. In 1517 the university produced Europe's first polyglot bible, which had parallel texts in Latin, Greek, Hebrew and Chaldean.

Alcalá's other sights are the cathedral, the **Casa-Museo de Cervantes**, birthplace of the author and now an intriguing museum, and the recently restored 19th-century Neo-Moorish **Palacio de Laredo**.

🏛 Casa-Museo de Cervantes
Calle Mayor. 📞 918 89 96 54.
🕐 Tue–Sun. ⬤ public hols.
🚩 Palacio de Laredo
Paseo de la Estación 18. 📞 918 82 13 54. 🕐 Tue–Sun. 📷 📷

MIGUEL DE CERVANTES

Miguel de Cervantes Saavedra, Spain's greatest literary figure *(see p26)*, was born in Alcalá de Henares in 1547. After fighting in the naval Battle of Lepanto (1571), he was held captive by the Turks for more than five years. In 1605, when he was almost 60 years old, the first of two parts of his comic masterpiece *Don Quixote* was published to popular acclaim. Cervantes continued writing novels and plays until his death in Madrid on 23 April 1616, the same day that Shakespeare died.

Lavish, finely woven 18th-century tapestry inside the Palacio de El Pardo

Palacio de El Pardo ⑬

El Pardo, northwest of Madrid on N605.
📞 91 376 15 00. 🚌 from Moncloa.
🕐 10:30am–6pm Mon–Sat (till 5pm Oct–Apr), 9:25am–1:40pm Sun and public hols (from 9:55am Oct–Apr).
⬤ during royal visits. 📷 (free Wed).
🌐 www.patrimonionacional.es

THIS ROYAL HUNTING lodge and palace, set in parkland, includes General Franco among its former residents. A tour takes visitors around the palace's original Habsburg wing and identical 18th-century extension by Francesco Sabatini.

The Bourbon interior is decorated with frescoes, gilt mouldings and tapestries, many of which were woven at the Real Fábrica de Tapices (see p112). Today the palace is used to entertain heads of state and royalty. Surrounding the palace and the village of El Pardo is an enormous oak forest, where you can eat at a restaurant or enjoy a picnic.

Museo del Aire ⑭

Carretera de Extremadura, km 10.5.
📞 91 509 16 90. 🚌 from Estación del Príncipe Pío (Norte) any bus towards Alcorcón or Móstoles. 🕐 10am–2pm Tue–Sun. 🔴 1 Jan, Easter Thu & Good Fri, 10 & 25 Dec. 📷 (free Wed). ♿

AMONG THE MANY magnificent flying machines on display at the museum of Spanish aviation, the star exhibit is the Breguet-XIX Jesús del Gran Poder, which made the first Spanish transatlantic flight in 1929. Others include the 1911 Vilanova-Acedo, one of the first planes made in Spain, and the Henkel 111 German warplane, the only one ever made. Also on display is La Cierva – half-plane, half-helicopter.

Some of the planes are linked with famous people. For example, in 1936 General Franco flew from the Canary Islands to Tetuán to start the Spanish Civil War in the De Havilland Dragon Rapide; Juan Carlos I flew a Bell 47G solo; Prince Felipe made his first solo flight in a T-Mentor; and in the Trener Master, Tomás Castaños won the 1964 World Aerobatic Championships.

Prototypes of various Spanish aircraft include the Saeta, Super Saeta and the Casa C–101 Aviojet. The F–104 Starfighter, notorious for its tendency to crash, is one in which Spanish pilots flew a record 10,000 hours without accidents.

On the runway you may see the bulbous Boeing Guppy, which flies part of the fuselage (made nearby) of the Airbus to its assembly plant in France.

In addition to aircraft, the museum provides information on the lives of famous aviators, and features displays of Air Force regalia, flight plans and models. There are also films, videos, drawings, documents, photographs and paintings.

Early Lufthansa aircraft at the Museo del Aire

◁ Cattle grazing on the isolated plains of La Mancha

Chinchón

Madrid. 🏘 *4,300.* 🚌 🛈 *Plaza Mayor 3 (91 894 00 84).* 🚂 *Sat.* 🎉 *Semana Santa (Easter Week), San Roque (12–18 Aug).* 🌐 www.ciudadchinchon.com

CHINCHÓN IS ARGUABLY Madrid province's most picturesque town. The 16th-century, typically Castilian, porticoed **Plaza Mayor** has a splendidly theatrical air. It comes alive for the Easter passion play (*see p34*) and during the August bullfights. The 16th-century church, perched above the square, has an altar painting by Goya (*see p26*), whose brother was a priest here. Just off the square an 18th-century Augustinian monastery has been converted into a parador with a peaceful patio garden (*see p150*). There is a ruined 15th-century castle on a hill to the west of town. It is closed to the public but, from the outside, there are excellent views of Chinchón and the surrounding countryside.

Madrileños often come to the town at weekends to sample the superb chorizo and locally produced *anís* (*see p157*) in the town's many taverns.

Chinchón's unique porticoed Plaza Mayor, occasionally used for bullfights

Palacio Real de Aranjuez

Plaza de Parejas, Aranjuez. 📞 *91 891 13 44.* 🚌 🚆 🔵 *Apr–Sep: 10am–6:15pm Tue–Sun; Oct–Mar: 10am–5:15pm; gardens until 8:30pm, (6:30pm Oct–Mar) by appointment for Casa del Labrador.* 🎫 *(free Wed to EU residents).* 📷 ♿ 🌐 www.patrimonionacional.es

THE ROYAL SUMMER PALACE and gardens of Aranjuez grew up around a medieval hunting lodge standing beside a natural weir, the meeting point of the Tagus and Jarama rivers.

Today's palace was built by Carlos III in the 18th century to restore an earlier Habsburg palace commissioned by Felipe II, which burned down. A guided tour takes you through numerous Baroque rooms, including the Chinese Porcelain Room, the Hall of Mirrors and the Smoking Room, modelled on the

Alhambra in Granada. It is worth visiting Aranjuez for the simple pleasure of walking in the 3 sq km (1 sq mile) of shady royal gardens which inspired Joaquín Rodrigo's *Concierto de Aranjuez*. The Parterre Garden and Island Garden survive from the original 16th-century palace.

The 18th-century Prince's Garden is decorated with fountains and trees from the Americas. The Casa de Marinos (Sailors' House) is a small museum housing boats once used by the royal family.

At the far end of the garden stands the Casa del Labrador (Labourer's Cottage), a richly decorated royal pavilion built by Carlos IV (*see p16*).

The restaurants in the town of Aranjuez are very popular. In summer, a 19th-century

Pleasant grounds at the Palacio Real de Aranjuez

steam train, built to take strawberries to the market in Madrid, runs between here and the capital.

Illescas 🅰

Toledo. 🏘 *14,000.* 🚌 🛈 *Plaza Mayor 1 (925 51 10 51).* 🚂 *Thu.* 🎉 *Fiesta de Milagro (11 Mar), Fiesta Patronal (31 Aug).*

THE TOWN OF ILLESCAS was the summer venue for the court of Felipe II (*see p15*). While there is little to see of the old town, it does have two interesting churches. The **Parroquial de la Asunción**, built between the 13th and 16th centuries, is easily identified by its Mudéjar tower, one of the best examples of its kind in the region. Nearby is the 16th-century church of the **Hospital de Nuestra Señora de la Caridad**, which boasts an important art collection. The church owns five outstanding works by El Greco (*see p139*), the most famous being *The Virgin Dictating to Saint Ildefonso*. In its Chapel of Relics there is a portrait of Francisco Pacheco de Toledo by Pantoja de la Cruz and, in the sacristy, there is an original Ecce Homo by Luis de Morales.

🏛 **Hospital de Nuestra Señora de la Caridad**
Calle Cardenal Cisneros 2.
📞 *925 54 00 35.*
🔵 *daily.* 📷 ♿

Street-by-Street: Toledo ⓲

Damascene work, typical of Toledo

PICTURESQUELY SITED on a hill above the River Tagus is the historic centre of Toledo. Behind the old walls lies much evidence of the city's rich history. The Romans built a fortress on the site of the present-day Alcázar. The Visigoths made Toledo their capital in the 6th century AD, and left behind several churches. In the Middle Ages, Toledo was a melting pot of Christian, Muslim and Jewish cultures, and it was during this period that the city's most outstanding monument – its cathedral – was built. In the 16th century the painter El Greco came to live in Toledo, and today the city is home to many of his works.

The Iglesia de San Román, of Visigothic origin, now contains a museum relating the city's past under the Visigoths.

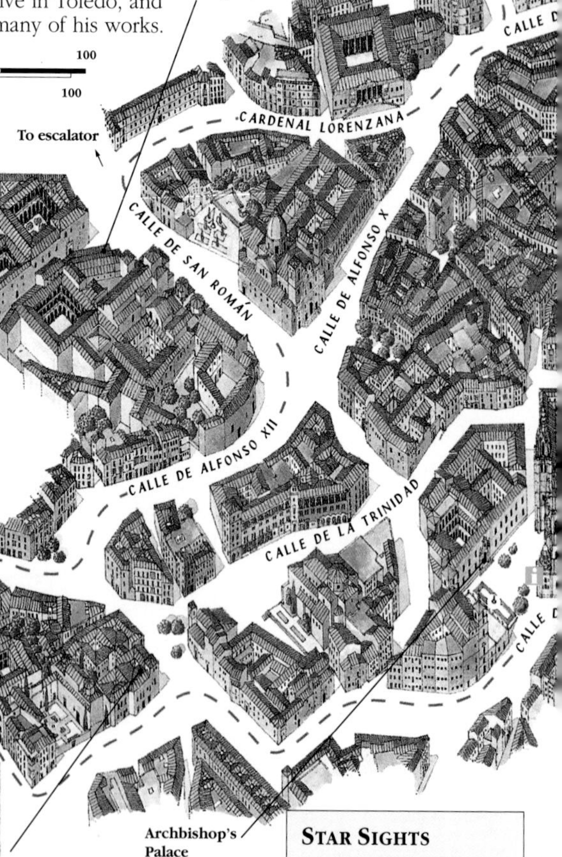
Puerta de Valmardón
0 metres 100
0 yards 100
To escalator
CALLE D
CARDENAL LORENZANA
CALLE DE SAN ROMÁN
CALLE DE ALFONSO X
CALLE DE ALFONSO XII
CALLE DE LA TRINIDAD
CALLE D
Sinagoga de Santa María la Blanca; Monasterio de San Juan de los Reyes
Sinagoga del Tránsito; Casa-Museo de El Greco
Archbishop's Palace

★ Iglesia de Santo Tomé
This church, with a beautiful Mudéjar tower, houses El Greco's The Burial of the Count of Orgaz.

Taller del Moro
Once used as a workshop by craftsmen building the cathedral, this Mudéjar palace now houses a museum of Mudéjar ceramics and tiles.

STAR SIGHTS

- **★ Iglesia de Santo Tomé**
- **★ Museo de Santa Cruz**
- **★ Cathedral**

**The Puerta del
ol** has a double
loorish arch and
two towers.

Ermita del Cristo
de la Luz
*This small mosque, the
city's only remaining
Muslim building, dates
from around AD 1000.*

Tourist information;
Estación de
Autobuses & RENFE

The Plaza de Zocodover
is named after the market
which was held here in
Moorish times. It is still the
city's main square, with
many cafés and shops.

ALFILERITOS

PLAZA DE
ZOCODOVER

CALLE DEL COMERCIO

CUESTA DE CARLOS V

SIXTO RAMÓN PARRO

ENAL CISNEROS

★ Museo de Santa Cruz
*The city's main fine arts
collection includes several
tapestries from Flanders.
Among them is this
15th-century zodiac
tapestry, with well-
preserved rich colours.*

KEY

– – – Suggested route

★ Cathedral
*Built on the site of a Visigothic
cathedral and a mosque, this
impressive structure is one
of the largest cathedrals in
Christendom (see pp140–41).
The Flamboyant Gothic high
altar reredos (1504) is the
work of several artists.*

Alcázar
*Inside the fortress, a statue
of Carlos V portrays him
triumphant over a Moor.
The original is on display
in the Museo de Prado.*

Toledo cathedral rising above the rooftops of the medieval part of the city

Exploring Toledo

Toledo is easily reached from Madrid by rail, bus or car, and is then best explored on foot. To visit all the main sights you need at least two days, but it is possible to walk around the medieval and Jewish quarters in a long morning. To avoid the heavy crowds, go midweek and stay for a night, when the city is at its most atmospheric.

♣ Alcázar

Cuesta de Carlos V. ☎ 925 22 16 73. ◐ until 2006. ☒ (free Wed). ✉ Library ☎ 925 25 66 80. ◯ 9am–9pm Mon–Fri, 9am–2pm Sat.

The fortified palace of Carlos I (Holy Roman Emperor Charles V) stands on the site of former Roman, Visigothic and Muslim fortresses. Its severe square profile suffered fire damage before being nearly destroyed in 1936 when the Nationalists survived a 70-day siege by the Republicans. Restoration followed the original plans and the building now houses an army museum. The museum is closed pending the move of the Museo del Ejército (see p77) from Madrid to the Alcázar in 2006. The Alcázar **library** contains the Borbón-Lorenzana collection with more than 100,000 books dating from the 16th to the 19th century and 1,000 manuscripts from the 11th to the 19th century.

🏛 Museo de Santa Cruz

Calle Cervantes 3. ☎ 925 22 10 36. ◯ daily. ◐ Sun pm. ☒ (free Sat pm & Sun am to EU residents).

This museum is housed in a 16th-century hospital founded by Cardinal Mendoza. The building has some outstanding Renaissance features, including the main doorway, staircase and cloister. The four wings, in the shape of a Greek cross, are dedicated to the fine arts. The collection is strong in medieval and Renaissance works of art. There are also paintings by El Greco, including one of his last, *The Assumption* (1613), still in its original altarpiece. Displays include two typical Toledan crafts: armour and

The Assumption (1613) by El Greco in the Museo de Santa Cruz

damascened swords, made by inlaying blackened steel with gold wire. Damascene work, including swords, plates and jewellery, is still made in the city. An extension is currently being built, which is due to open at the end of 2005.

🔒 Iglesia de Santo Tomé

Plaza del Conde 4. ☎ 925 25 60 98. ◯ daily. ☒ (free Wed pm to EU residents).

Visitors come to Santo Tomé mainly to admire El Greco's masterpiece, *The Burial of the Count of Orgaz*. An important patron of the church, the Count paid for much of the 14th-century building that stands today. The painting, commissioned in his memory by a parish priest, depicts the miraculous appearance of St Augustine and St Stephen at his burial, to raise his body to heaven. It has never been moved from the setting for which it was painted, nor restored. Nevertheless, it is remarkable for its contrast of colours. In the foreground, allegedly, are the artist and his son (both looking out) as well as Cervantes. The church is thought to date back to the 12th century, and its tower is one of the best examples of Mudéjar architecture in the city.

Nearby is the **Pastelería Santo Tomé**, a good place to buy locally made marzipan.

🕎 Sinagoga de Santa María la Blanca

Calle de los Reyes Católicos 4.
📞 925 22 72 57. ⭘ daily. 💷 (free Wed pm).

The oldest and largest of the city's eight original synagogues, this monument dates back to the 12th century. In 1405 it was taken over as a church by the military-religious Order of Calatrava. Restoration has returned it almost to its original beauty – finely carved stone capitals and wall panels stand out against plain white arches and plasterwork. In the chapel is a Plateresque altarpiece. In 1391 a massacre of Jews took place here, a turning point after years of religious tolerance in the city.

Mudéjar arches in the Sinagoga de Santa María la Blanca

🕎 Sinagoga del Tránsito

Calle Samuel Levi. 📞 925 22 36 65.
⭘ Tue–Sun am. 💷 (free Sat pm & Sun am). ⬤ 1 Jan, 1 May, 24, 25 & 31 Dec. 🆆 www.museosefardi.net

The most elaborate Mudéjar interior in the city is hidden behind the deceptively humble façade of this former synagogue, built in the 14th century by Samuel Ha-Leví, the Jewish treasurer to Pedro the Cruel. The interlaced frieze of the lofty prayer hall harmoniously fuses Islamic, Gothic and Hebrew geometric motifs below a wonderful coffered ceiling.

Adjoining the synagogue is a museum of Sephardi (Spanish Jewish) culture. The manuscripts, costumes and sacred objects on display date from both before and after the Jews' expulsion from Spain at the end of the 15th century.

Ornate ceiling in the Monasterio de San Juan de los Reyes

🔒 Monasterio de San Juan de los Reyes

Calle de los Reyes Católicos 17.
📞 925 22 38 02. ⭘ daily. 💷

A wonderful mixture of architectural styles, this monastery was commissioned by the Catholic Monarchs in honour of their victory over the Portuguese at the battle of Toro (near Salamanca) in 1476. It was intended to be their burial place, but they were actually laid to rest in Granada. Largely the work of Juan Guas, the church's main Isabelline structure was completed in 1492. Although badly damaged by Napoleon's troops in 1808 *(see p16)*, it has been restored to its original splendour. It retains superb features such as a Gothic cloister (1510) which has a beautiful multi-coloured Mudéjar ceiling. Near to the church is a stretch of the Jewish quarter's original wall.

🏛 Casa-Museo de El Greco

Calle Samuel Leví. 📞 925 22 40 46.
⭘ Tue–Sun am. 💷 (free Sat pm & Sun am).

It is not clear whether El Greco actually lived in or simply near to this house, in the heart of the Jewish quarter, which has been turned into a museum containing an important collection of his works. Canvases on display include *View of Toledo*, a detailed depiction of the city at the time, and the superb series *Christ and the Apostles*. Underneath the museum is a chapel with a fine Mudéjar ceiling and a collection of art by painters of the Toledan School, such as Luis Tristán, a student of El Greco.

🔒 Iglesia de Santiago del Arrabal

Calle Arrabal.

This is one of Toledo's most beautiful Mudéjar monuments. It can easily be identified by its tower, reminiscent of a minaret, which is said to date back to the 12th-century Reconquest *(see p13)*. The church, which was built slightly later, has a beautiful woodwork ceiling. The ornate Mudéjar pulpit and Plateresque altarpiece stand out against the plain interior.

🕎 Puerta Antigua de Bisagra

When Alfonso VI conquered Toledo in 1085, he entered it through this gateway, alongside El Cid. It is the only gateway in the city to have kept its original 10th-century military architecture. The huge towers are topped by a 12th-century Arab gatehouse.

EL GRECO

Born in Crete in 1541, El Greco ("the Greek") came to Toledo in 1577 to paint the altarpiece in the convent of Santo Domingo el Antiguo. Enchanted by the city, he stayed here, painting religious portraits and altarpieces for other churches. Although El Greco was trained in Italy and influenced by masters such as Tintoretto, his works are closely identified with the city where he settled. He died in Toledo in 1614.

Domenikos Theotocopoulos, better known as El Greco

Toledo Cathedral

THE SPLENDOUR OF TOLEDO'S massive cathedral reflects its history as the spiritual heart of the Spanish church and the seat of the Primate of all Spain. Still today, the Mozarabic Mass, which dates back to Visigothic times, is said here. The present cathedral was built on the site of a 7th-century church. Work began in 1226 and spanned three centuries, until the completion of the last vaults in 1493. This long period of construction explains the cathedral's mixture of styles: pure French Gothic – complete with flying buttresses – on the exterior and Spanish decorative styles, such as Mudéjar and Plateresque work, in the interior.

Sacristy
El Greco's The Denuding of Christ, above the marble altar, was painted especially for the cathedral. Also here are works by Titian, Van Dyck and Goya.

The Cloister, on two floors, was built in the 14th century on the site of the old Jewish market.

View of Toledo Cathedral
Dominating the city skyline is the Gothic tower at the west end of the nave. The best view of the cathedral, and the city, is from the parador (see p151).

The belfry in the tower contains a heavy bell known as *La Gorda* ("the Fat One").

The Puerta del Mollete, on the west façade, is the main entrance to the cathedral. From this door, *mollete* (soft bread) was distributed to the poor.

★ Monstrance
The 16th-century Gothic silver and gold monstrance is over 3 m (10 ft) high. It is carried through the streets during the Corpus Christi celebrations (see p34).

STAR FEATURES

★ **Monstrance**

★ **Transparente**

★ **High Altar Reredos**

★ **Choir**

★ **Transparente**
This Baroque altarpiece of marble, jasper and bronze, by Narciso Tomé, is illuminated by an ornate sky-light. It stands out from the mainly Gothic interior.

VISITORS' CHECKLIST

Calle Arco Palacio 2. **[** 925 22 22 41. ◯ 8am–6:30pm daily. **✝** 8am, 9am, 9:45am (Mozarabic Mass), 10am, 5:30pm, 6:30pm daily (also 11am, noon & 1pm Sun). **Choir, Treasury, Sacristy and Chapterhouse** ◯ 10:30am–6:30pm Mon–Sat, 2pm–6:30pm Sun (last tickets sold at 6pm).

Capilla de Santiago

The Capilla de San Ildefonso contains the superb Plateresque tomb of cardinal Alonso Carrillo de Albornoz.

Chapterhouse
Above beautiful 16th-century frescoes by Juan de Borgoña is this spectacular, multi-coloured Mudéjar ceiling.

Puerta de los Leones

★ **High Altar Reredos**
The polychrome reredos, one of the most beautiful in Spain, depicts scenes from Christ's life.

Puerta Llana (entrance)

The Puerta del Perdón, or Door of Mercy, has a tympanum decorated with religious characters.

The Capilla Mozárabe has a beautiful Renaissance ironwork grille, carved by Juan Francés in 1524.

★ **Choir**
The carvings on the wooden lower stalls depict scenes of the fall of Granada. The alabaster upper ones show figures from the Old Testament.

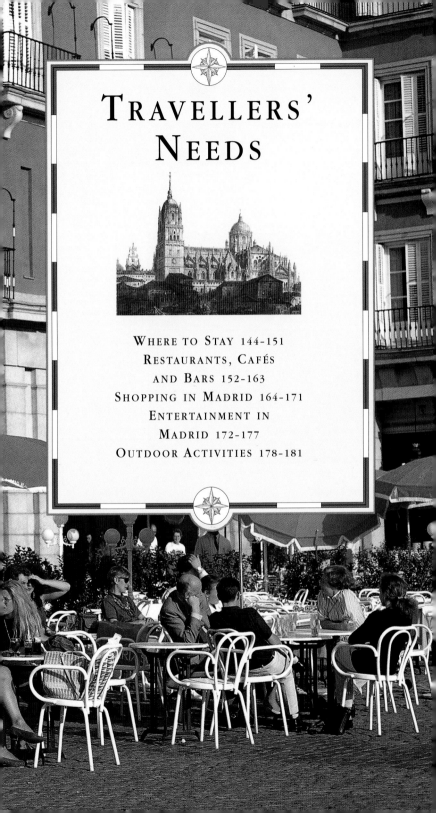

TRAVELLERS'
NEEDS

WHERE TO STAY

W HEN ALFONSO XIII *(see p17)* was married in 1906, he was embarrassed that his city, unlike other European capitals, did not have elegant hotels to accommodate his wedding guests. He decided to put things right, and personally instigated the building of the luxurious Ritz and Palace, which are still two of the best hotels in Europe. But, centuries before, Madrid already had a strong tradition of more modest hostelries and guest houses offering shelter to the multitude of visitors from the provinces and from other countries. Today, the city continues to provide an abundance of comfortable lodgings, be they simple *pensiones*, pleasant three-star hotels in converted town houses, or palatial five-star establishments with every possible amenity.

Hotel doorman

Stately façade of the Reina Victoria *(see p147)* from the Plaza de Santa Ana

WHERE TO LOOK

C ENTRAL MADRID has plenty of hotels, in every price category, close to the major sights. Some areas, such as Gran Vía and around Puerta del Sol, can be very noisy, both day and night, so soundproofing is a big consideration. If you are driving, parking in central Madrid is difficult, and a hotel with parking facilities is essential. If it is tranquillity you want, and you do not mind having to take a taxi or the metro to go sightseeing, there are some good hotels in the residential districts of Salamanca (east) or Chamberí (north). A few modern luxury hotels, aimed mainly at business travellers, are located along the Paseo de la Castellana, and on the eastern side of the M30 ring road, convenient for those needing easy access to the airport.

GRADING AND FACILITIES

S PANISH HOTELS are rated from one to five stars. The top category is Gran Lujo (GL), indicated by five stars. Madrid has 13 hotels in this category – the Ritz, the Palace *(see p148)* and the modern Villamagna *(see p149)* are among the best.

Suite at the Ritz – one of Madrid's most exclusive and expensive hotels *(see p148)*

Although the star-rating gives a rough indication of standards and prices, it is not an exact science. Three-star hotels, for example, can include anything from charmless grey establishments in need of repair, to real gems with friendly staff and interesting decor. Both four- and five-star hotels should have a good range of extra facilities, and they will be fairly smart, but often less so than a similarly-priced hotel located in a rural part of Spain. Most Madrid hotels in the three- to five-star category have air conditioning and televisions. Very few have gardens or swimming pools.

One- and two-star hotels offer basic facilities, although most now have a telephone and television in the rooms, as well as individual bathrooms. The better ones will have friendly staff, high standards of cleanliness, direct-dial phones and air-conditioning, which is essential in summer.

Hostal-residencias (HR) are hotels without a meal service; otherwise, they are the same as other hotels. Accommodation with basic facilities is also offered in *bostales* (Hs) and *pensiones* (P) at much lower prices than hotels. The two types are essentially the same.

A double room for one person *(habitación doble uso individual)*, which will cost slightly more than a single room, is an option for single travellers needing more space.

Some hotels have their own parking area. Those without often have an arrangement with neighbouring public car parks. There is an additional charge for this service, and it can be quite expensive.

One of Madrid's many inexpensive *hostales* scattered around the centre

PARADORS

PARADORS ARE the deservedly famous state-run hotels in Spain. The best of them are located in converted historic buildings, and many are worth a visit in their own right. Madrid itself has none, but some of the most picturesque paradors are in striking distance of the city, including the first one to open, in 1928, in the Sierra de Gredos. A 17th-century palace in Chinchón *(see p150)*, a Moorish castle in Sigüenza *(see p151)* and a luxury parador in Segovia *(see p151)* offer unique accommodation.

Guest room in the spacious Crowne Plaza *(see p146)*

HOW TO BOOK

WHILE MADRID HAS ample hotel options, you never know whether an important trade fair or conference is going to cause greater demand, so prior booking is advisable. This can be done through a travel agent or directly by fax, phone or email. If you have any special requirements, such as a twin or double bed, interior room or one facing the street, make these known when booking. The receptionist will specify the hour until which your reservation will be held. Few hotels

demand a credit card number or deposit to guarantee a booking. When checking in, you will be asked for ID (a national identity card or passport) and to sign a registration form. Deposit valuables in the safe and tip the porter a few euros.

When leaving, rooms must be vacated before noon, but hotels will look after your luggage if your travel plans call for a later departure.

PAYMENT AND DISCOUNTS

PRACTICALLY ALL hotels take major credit cards, but not personal cheques. Rates are increased by seven per cent value-added tax (IVA). Madrid hotels often offer discounts on weekend stays and in August, and it is also possible to buy discount vouchers at travel agents. Companies can usually get a corporate rate – *precio de empresa* – which may mean a reduction of up to a third.

When booking, ask for the room rate, as this is often lower than the listed price. It is even worth asking for a discount.

SPECIAL NEEDS

ON THE WHOLE Spain is not wheelchair friendly, but newer hotels have ramps, wide elevators (lifts) and certain rooms adapted for disabled people. Enquire with the hotel beforehand, and be specific about your needs; a receptionist might think a ramp up the front steps makes the hotel "wheelchair accessible".

Few Madrid hotels, and only those with four or five stars, provide non-smoking rooms.

SELF CATERING

SOME HOTELS, known as *hotel apartamentos* or *apart-hotels*, contain a number of limited self-catering apartments (efficiency units). A few other establishments are entirely self-catering. These are called *apartamentos turísticos*, and usually require a minimum stay of one week.

CHILDREN

CHILDREN ARE WELCOME in most Madrid hotels, whatever the category. For small children, a cot or an extra bed will be put in the parents' room, often at no additional cost. But, as a rule, hotels provide few facilities for children, and only some of the more expensive offer babysitting – in Spain children tend to go everywhere with their parents.

HOSTELS

THE SPANISH *HOSTAL* is not a hostel, but a modest hotel. Madrid has two youth hostels, known as *albergues juveniles*: one on Calle de Santa Cruz de Marcenado in central Madrid, the other in the Casa de Campo *(see p114)*. Space is at a premium; to secure a place, book ahead through www.madrid.org/inforjoven, or the **Instituto de Albergues Juveniles** on Gran Vía 10, 3rd floor, telephone: 91 720 11 65.

The opulent Ritz hotel *(see p148)* facing Plaza Canovas del Castillo

Choosing a Hotel

THE HOTELS in this guide have been selected across a wide price range for excellent facilities and location. Many also have a highly recommended restaurant, pretty gardens or bedrooms with balcony views. The chart is divided into chapter areas for easy reference. For details on restaurants see pages 152–163.

		CREDIT CARDS	NUMBER OF ROOMS	PRIVATE PARKING	SWIMMING POOL	GARDEN OR TERRACE

OLD MADRID

		CREDIT CARDS	NUMBER OF ROOMS	PRIVATE PARKING	SWIMMING POOL	GARDEN OR TERRACE
HOSTAL BUENOS AIRES. Map 2 D5. W www.hotelshn.com € Gran Vía 61, 28013. 91 542 01 02. FAX 91 542 28 69. A simple and economical hotel conveniently located on the busy Gran Vía. Each of the bedrooms has its own balcony or small terrace. 📻 🍽 TV		DC MC V	25			
CARLOS V. Map 4 E2. W www.bestwestern.es/carlosv €€ Calle Maestro Victoria 5, 28013. 91 531 41 00. FAX 91 531 37 61. A city-centre hotel in a pedestrian street beside the Puerta del Sol, run by a family. There are interconnecting bedrooms, family rooms, rooms with balconies and top-floor rooms with sizeable sun terraces. 📻 🍽 TV		AE DC MC V	67			
REGENTE. Map 4 F1. W www.hotelregente.com €€ Calle de Mesonero Romanos 9, 28013. 91 521 29 41. FAX 91 532 30 14. Convenient, centrally located hotel combining new facilities with old-style furniture. Rooms facing the Gran Vía can be noisy. 📻 🍽 TV		AE DC MC V	145			
REYES CATÓLICOS. Map 3 C4. W www.domus-hoteles.es €€ Calle del Ángel 18, 28005. 91 365 86 00. FAX 91 365 98 67. This modern, central hotel is popular and always very busy. Children are made welcome. The bedroom windows are double-glazed for sound-proofing. There are views of the city from the roof terrace. 📻 🍽 TV		AE DC MC V	38	▪		▪
PUERTA DE TOLEDO. Map 3 C5. W www.hotel-puertadetoledo.es €€€ Glorieta Puerta de Toledo 4, 28005. 91 474 71 00. FAX 91 474 07 47. Functional, reasonably priced hotel facing the Glorieta Puerta de Toledo. Close to El Rastro (see p61), typical Spanish taverns in Cava Alta and Cava Baja and a short walk from the Palacio Real (see pp54–7). 📻 🍽 TV 🅰		AE DC MC V	152	▪		▪
REGINA. Map 7 A2. W www.hotelreginamadrid.com €€€ Calle de Alcalá 19, 28014. 91 521 47 25. FAX 91 522 40 88. This modern hotel has a very elegant address near to the Real Academia de Bellas Artes on Calle de Alcalá, and close to the Puerta del Sol. 📻 🍽 TV		AE DC MC V	142	▪		
HOTEL GAUDÍ. Map 7 A1. W www.hoteles-catalonia.es €€€€ Gran Vía 9, 28013. 91 531 22 22. FAX 91 531 54 69. This central hotel, set in a Modernist building of the 1920s, is attractively decorated with Gaudí details. The five top-floor suites have their own balconies and Jacuzzis. 📻 🍽 TV 🅰			185		●	
SANTO DOMINGO. Map 4 D1. W www.hotelsantodomingo.net €€€€ Plaza de Santo Domingo 13, 28013. 91 547 98 00. FAX 91 547 59 95. Stylish, mid-1990s establishment one block south of the Gran Vía and close to the Puerta del Sol and the Teatro Real. Modern interior decor. Each room is different; some non-smoking rooms. 📻 🍽 TV			120	▪		▪
TRYP AMBASSADOR. Map 4 D1. W www.solmelia.com €€€€ Cuesta de Santo Domingo 5, 28013. 91 541 67 00. FAX 91 559 10 40. Modern hotel in a 19th-century palace. Stylish and comfortable, with large rooms. Close to the Teatro Real and the Palacio Real (see pp54–7). Pleasant greenhouse-style bar with tropical plants. 📻 🍽 TV			182			
TRYP CAPITOL. Map 4 E1. W www.solmelia.com €€€€ Gran Vía 41, 28013. 91 521 83 91. FAX 91 521 77 29. Right in the middle of the action on the Gran Vía, next to the Plaza Callao, this hotel occupies one of Madrid's most architecturally interesting modern buildings. 📻 🍽 TV ● until mid-2005 for refurbishment.		AE DC MC V	143			
TRYP GRAN VÍA. Map 4 F1. W www.solmelia.com €€€€ Gran Vía 25, 28013. 91 522 11 21. FAX 91 521 24 24. A chain hotel located in one of the city's busiest streets. Some of the furniture is in the style of the 1960s and 1970s. 📻 🍽 TV		AE DC MC V	175			

Price categories for a standard double room per night, with tax, breakfast and service included:

€ under 80 euros
€€ 80–130 euros
€€€ 130–170 euros
€€€€ 170–230 euros
€€€€€ over 230 euros

CREDIT CARDS
Indicates which credit cards are accepted: *AE* American Express; *DC* Diners Club; *MC* MasterCard/Access; *V* VISA.
PARKING
Parking provided by the hotel in a private car park or a private garage on the hotel site or very close by. Some hotels charge for use of private parking facilities.
SWIMMING POOL
Hotel pool outdoors unless otherwise stated.
GARDEN
Hotel with garden, courtyard or terrace, often providing tables for eating outdoors.

	CREDIT CARDS	NUMBER OF ROOMS	PRIVATE PARKING	SWIMMING POOL	GARDEN OR TERRACE
TRYP REX. Map 4 E1. W www.solmelia.com €€€€ Gran Vía 43, 28013. 91 547 48 00. FAX 91 547 12 38. A chain hotel in an old building between the Plaza del Callao and the Plaza de España, close to a large public car park. It has spacious public rooms and well-equipped bedrooms, each with its own safe. 🖥 ▤ TV	AE DC MC V	145			
AROSA. Map 4 F1. W www.bestwestern.com/es/arosa €€€€€ Calle de la Salud 21, 28013. 91 532 16 00. FAX 91 531 31 27. This central hotel is popular with international and business visitors to Madrid. All the bedrooms are comfortable and well soundproofed. 🖥 ▤ TV	AE DC MC V	134	▪		
CROWNE PLAZA. Map 2 D5. €€€€€ Gran Vía 84, 28013. 91 547 12 00. FAX 91 548 23 89. W www.madrid_citycentre.crowneplaza.com Newly refurbished, American-style hotel in the Edificio España, facing the Plaza de España. Close to the action on the Gran Vía. Spacious common areas and large rooms. 🖥 ▤ TV �		306	▪		
TRYP MENFIS. Map 2 D5. W www.solmelia.com €€€€€ Gran Vía 74, 28013. 91 547 09 00. FAX 91 547 51 99. In a modern building next to the Plaza de España. The service is professional, and the rooms were completely renovated in 1997. 🖥 ▤ TV	AE DC MC V	115			
TRYP REINA VICTORIA. Map 7 A3. W www.solmelia.com €€€€€ Plaza de Santa Ana 14, 28012. 91 531 45 00. FAX 91 522 03 07. Ernest Hemingway once lodged in this historic hotel, a graceful edifice and a traditional haunt of bullfighting aficionados. 🖥 ▤ TV �		201	▪		

BOURBON MADRID

	CREDIT CARDS	NUMBER OF ROOMS	PRIVATE PARKING	SWIMMING POOL	GARDEN OR TERRACE
HOSTAL-RESIDENCIA LISBOA. Map 7 A2. W www.hostallisboa.com € Calle de Ventura de la Vega 17, 28014. 91 429 46 76. FAX 91 429 46 76. Clean and centrally located near the Plaza de Santa Ana and one block east of Calle Echegaray. The rooms are simply furnished. 🖥 ▤ TV	AE DC MC V	27			
MEDIODÍA. Map 7 C4. € Plaza del Emperador Carlos V 8, 28012. 91 527 30 60. FAX 91 527 30 66. This great bargain hotel lies in a stately 19th-century building near the Centro de Arte Reina Sofía (*see pp86–9*). Comfortable, wooden-floored rooms, some with splendid views over Atocha station, and friendly service. 🖥 TV	AE MC V	170			
MORA. Map 7 C4. € Paseo del Prado 32, 28014. 91 420 15 69. FAX 91 420 05 64. This 1930s hotel has an attractive entrance. Its rooms and facilities are functional, but its prices are low and it is centrally located, near the Jardín Botánico and the Museo del Prado (*see pp80–83*). 🖥 ▤ TV	AE DC MC V	75			
SANTANDER. Map 7 A3. € Calle de Echegaray 1, 28014. 91 429 46 44. FAX 91 369 10 78. This small, friendly family hotel offering neat, comfortable, simple rooms has been popular with travellers since it opened in the 1920s. Good location – close to the Puerta del Sol and handy for the sights in central Madrid. 🖥 TV		35			
INGLÉS. Map 7 A3. @ comercial@ingleshotel.com €€ Calle de Echegaray 8, 28014. 91 429 65 51. FAX 91 420 24 23. A good-value, family-run hotel with its own garage. The bedrooms facing the street are sunny but the back rooms are quieter. 🖥 TV	AE DC MC V	58	▪		
AGUMAR. Map 8 E5. W www.h-santos.es €€€€ Paseo de la Reina Cristina 7, 28014. 91 552 69 00. FAX 91 433 60 95. A stylish hotel near the big museums, with its own collection of good paintings and carpets from the Real Fábrica de Tapices. 🖥 ▤ TV	AE DC MC V	245	▪		

For key to symbols see back flap

<table>
<tr><td colspan="5">
Price categories for a standard double room per night, with tax, breakfast and service included:

€   under 80 euros
€€   80–130 euros
€€€   130–170 euros
€€€€   170–230 euros
€€€€€   over 230 euros
</td></tr>
</table>

CREDIT CARDS
Indicates which credit cards are accepted: *AE* American Express; *DC* Diners Club; *MC* MasterCard/Access; *V* VISA

PARKING
Parking provided by the hotel in a private car park or a private garage on the hotel site or very close by. Some hotels charge for use of private parking facilities.

SWIMMING POOL
Hotel pool outdoors unless otherwise stated.

GARDEN
Hotel with garden, courtyard or terrace, often providing tables for eating outdoors.

	CREDIT CARDS	NUMBER OF ROOMS	PRIVATE PARKING	SWIMMING POOL	GARDEN OR TERRACE
EL PRADO. Map 7 B3. [w] www.green-hoteles.com €€€€ Calle del Prado 11, 28014. [91 369 02 34. FAX 91 429 28 29. Modern and efficiently run small hotel with spacious rooms, located along a narrow street close to Plaza de Santa Ana. Business facilities. ▦ ▤ TV	AE DC MC V	45	▪		
SUECIA. Map 7 B2. [w] www.hotelsuecia.com €€€€ Calle del Marqués de Casa Riera 4, 28014. [91 531 69 00. FAX 91 521 71 41. Centrally located near the Puerta del Sol, the Suecia has a small, seventh-floor terrace where guests can relax and soak up the sun. ▦ ▤ TV	AE DC MC V	128	▪		▪
SUITE PRADO. Map 7 A3. [w] www.suiteprado.com €€€€ C/ Manuel Fernández y González 10, 28014. [91 420 23 18. FAX 91 420 05 59. A stylish apartment hotel of luxury suites a short distance from the Prado *(see pp80–83)* and the Museo Thyssen-Bornemisza *(see pp70–73)*. ▦ ▤ TV	AE DC MC V	18	▪		
VILLA REAL. Map 7 B2. [w] www.derbyhotels.es €€€€ Plaza de las Cortes 10, 28014. [91 420 37 67. FAX 91 420 25 47. A stylish hotel near the Prado *(see pp80–83)*, built in the 19th-century. The public areas have mahogany furniture and embroideries. ▦ ▤ TV	AE DC MC V	115	▪		
HOTEL RITZ. Map 7 C3. [w] www.ritz.es €€€€€ Plaza de la Lealtad 5, 28014. [91 521 28 57. FAX 91 532 87 76. Inaugurated in 1910 as a hotel for aristocrats, the Ritz is still one of Spain's most elegant hotels *(see p68)*. It has an ornate, circular foyer and a terrace garden, and offers musical teas and brunches. ▦ ▤ TV	AE DC MC V	158	▪		▪
NH ALCALÁ. Map 8 E1. [w] www.nh-hotels.com €€€€€ Calle de Alcalá 66, 28009. [91 435 10 60. FAX 91 435 11 05. A hotel with a friendly atmosphere across the street from the Parque del Retiro. The back bedrooms overlook a pretty garden. ▦ ▤ TV	AE DC MC V	146	▪		▪
NH NACIONAL. Map 7 C4. [w] www.nh-hotels.com €€€€€ Paseo del Prado 48, 28014. [91 429 66 29. FAX 91 369 15 64. This renovated 19th century mansion is close to the Prado *(see pp80–83)* and the Museo Thyssen-Bornemisza *(see pp70–73)*. ▦ ▤ TV ♿	AE DC MC V	214	▪		
WESTIN PALACE. Map 7 B2. [w] www.palacemadrid.com €€€€€ Plaza de las Cortes 7, 28014. [91 360 80 00. FAX 91 360 81 00. This gracious Belle Epoque hotel *(see p69)*, with a glass dome and a colonnade, has accommodated statesmen as well as the spy Mata Hari. The bedrooms are elegant and the service welcoming. ▦ ▤ TV ♿	AE DC MC V	465	▪		

AROUND LA CASTELLANA

	CREDIT CARDS	NUMBER OF ROOMS	PRIVATE PARKING	SWIMMING POOL	GARDEN OR TERRACE
HOSTAL SANTA BÁRBARA. Map 5 B4. € Plaza de Santa Bárbara 4, 28004. [91 446 93 08. FAX 91 446 23 45. A simple and clean low-budget option in one of the liveliest spots in Madrid. Some rooms have balconies. The interior rooms are quieter. ▦ TV	AE DC MC V	15			
HOSTAL SIL. Map 5 A5. [@] info@silserranos.com € Calle de Fuencarral 95, 28004. [91 448 89 72. FAX 91 447 48 29. In a lively part of town, this is a comfortable, convenient hotel with quality bedroom and bathroom furnishings, but low prices. ▦ TV	MC V	50			
DON DIEGO. Map 6 F4. [w] www.hostaldondiego.com €€ Calle de Velázquez 45, 28001. [91 435 07 60. FAX 91 431 42 63. Reasonably priced, friendly hotel in the elegant Salamanca district *(see p99)*. Some rooms have balconies; interior rooms are quieter. ▦ ▤ TV	AE DC MC V	58			
GALIANO. Map 6 D4. [w] www.hotelgaliano.com €€ Calle de Alcalá Galiano 6, 28010. [91 319 20 00. FAX 91 319 99 14. A surprising little hotel in a Neo-Classical building, one block west of Plaza de Colón. Quirky service, but spacious and comfortable rooms. ▦ ▤ TV	AE DC MC V	29	▪		

MÓNACO. Map 7 B1. €€ AE DC MC V 34
Calle de Barbieri 5, 28004. **[** 91 522 46 30. **FAX** 91 521 16 01.
The decor of this hotel, formerly Madrid's most famous high-class brothel, is
unashamedly kitsch. The bedrooms retain some decadent features.

NH ZURBANO. www.nh-hotels.com €€€€ AE DC MC V 267
Calle de Zurbano 79–81. **[** 91 441 45 00. **FAX** 91 441 32 24.
Modern, efficient and comfortable, if somewhat impersonal, this hotel is
located in two separate buildings one block from La Castellana, on a
quiet street. It is very popular with business travellers.

CASTELLANA INTERCONTINENTAL. Map 6 D1. €€€€€ AE DC MC V 307
Paseo de la Castellana 49, 28046. **[** 91 700 73 00. www.madrid.intercontinental.com
This hotel in Madrid's commercial centre is a favourite with business
travellers. Guests can choose between two restaurants.

HESPERIA MADRID. Map 6 D1. www.hesperia-madrid.com €€€€€ DC MC V 171
Paseo de la Castellana, 57, 28046. **[** 91 210 88 00. **FAX** 91 210 88 99.
A fashionable and well-equipped new hotel in a modern building close
to the financial area and the smart shopping street Calle de Serrano. Some of
the suites have their own balconies and Jacuzzis.

MELIÁ FENIX. Map 6 D4. www.solmelia.com €€€€€ AE DC MC V 215
Calle de Hermosilla 2, 28001. **[** 91 431 67 00. **FAX** 91 576 06 61.
This is one of Madrid's most elegant addresses. The communal areas are
stylish, and the lobby has a magnificent spiral staircase. Most rooms have
good views of the Paseo de la Castellana or Plaza de Colón.

NH SANVY. Map 6 D4. www.nh-hotels.com €€€€ AE DC MC V 149
Calle de Goya 3, 28001. **[** 91 576 08 00. **FAX** 91 575 24 43.
This very modern hotel, in a side street off Plaza de Colón, is the flagship of
the NH chain, which caters for the business traveller. Modern and functional. Facilities for business meetings. Non-smoking rooms.

OCCIDENTAL MIGUEL ÁNGEL. Map 6 D1. www.occidental-hoteles.com €€€€€ AE DC MC V 263
Calle de Miguel Ángel 31, 28010. **[** 91 442 81 99. **FAX** 91 442 53 20.
Located beside the Paseo de la Castellana, the Miguel Ángel combines
modern comfort with classic style. One of the hotel's two fine restaurants
holds dinner dances until 3am.

SANTO MAURO. Map 5 C2. www.ac-hoteles.com €€€€€ AE DC MC V 51
Calle de Zurbano 36, 28010. **[** 91 319 69 00. **FAX** 91 308 54 77.
This palace, built in 1894 in one of Madrid's most elegant streets, has
housed embassies. It has a swimming pool beneath a vaulted basement
ceiling, and a restaurant occupies the former library.

TRYP STYLE ESCULTOR. Map 6 D2. www.solmelia.com €€€€€ AE DC MC V 63
Calle de Miguel Ángel 3, 28010. **[** 91 310 42 03. **FAX** 91 319 25 84.
Good price for a hotel of this category in this location, a block west of Paseo
de la Castellana in the Chamberí area. All rooms have balconies.

VILLAMAGNA. Map 6 D3. www.madrid.hyatt.com €€€€€ AE DC MC V 182
Paseo de la Castellana 22, 28046. **[** 91 587 12 34. **FAX** 91 431 22 86.
The Villamagna combines 18th-century decor with modern luxury, and is
ringed by gardens. It is popular with business people.

WELLINGTON. Map 8 F1. www.hotel-wellington.com €€€€€ AE DC MC V 260
Calle de Velázquez 8, 28001. **[** 91 575 44 00. **FAX** 91 576 41 64.
A stylish hotel built in the early 1950s close to the Parque del Retiro. It is
a meeting place for people interested in bullfighting.

FURTHER AFIELD

RAMÓN DE LA CRUZ. www.hotelramondelacruz.com €€ MC V 103
C/ de Don Ramón de la Cruz 94, 28006. **[** 91 401 72 00. **FAX** 91 402 21 26.
Very good value at this hotel in a quiet street off Plaza Manuel Becerra, at
the top of Calle de Alcalá and close to the Ventas bullring *(see p110)*. Rooms
are large, comfortably furnished and have wooden floors.

ARISTOS. www.elchaflan.com €€€ AE DC MC V 23
Avenida de Pío XII 34, 28016. **[** 91 345 04 50. **FAX** 91 345 10 23.
If pleasant, tranquil surroundings take precedence over proximity to the
centre, this delightful small hotel in a leafy northern residential area is a good
choice. Its restaurant serves modern Mediterranean cuisine.

For key to symbols see back flap

Price categories for a standard double room per night, with tax, breakfast and service included:

€ under 80 euros
€€ 80–130 euros
€€€ 130–170 euros
€€€€ 170–230 euros
€€€€€ over 230 euros

CREDIT CARDS
Indicates which credit cards are accepted: *AE* American Express; *DC* Diners Club; *MC* MasterCard/Access; *V* VISA
PARKING
Parking provided by the hotel in a private car park or a private garage on the hotel site or very close by. Some hotels charge for use of private parking facilities.
SWIMMING POOL
Hotel pool outdoors unless otherwise stated.
GARDEN
Hotel with garden, courtyard or terrace, often providing tables for eating outdoors.

		CREDIT CARDS	NUMBER OF ROOMS	PRIVATE PARKING	SWIMMING POOL	GARDEN OR TERRACE
TIROL. W www.hotel-tirol.com €€€ Calle del Marqués de Urquijo 4, 28008. (91 548 19 00. FAX 91 541 39 58. A good-value hotel, conveniently located off the Plaza de España and near university district, so the area is always lively. The bedrooms are spacious and clean. 🖼 🗒 TV		AE DC MC V	103			
COLÓN. W www.fiesta-hotels.com €€€€ Calle del Doctor Esquerdo 119, 28007. (91 573 59 00. FAX 91 573 08 09. A comfortable hotel in a tower block between the Parque del Retiro and the Parque de Roma. It has a gym and business facilities. 🖼 🗒 TV		AE DC MC V	359	▦		▦
CONDE DE ORGAZ. W www.zenithhoteles.com €€€€ Avenida del Moscatelar 24, 28043. (91 748 97 60. FAX 91 388 00 09. A modern hotel, with big, comfortable bedrooms, near to the airport and the Campo de las Naciones Exhibition Centre. 🖼 🗒 TV 🅿		AE DC MC V	91	▦		
GRAN ATLANTA. W www.granatlanta.com €€€€ Calle del Comandante Zorita 34, 28020. (91 553 59 00. FAX 91 533 08 58. A large, bright, attractively decorated lobby welcomes you to this modern hotel in the heart of Madrid's business district. Catering mainly to business travellers, it is near some of Madrid's best-known restaurants. 🖼 🗒 TV		AE DC MC V	180	▦		
RAFAEL VENTAS. W www.rafaelhotels.com €€€€ Calle de Alcalá 269, 28027. (91 326 16 20. FAX 91 326 18 19. Modern building with marble exterior, and efficiently run. Convenient for the airport and a favourite with business travellers. 🖼 🗒 TV 🅿		AE DC MC V	111	▦		
BAUZA. W www.hotelbauza.com €€€€€ Calle de Goya 79, 28001. (91 435 75 45. FAX 91 431 09 43. The lobby of this hotel, a short walk from the Plaza de Colón or the Parque del Retiro, has been remodelled in a modernist style. 🖼 🗒 TV		AE DC MC V	177	▦		
CUZCO. W www.hotelcuzco.net €€€€€ Paseo de la Castellana 133, 28046. (91 556 06 00. FAX 91 556 03 72. Flashy, American-style hotel near the Santiago Bernabeu stadium. Occupies a high-rise block in the business district on La Castellana. Spacious common areas, health centre, sauna and gym, and modern, large rooms. 🖼 🗒 TV		AE DC MC V	330	▦		
MONTE REAL. W www.hotelmontereal.com €€€€€ Camino del Arroyo Fresno 17, 28035. (91 316 21 40. FAX 91 316 39 34. Situated in a residential area near the Puerta de Hierro golf course, this imposing modern hotel has a peaceful atmosphere. Its balconies over-look the swimming pool and gardens. 🖼 🗒 TV		AE DC MC V	80	▦		
NH BALBOA. W www.nh-hotels.com €€€€€ Núñez de Balboa 112, 28006. (91 563 03 24. FAX 91 562 69 80. Modern and comfortable, with an efficient, professional staff, this hotel on the corner of Núñez de Balboa and General Oráa is in the elegant Salamanca district *(see p99)* near the fashionable shops. 🖼 🗒 TV 🅿		AE DC MC V	122	▦		

BEYOND MADRID

		CREDIT CARDS	NUMBER OF ROOMS	PRIVATE PARKING	SWIMMING POOL	GARDEN OR TERRACE
GUADALAJARA: *España* @ hegu@he.e.telefonica.net € Calle Teniente Figueroa 3, 19001. (949 21 13 03. FAX 949 21 13 05. Family-run hotel in a 19th-century mansion in the city centre. Modern interior with original touches, such as the mural on the staircase. 🖼 TV 🅿		AE DC MC V	40	▦		
TOLEDO: *La Almazara* W www.hotelalmazara.com € Carretera Toledo-Cuerva km 3.4, 45080. (925 22 38 66. FAX 925 25 05 62. This 16th-century country house hotel is high on a wooded hilltop outside Toledo, and has a magnificent view. Obliging and informal staff compensate for simple bedrooms and limited facilities. 🖼 🅿		AE DC MC V	28	▦		▦

ALAMEDA DEL VALLE: *La Posada de Alameda* Ⓦ www.laposadadealameda.com €€
Calle Grande 34, 28749. **[** 91 869 13 37. **FAX** 91 869 01 63.
A sensitively restored farmhouse in the tranquil Lozoya valley, about an
hour's drive from Madrid. All the bedrooms are well equipped and some
have views of the countryside. 🚗 📺
Cards: DC MC V — *Rooms:* 22

PEDRAZA DE LA SIERRA: *El Hotel de la Villa* Ⓦ www.elhoteldelavilla.com €€
Calle Calzada 5, 40172 (Segovia). **[** 921 50 86 51. **FAX** 921 50 86 53.
All the rooms in this charming hotel are exquisitely decorated with floral
wallpaper and furnished with antiques and four-poster beds. 🚗 📋 📺
Cards: AE DC MC V — *Rooms:* 38

PEDRAZA DE LA SIERRA: *La Posada de Don Mariano* €€
Calle Mayor 14, 40172 (Segovia). **[** 921 50 98 86. **FAX** 921 50 98 86.
It is hard to nominate the best hotel in this lovely village. Every room
here looks like something out of a decor magazine. 🚗 📺
Cards: AE DC MC V — *Rooms:* 18

SAN LORENZO DE EL ESCORIAL: *El Botánico* Ⓦ www.valdesimonte.com €€
Timoteo Padrós 16, 28200. **[** 91 890 78 79. **FAX** 91 890 81 58.
A small and pleasant hotel near the famous palace of El Escorial *(see
pp122–5)*, located opposite a golf course. 🚗 📋 📺
Cards: AE DC MC V — *Rooms:* 20

SEGOVIA: *Infanta Isabel* Ⓦ www.hotelinfantaisabel.com €€
Plaza Mayor, 40001. **[** 921 46 13 00. **FAX** 921 46 22 17.
This modern hotel in *fin de siècle* style is complemented by traditional
Segovian decor. The bedrooms are cosy. 🚗 📋 📺
Cards: AE DC MC V — *Rooms:* 37

SEGOVIA: *Los Linajes* Ⓦ www.loslinajes.com €€
Calle Doctor Velasco 9, 40003. **[** 921 46 04 75. **FAX** 921 46 04 79.
Hidden behind an ancient half-timbered, red-brick façade is a modern
hotel which steps down the hillside beside the city walls in eight levels.
The higher your room level, the better the view. 🚗 📺
Cards: AE DC MC V — *Rooms:* 53

SIGÜENZA: *Parador de Sigüenza* Ⓦ www.parador.es €€
Plaza del Castillo, 19250 (Guadalajara). **[** 949 39 01 00. **FAX** 949 39 13 64.
Sigüenza's massive castle overlooks the town from a hilltop. Its former
VIP guests include the Catholic Monarchs *(see p20)*. It is furnished in
regal style and the bedrooms surround a courtyard. 🚗 📋 📺 ♿
Cards: AE DC MC V — *Rooms:* 81

TOLEDO: *Hostal del Cardenal* Ⓦ www.hostaldelcardenal.com €€
Paseo de Recaredo 24, 45004. **[** 925 22 49 00. **FAX** 925 22 29 91.
Now a historic hotel by the city walls, this 18th-century mansion was
formerly the residence of the archbishop of Toledo. It has splendid,
sculpted ceilings and pretty brick courtyards. 🚗 📋 📺
Cards: AE DC MC V — *Rooms:* 27

TOLEDO: *Pintor El Greco* Ⓦ www.hotelpintorelgreco.com €€
Calle Alamillos del Tránsito 13, 45002. **[** 925 28 51 91. **FAX** 925 21 58 19.
A 17th-century house in Toledo's former Jewish quarter has been
discreetly extended behind the original façade and patio. Wrought iron
and traditional ceramics add character to the hotel. 🚗 📋 📺 ♿
Cards: AE DC MC V — *Rooms:* 33

CHINCHÓN: *Parador de Chinchón* Ⓦ www.parador.es €€€
Avenida del Generalísimo 1, 28370. **[** 91 894 08 36. **FAX** 91 894 09 08.
This converted 17th-century monastery with immensely thick walls is built
round an airy courtyard. Delightful tiles, frescoes and antiques. 🚗 📋 📺
Cards: AE DC MC V — *Rooms:* 38

RASCAFRÍA: *Santa María de El Paular* Ⓦ www.sierranorte.com/paular €€€
Carretera M604 km 26.5, El Paular, 28741. **[** 91 869 10 11. **FAX** 91 869 10 06.
Hotel occupying part of a Benedictine monastery in the Guadarrama moun-
tains. The bar offers an informal alternative to the dining room. ● Jan. 🚗 📺
Rooms: 58

SAN LORENZO DE EL ESCORIAL: *Victoria Palace* **FAX** 91 896 98 96 €€€
Calle Juan de Toledo 4, 28200. **[** 91 896 98 90. Ⓦ www.hotelvictoriapalace.com
A short walk from the 16th-century palace of El Escorial, this stylish and
elegant hotel offers magnificent views from the bedrooms. 🚗 📺
Cards: AE DC MC V — *Rooms:* 87

SEGOVIA: *Parador de Segovia* Ⓦ www.parador.es €€€
Carretera de Valladolid, 40003. **[** 921 44 37 37. **FAX** 921 43 73 62.
Luxury parador strategically sited just outside Segovia where guests can
enjoy splendid views from the gardens. Gym and indoor pool. 🚗 📋 📺 ♿
Cards: AE DC MC V — *Rooms:* 113

TOLEDO: *Parador de Toledo* Ⓦ www.parador.es €€€
Cerro del Emperador, 45002. **[** 925 22 18 50. **FAX** 925 22 51 66.
There is a spectacular view of Toledo from the terrace of this parador on the
brow of a hill overlooking the city. Popular with photographers. 🚗 📋 📺
Cards: AE DC MC V — *Rooms:* 76

RESTAURANTS, CAFÉS AND BARS

E VEN IF MADRID didn't have its wealth of fabulous museums, palaces and monuments, it would be worth coming here just to experience its abundance of restaurants, cafés and bars. *Madrileños* spend a signifi-cant amount of time away from home with family, friends or colleagues, enjoy-ing breakfast, pre-meal *tapas (see pp30–31)* or lunch. For the visitor, it is very easy to slip into this unhurried style of eating and drinking.

Tiles at La Chata, a bar in Old Madrid's Calle de la Cava Baja

Regional food from all over Spain is served in picturesque *tabernas (see pp28–9)*, including some of the oldest existing in Europe, modest *casas de comidas* (local restaurants) and some of the continent's most ele-gant and creative culinary establishments. Whatever the ambience, whatever the price, tasty food is guaran-teed – a restaurant serving mediocre fare is unlikely to survive long in this city of discerning eaters.

Interior view of the finely polished bar at El Espejo (see p160)

RESTAURANTS AND BARS

M ADRID IS POPULATED by legions of executives and white-collar workers who are the mainstay of the city's restaurant trade. They demand good food, fast service and like to linger at the table after the meal. Lunchtime and the *sobremesa* – the casual conver-sation that follows the meal – are sacred in this city. To serve this market, there are hundreds of places to eat, from simple bistros that offer home cook-ing and daily menus at low prices, to some of Europe's most stylish establishments.

Some of the most famous restaurants are run by Basques, the acknowledged gastronomic masters of Spain. Every other Spanish region is represented as well, and Madrid also has restaurants serving international food, from Japanese to Russian, but to a lesser degree than other major European cities.

As the majority of their clients are business people, most restaurants close on Sunday. Many close Saturday lunch-time too, and a large number close for the whole of August.

FAST FOOD

I N ADDITION TO home-grown bars serving *tapas*, Madrid has branches of most of the international franchises, offer-ing American-style hamburg-ers. Successful Spanish chains include Pans & Co (sandwich-es) and Telepizza (pizzas, sandwiches and salads). One of the best is the Museo del Jamón, which serves cured ham and sausages *(see p161)*.

EATING HOURS IN SPAIN

M ADRID IS NOTORIOUS for its late meal times, with lunch around 2–3pm and din-ner around 10–11pm. For many travellers, eating times take some getting used to.

Madrileños usually have two breakfasts *(desayunos)*. The first may be a perfunctory coffee at home. The second, around 10 or 11am, is often eaten in a bar or a café. It might consist of coffee with *churros* – sticks of fried batter for dunking, a thick slice of *tortilla* (potato omelette) or a sandwich *(bocadillo)*. Most hotels offer either a continental breakfast of coffee or tea with a roll, or a breakfast buffet.

At lunchtime *Madrileños* adjourn to a bar for a *tapa* – an appetizer served with beer or a *vino* (glass of wine). This is followed by the midday *comida* or *almuerzo* (lunch), often eaten at a restaurant.

A late-afternoon *merienda* (tea) of sandwiches or pastries with coffee, tea or juice tides *Madrileños* over until the time comes for a second round of *tapas* at a bar in the evening, before returning home for the *cena* (dinner) or enjoying another meal at a restaurant.

Dining room at Hostería Pintor Zuloaga in Pedraza de la Sierra (see p163)

An enticing place to rest – a terrace bar on Paseo de Recoletos

READING THE MENU

THE SPANISH WORD *menú* refers to the attractively-priced daily fixed menu. Some gourmet restaurants also offer a *menú de degustación* – a sampler menu which might include several small portions of the house specialities.

On a set day of the week some restaurants may serve an elaborate, traditional dish such as *fabada* (bean stew) or *cocido madrileño*, the classic hearty local dish *(see p155)*.

The Spanish word for menu is *la carta*. It starts with *sopas* (soups), *entremeses* (hors d'oeuvres), *ensaladas* (salad), *huevos y tortillas* (eggs and omelettes) and *verduras y legumbres* (vegetable dishes). The *plato principal* (main course) may be *pescados y mariscos* (fish and shellfish) or *carnes y aves* (meat and poultry). Dessert is *postre*.

PRICES AND TIPPING

ALL SPANISH RESTAURANTS must offer a *menú del día*, a comparatively inexpensive daily fixed-price menu comprising two courses and a dessert. Some restaurants do not reveal their daily menu unless it is requested.

Certain dishes, especially seafood, are not priced on the menu. They might be labelled as *según peso* (according to weight) or *según mercado* (according to the market price that day). It is a good idea to ask for an estimate. Seven per cent value-added tax (IVA) is added to *la cuenta* (the bill)

as well as service, but tips in cash are customary – around five per cent of the bill. Almost all restaurants take credit cards, though MasterCard and VISA are the most commonly used.

Bodega de Angel Sierra, a local bar in the Plaza de Chueca *(see p92)*

BOOKING

AS A RULE, BOOKING is essential in Madrid, especially at midday. Phoning a few hours ahead will usually secure a table. At the most popular or fashionable restaurants, however, you should reserve a table one or more days in advance. Arriving early may be no guarantee of a place.

ETIQUETTE AND SMOKING

APART FROM THE inexpensive and the tourist restaurants, smart casual dress is best in most places, and smart dress should be worn in more exclusive establishments, especially in the evening. Few restaurants have non-smoking sections.

CHILDREN

CHILDREN ARE WELCOME in most restaurants, even the more exclusive during the day, but they do not receive the royal treatment they get in other parts of Spain, nor are children's menus or high chairs likely to be offered. Children might feel happiest in an informal restaurant, especially if it has an outdoor terrace.

DISABLED PERSONS

FACILITIES FOR disabled people are rare in Spanish restaurants and it is always worth phoning in advance (or asking the hotel staff to phone) to enquire about their provision.

WINE CHOICES

YOUR WAITER MIGHT offer you an *aperitivo* (aperitif), in which case an excellent choice would be a sherry – a pale, dry *fino* or darker *oloroso* – accompanied perhaps by olives or a *tapa*. Wine is usually served with the main course. Spain has a formidable selection of wines *(see pp156–7)*. Although there is a significant mark-up in restaurants, they can still be reasonably priced, especially *vino de la casa* (house wine).

VEGETARIANS

WITH FEW VEGETARIAN establishments in Madrid, you may decide to opt for the egg, salad or vegetable dishes at an ordinary restaurant, but always check the ingredients first.

The entrance to Combarro, with its medieval charm *(see p162)*

What to Eat in Madrid

T HROUGHOUT MADRID'S HISTORY, people have flocked to the capital from every region of Spain, bringing their recipes with them. Thus, Madrid's restaurants offer the perfect chance for a complete culinary tour of Spain. In addition to Madrid's own classics, such as *cocido madrileño* or *besugo a la madrileña* (red bream), you'll find seafood as fresh as any in Galicia, *paella* as tasty as Valencia's, refreshing Andalusian *gazpacho*, filling *fabada* from Asturias, roast suckling-pig from Castile and culinary delights from the Basque country. Spanish cuisine is based on the freshest of ingredients. A first course may consist of a rich soup or vegetable dish, followed by fish or meat. The choice of desserts, however, is often limited to fruit, *flan* (caramel custard) or ice cream.

Garlic

Fritura de pescado *is a typical dish from Málaga and Cádiz, where fried fish and squid* (calamares) *are served with wedges of fresh lemon.*

Fish and seafood *are popular ingredients in many Spanish recipes and in a vast range of* tapas *(see pp30– 31). It is never a problem to find high quality fish* (pescado) *and seafood* (mariscos), *even in a city like Madrid which is a long way from the sea. Although it tends to be on the expensive side, it is a price worth paying.*

Scallops (veneras)

Spider crab (centollo)

Pimientos rellenos, *the regional dish of Navarra, are the local spicy pointed red peppers stuffed with fish, seafood or meat* (carne).

Saffron rice (arroz con azafrán)

Prawns (gambas)

Mussels (mejillones)

Fabada *is stew from Asturias with broad beans* (fabes), *salt pork* (tocino), *black sausage* (morcilla), *spicy* chorizo *sausage and ham.*

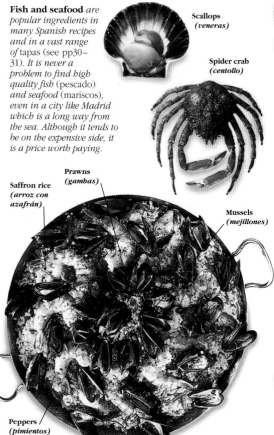

Peppers (pimientos)

Paella

This Valencian rice dish is cooked in a large, shallow pan, traditionally over an open fire. Short-grain Spanish saffron rice is simmered with a variety of ingredients: seafood, chicken, rabbit (conejo), *peas* (guisantes), *tomatoes, peppers and beans.*

Pisto, *which originated in La Mancha, is the Spanish version of* ratatouille. *It is a delicious combination of peppers, tomatoes, onions, garlic and zucchini* (courgettes).

COCIDO MADRILEÑO

The *cocido*, a full meal cooked in a pot, is available in one variation or another in many Spanish regions, but nowhere is it as revered as in Madrid, where *cocido madrileño* occupies a special place in people's hearts – and on their tables. To prepare this traditional dish, all the ingredients – *garbanzos* (chickpeas), *puerros* (leeks), cabbage, potatoes, *nabos* (turnips) and *zanahorias* (carrots), sausages, beef, chicken, *jamón serrano* (cured ham), bay leaves, cloves, and more – simmer together for many hours. The broth is served as a first course, then the vegetables and meat as a second course. As it takes so long to cook and cannot be prepared in small quantities, Madrid restaurants tend to offer *cocido* on a particular day of the week, usually Thursday.

Sopa de ajo *is a warming garlic soup thickened with bread. The Spanish often eat this soup with a poached egg and some paprika.*

Chicken (pollo)

Chickpeas (garbanzos)

Beef (ternera)

Cabbage (col)

Salt pork belly

Sausage

Rabo de toro *is the tail of a bull braised with vegetables and red wine. Of all the dishes that use bull's meat, this is one of the best.*

Pollo al ajillo *is fried chicken with garlic. It is served with a white wine or sherry sauce made with the juices from the chicken.*

Red pepper

Cold *gazpacho* soup

Croutons

Cucumber

Tocino de cielo, *which is translated as "heavenly bacon", is the richest and most mouthwateringly delicious of Spain's custard and caramel desserts.*

Gazpacho *is a chilled raw soup that is made by pounding bread and garlic with tomatoes, cucumber and peppers. Olive oil makes it creamy and vinegar gives it a refreshing tang. It is usually garnished with diced vegetables and croutons.*

What to Drink in Madrid

SPAIN IS ONE OF THE WORLD's largest wine-producing countries and many fine wines are made here, in addition to the famous sherries of southern Spain and the *cavas* (sparkling wines) of Catalonia. Beer is produced throughout Spain, and Madrid's *cervecerías* (beer bars) are especially adept at pulling a refreshing half pint. Some offer *sidra* (apple cider) from northern Spain. The full range of non-alcoholic drinks is available, including mineral water. Spanish coffee is rich and strong and, to round off a meal, many restaurants offer traditional liqueurs such as brandy and *anís*.

Customers enjoying a pre-meal drink at an outdoor terrace bar

Hot chocolate

A plate of *churros* (batter sticks)

Café con leche

Camomile   Lime flower

HOT DRINKS

COFFEE SERVED in Spanish bars is usually *espresso*. The traditional start to the day is a big cup of *café con leche* (with milk). *Café cortado* has a dash of milk, *café sólo* is black and *café americano* is weaker. Another popular breakfast drink is thick hot chocolate served with *churros* (fried batter sticks). A good cup of tea is hard to find, but herbal teas to try are *manzanilla* (camomile) and *tila* (lime flower).

COLD DRINKS

MADRID'S TAP WATER is safe to drink, but Spaniards prefer bottled water *(agua mineral)*, either still *(sin gas)* or sparkling *(con gas)*. Summer favourites include Valencian *horchata*, a sweet milky drink made from ground *chufas* (earth almonds), and *granizado de limón* (iced lemon). *Gaseosa*, or sparkling lemonade, can be drunk either on its own or as *tinto de verano*, mixed with red wine *(see Mixed Drinks)*. Soft drinks and orange juice *(zumo de naranja)* are also widely available.

Horchata, made from *chufas*

Sparkling and still mineral water

WINE

SPAIN PRODUCES SOME of the best wines in the world. The key standard for the industry is the *Denominación de Origen* (DO) classification, a guarantee of a wine's origin and quality. *Vino de la Tierra* is a classification of wines below that of DO in which over 60 per cent of the grapes come from a specified region. *Vino de Mesa*, the lowest category, covers basic unclassified wines. Spanish *cavas* include best-selling sparkling wines, Freixenet and Codorniú, which are *brut* (dry) or *semi-seco* (slightly sweet). In restaurants, wine is served by the glass, bottle or half-bottle. House wines are sometimes decanted into a carafe.

Penedès white wine   **Rioja red wine**   **Sparkling wine *(cava)***

SPIRITS AND LIQUEURS

Not all of Spain's grapes go into making wine. Much of the harvest is distilled to make clear spirits, the basis of Spain's many liqueurs. These include the aniseed flavoured *anís* which can either be extremely dry *(seco* or *orujo)* or syrupy sweet *(dulce)*. Brandy *(coñac)* de Jeréz, an aged wine spirit, is another popular digestive; the price is a good indication of quality. Fruits are also used to flavour liqueurs. One of the most popular variations is *pacharán*, a Navarrese drink using sloes. Spain, and especially the Canary Islands, has always produced *ron* (rum) from sugar cane that grows in the south. *Ginebra* (gin) was introduced by the British when they occupied the island of Menorca in the 18th century. Whisky is also a favourite, though imported Scotch is preferred to the domestic brands. A popular drink with younger people is *cuba-libre*, a rum with cola *(see Mixed Drinks)*.

Anís　　*Pacharán*

BEER

Spaniards love their *cerveza* (beer) and Mahou is a popular brand in Madrid. Bars serve *cerveza del barril* (draught beer) in a *caña* (small glass) or larger *jarra*. Beer also comes in bottles of 25 cl, 33 cl or one litre *(litronas)*. Alcohol-free lager *(cerveza sin alcohol)* is sold in many bars.

Bottled beers

SHERRY

Sherry is produced in *bodegas* in Jeréz de la Frontera, Sanlúcar de Barrameda and El Puerto de Santa María. Similar wines are produced in Montilla near Córdoba, although they are not officially called sherry. Pale *fino* is dry and light and makes an excellent aperitif. Amber *amontillado* (aged *fino*) has a strong earthy taste while *oloroso* is full-bodied and ruddy.

Two brands of *fino* sherry

MIXED DRINKS

Sangría is a refreshing blend of red wine and *gaseosa* (lemonade). Other ingredients include pieces of freshly chopped fruit, sugar and liqueurs. Another favourite drink is *Agua de Valencia*, which is an invigorating combination of *cava* (sparkling wine) and orange juice. A wide range of cocktails is available, including the ever popular *cuba-libre*.

Red wine and lemonade

Cuba-libre　　*Tinto de verano*

Sangría

HOW TO READ A WINE LABEL

As well as the wine's name and its producer, the label will tell you the region it comes from, usually a *Denominación de Origen*, and the vintage year. Wines labelled *cosecha* are recent vintages and the least expensive, while *crianza* and *reserva* wines are aged a minimum of two or three years, part of that time in oak casks. *Blanco* (white) can be *seco* (dry), *semi-seco* (semi-dry) or *dulce* (sweet). *Rosado* is rosé and *tinto* is red. The label also gives the content (usually 75 cl), the alcohol level (around 12–13 per cent volume) and sometimes specifies the grape variety.

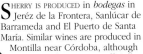

Brand name　　**Company's crest**

Capacity of the bottle

Estate-bottled rather than cooperative

The wine's *Denominación de Origen*

75 cl.　　　13% Alc.

MARQUES DE MURRIETA
Embotellado por: BODEGAS MARQUES DE MURRIETA, S.A. - YGAY
Vinos de Rioja

YGAY

(LOGROÑO)

RESERVA
COSECHA 1970

The vintage　　**Symbol for region**

Choosing a Restaurant

THE RESTAURANTS in this guide have been selected across a wide range of price categories for their good value, exceptional food and interesting location. Some offer tables outside and special menus. The restaurants are listed by area, starting with Old Madrid, then Bourbon Madrid, Around La Castellana, Further Afield and Beyond Madrid.

	CREDIT CARDS	TAPAS BAR	FIXED-PRICE MENU	GOOD WINE LIST	OUTDOOR TABLES

OLD MADRID

MALACATÍN. Map 4 E4. €
Calle de la Ruda 5. ☎ 91 365 52 41.
This old bar in the centre of the Rastro is decorated in bullfighting style and has only one item on the menu: *cocido madrileño (see p155)*, served in three separate stages. Book a day ahead. ● *Sun & Aug.* ▤

	V	●	▤		

LA TRUCHA. Map 7 A3. €
Calle de Núñez de Arce 6. ☎ 91 532 08 90.
This inexpensive restaurant one block from Plaza de Santa Ana offers simple Spanish fare, including three recipes for *trucha* (trout). The *verbena de ahumados* (selection of smoked fish) is famous. ● *Sun & Mon.* ▤

	AE DC MC V	●	▤		

LA BARRACA. Map 7 A1. €€
Calle de la Reina 29. ☎ 91 532 71 54.
Over ten different Valencia-style rice dishes and paellas are on offer here, made with first-class ingredients. Good home-made desserts. ▤

	AE DC MC V		▤	●	

LA BOLA. Map 4 D1. €€
Calle de la Bola. ☎ 91 547 69 30.
A true bastion of the *cocido madrileño (see p155)*, this restaurant dates back to 1870. Since then, little has changed in the preparation of the hearty stew, served at lunchtimes only. ● *Sat & Sun dinner in Jul, Aug.* ▤ &

			▤	●	

CASA CIRIACO. Map 3 C3. €€
Calle Mayor 84. ☎ 91 548 06 20.
A traditional tavern near the Palacio Real, renowned for its *gallina en pepitoria* (a chicken stew with egg and saffron). ● *Wed & Aug.* ▤ &

	DC MC V	●	▤	●	

CASA PATAS. Map 7 A3. €€
Calle de Cañizares 10. ☎ 91 369 04 96.
Known for its flamenco shows in the evening, Casa Patas has a well-stocked *tapas* bar and unbeatable fixed-price menu. ● *Sun.* ▤ &

	AE DC MC V	●	▤	●	

CORNUCOPIA. Map 4 E2. €€
Calle de la Flora 1. ☎ 91 547 64 65.
Pleasant dining rooms in a 19th-century building facing the Monasterio de las Descalzas Reales *(see p52)*. Creative cuisine with an American influence, friendly service and excellent value menu of the day. ● *Mon.* ▤

	AE DC MC V		▤		

RASPUTIN. Map 3 C2. €€
Calle de San Nicolás 8. ☎ 91 366 39 62.
This well-known Russian restaurant is decorated with lace curtains and regal red drapes and carpets, evoking Imperial Russia. ● *Mon.* ▤

	MC V		▤		

TABERNA BILBAO. Map 4 D3. €€
Calle Costanilla de San Andrés 8. ☎ 91 365 61 25.
Quality Basque tavern located in the medieval Plaza de la Paja, serving home-made specialities, including *bacalao* (codfish) in several different dishes and baby squid prepared in their own ink. ● *Mon.* ▤ &

	MC V	●		●	

VIUDA DE VACAS. Map 4 D4. €€
Calle de la Cava Alta 23. ☎ 91 366 58 47.
The menu at this old rustic tavern in the lively La Latina district includes typical Spanish specialities, delicious *bacalao* (codfish) and traditionally roasted meats such as *rabo de toro* (bull's tail). ● *Thu & Sun dinner, mid-Sep.*

	MC V	●		●	

ASADOR FRONTÓN. Map 4 F3. €€€
Tirso de Molina 7. ☎ 91 369 23 25.
One of Madrid's oldest Basque *asadores* (roasting houses). The menu features an enormous *chuletón de buey*, or beef chop (it's okay to share), and fish dishes. ● *Sun dinner, Easter, every Sun Jul–Aug & some other days Aug.* ▤

	AE DC MC V				

	CREDIT CARDS	TAPAS BAR	FIXED-PRICE MENU	GOOD WINE LIST	OUTDOOR TABLES

Price categories for a three-course evening meal for one, including a half-bottle of house wine, tax and service:

€ under 20 euros
€€ 20–30 euros
€€€ 30–40 euros
€€€€ over 40 euros

CREDIT CARDS
Indicates which credit cards are accepted: *AE* American Express; *DC* Diners Club; *MC* MasterCard/Access; *V* VISA.
TAPAS BAR
In addition to the main dining room, there is a bar serving *tapas (see pp30–31)* and *raciones* (larger portions).
FIXED-PRICE MENU
A good-value menu is offered, usually with three courses.
GOOD WINE LIST
Denotes a wide range or specialized selection of wines.
OUTDOOR TABLES
Facilities for eating on a terrace, or in a garden or courtyard.

Restaurant	Credit Cards	Tapas Bar	Fixed-Price Menu	Good Wine List	Outdoor Tables
CASA LABRA. Map 4 F2. Calle de Tetuán 12. 91 531 00 81. In 1879 the Spanish Socialist party was founded in this classic Madrid tavern, also famous for its *tapas* of croquettes and fried codfish. ● *Sun & Aug.* €€€	AE MC V	●	■		
CAFÉ DE ORIENTE. Map 3 C2. Plaza de Oriente 2. 91 547 15 64/91 541 39 74. Splendidly located opposite the Palacio Real *(see pp54–7)*. As well as a large interior bar and cafeteria, there is a comfortable dining room serving innovative Basque-French cuisine. Reservations essential. €€€€	AE DC MC V	●	■	●	■
CASA LUCIO. Map 4 D3. Calle de la Cava Baja 35. 91 365 32 52. This historic tavern serves Castilian specialities. The fried eggs with potatoes are exquisite and the rice pudding renowned. ● *Sat lunch, Aug.* €€€€	AE DC MC V	●		●	
EL GRILL DE LA OPERA. Map 4 D2. Vergara 3. 91 548 18 05. Also known as Chez Margot, this tiny French restaurant off Plaza Isabel II has yet to be discovered by Madrid's gastronomic set. The pâté de foie gras makes a tasty starter, followed by fish or meat. ● *Sun.* €€€€	AE DC MC V				
JULIÁN DE TOLOSA. Map 4 D3. Calle de la Cava Baja 18. 91 365 82 10. The menu at this restaurant, pleasingly decorated in wood and unrendered brick, is quite small. Specialities include roast peppers and beef chops, but there is always something for fish eaters. ● *Sun.* €€€€	AE DC MC V			●	
LHARDY. Map 4 F2. Carrera de San Jerónimo 8. 91 521 33 85. Established in 1839 and conserving its true character with chandeliers, mirrors and dark wood panelling, Lhardy serves what is arguably the most classic *cocido madrileño (see p155)*. ● *Sun dinner, Aug, public hols. dinner.* €€€€	AE DC MC V	●	■		
LA POSADA DE LA VILLA. Map 4 D4. Calle de la Cava Baja 9. 91 366 18 60. Colourful restaurant, with extensive menu, in a building dating from 1642. One of the rooms has a dome-shaped roasting oven where lamb and roast suckling pig are cooked. A classic Madrid experience. ● *Sun dinner & Aug.* €€€€	AE DC MC V		■		
EL SOBRINO DEL BOTÍN. Map 4 E3. Calle de los Cuchilleros 17. 91 366 42 17. Reputedly the oldest restaurant in the world, dating back to 1725. The original wood-burning oven is still used to cook the traditional Castilian roast lamb and suckling pig. Reasonable fixed-price menu. €€€€	AE DC MC V		■	●	

BOURBON MADRID

Restaurant	Credit Cards	Tapas Bar	Fixed-Price Menu	Good Wine List	Outdoor Tables
CHAMPAGNERÍA GALA. Map 7 B3. Calle Moratín 22. 91 429 25 62. Admire the indoor patio and chandeliers and enjoy a generous set menu with Catalan specialities at an unbelievably reasonable price. €		●	■		■
LA FINCA DE SUSANA. Map 7 A2. Calle Arlaban 4. 91 369 35 57. Located in the town centre, close to the Museo Thyssen-Bornemisza *(see pp70–73)* and the Museo del Prado *(see pp80–83)*, this restaurant offers home-made Spanish cuisine. Its desserts are highly recommended. €	AE DC MC V				
EDELWEISS. Map 7 B2. Calle de Jovellanos 7. 91 532 33 83. Reputedly a hangout for spies during World War II, this popular German restaurant includes pork knuckles among its specialities. ● *Sun dinner.* €€€	AE DC MC V	●	■	●	

For key to symbols see back flap

Price categories for a three-course evening meal for one, including a half-bottle of house wine, tax and service:

€ under 20 euros
€€ 20–30 euros
€€€ 30–40 euros
€€€€ over 40 euros

CREDIT CARDS
Indicates which credit cards are accepted: *AE* American Express; *DC* Diners Club; *MC* MasterCard/Access; *V* VISA.
TAPAS BAR
In addition to the main dining room, there is a bar serving *tapas (see pp30–31)* and *raciones* (larger portions).
FIXED-PRICE MENU
A good-value menu is offered, usually with three courses.
GOOD WINE LIST
Denotes a wide range or specialized selection of wines.
OUTDOOR TABLES
Facilities for eating on a terrace, or in a garden or courtyard.

	CREDIT CARDS	TAPAS BAR	FIXED-PRICE MENU	GOOD WINE LIST	OUTDOOR TABLES

NICOLÁS. Map 8 D1. €€€
Calle de Villalar 4. (*91 431 77 37.*
This cosy, modern restaurant, panelled in wood, offers attentive service and good value fare. It serves Spanish classics such as *rabo de toro* (bull's tail) and *kokotxas de bacalao* (cod morsels). ● *Sun, Mon & Aug.* ▤ ⅷ
Credit cards: AE DC MC V. Good Wine List ●

PALACIO DE LINARES. Map 8 D1. €€€€
Paseo de Recoletos 2. (*91 575 45 40.*
Set in the Palacio de Linares *(see p66)*, this stylish restaurant features quality Catalan and Mediterranean dishes. ● *Sat lunch, Sun & public hols.* ▤
Credit cards: AE DC MC V. Good Wine List ●. Outdoor Tables ▪

PARADIS. Map 7 B2. €€€€
Calle del Marqués de Cubas 14. (*91 429 73 03.*
This restaurant is part of a successful Catalan chain offering quality Mediterranean cuisine. The grilled vegetables or rice dishes make delicious starters. ● *Sat lunch, Sun & public hols.* ▤ ⅷ
Credit cards: AE DC MC V. Good Wine List ●

VIRIDIANA. Map 8 D2. €€€€
Calle de Juan de Mena 14. (*91 523 44 78.*
Innovative Spanish cuisine complemented by an encyclopedic wine list is offered in this restaurant decorated with stills from Luis Buñuel's film *Viridiana*. The creative menu changes frequently. ● *Sun & Aug.* ▤
Credit cards: AE MC V. Good Wine List ●

AROUND LA CASTELLANA

LA BARDEMCILLA. Map 5 A5. €
Calle Augusto Figueroa 47. (*91 521 42 56.*
Situated in Chueca *(see p94)*, the city's gay district, this restaurant has a lively, young atmosphere. Owned by the family of actor Javier Bordem, the typically Spanish dishes are named after his films. ● *Sat lunch, Sun.* ▤
Credit cards: AE MC V. Tapas Bar ●. Good Wine List ●

TONY ROMA'S. Map 5 C4. €
Calle de Génova 17. (*91 310 14 88.*
An American-style rib house, popular with young Spaniards and a good place to take the children. Informal, fun atmosphere. ▤
Credit cards: AE MC V.

BOCAÍTO. Map 7 B1. €€
Calle de la Libertad 4–6. (*91 532 12 19.*
The combination bar and kitchen dominates this small, noisy restaurant. Good *tapas*; meals are served in the rear dining area. ● *Sat lunch & Sun.* ▤
Credit cards: MC V DC. Tapas Bar ●. Fixed-Price Menu ▪

CARMENCITA. Map 7 B1. €€
Calle de la Libertad 16. (*91 531 66 12.*
What was once a neighbourhood tavern (founded in 1850) patronized by impoverished intellectuals has become fashionable, serving refined home cooking. The menu of the day is excellent value. ● *Sat lunch & Sun.* ▤
Credit cards: AE DC MC V. Fixed-Price Menu ▪

CENTRO RIOJANO. Map 6 E5. €€€
Calle de Serrano 25. (*91 575 03 37.*
This is a social club for people from the Rioja region, but its restaurant is open to the public. Basic decor, large quantities of Rioja country cooking (and wine), and very good value. Packed at lunchtime. ● *Sun dinner.* ▤ ⅷ
Credit cards: DC MC V. Fixed-Price Menu ▪

EL ESPEJO. Map 6 D5. €€€
Paseo de Recoletos 31. (*91 308 23 47.*
This café offers a striking decorative blend of Toulouse Lautrec and Art Deco with plenty of mirrors. The dining room, behind, serves international cuisine. There is also a conservatory-style restaurant at the front. ▤
Credit cards: AE DC MC V. Tapas Bar ●. Fixed-Price Menu ▪. Outdoor Tables ▪

PIMIENTO VERDE. Map 6 F4. €€€
Calle Lagasca 46. (*91 576 41 35.*
A lively *taberna* with a wide range of *tapas*. The adjoining Basque restaurant, in a cider-house style, serves fish and meat dishes. ● *Sun.* ▤
Credit cards: AE MC V. Tapas Bar ●. Good Wine List ●

EL PUCHERO. Map 5 A4. €€€
Calle de Larra 13. ¶ 91 445 05 77.
Popular, unfussy restaurant offering hearty, home-style cooking. The baby
broad beans with ham, the roast suckling pig and the game stews are
legendary, along with the cantankerous waitresses. ● Sun & Aug. 🍽

	AE			●	
	MC				
	V				

TEATRIZ. Map 6 E4. €€€
Calle de Hermosilla 15. ¶ 91 577 53 79.
A restaurant in the stalls of an old theatre, with a cocktail bar on the stage.
Italian-inspired food, such as a salmon and sole *carpaccio*. 🍽 ♿

	AE	●	■	●	
	DC				
	MC				
	V				

ALKADE. Map 6 E5. €€€€
Calle Jorge Juan 10. ¶ 91 576 33 59.
Try Basque specialities in the dining room or at the *tapas* bar, such as spider
crab soup and *chipirones* (squid in its own ink). ● Sat & Sun in Jul & Aug. 🍽

	AE	●	■	●	
	DC				
	MC				
	V				

AL MOUNIA. Map 6 D5. €€€€
Calle de Recoletos 5. ¶ 91 435 08 28.
Madrid's finest Moroccan restaurant serving authentic couscous and *tajine*
(lamb stew). There is also the rich house dessert, made with honey,
almonds and orange blossom water. ● Sun, Mon, Easter & Aug. 🍽

	AE			●	
	DC				
	MC				
	V				

EL AMPARO. Map 6 E5. €€€€
Callejón de Puigcerdá 8. ¶ 91 431 64 56.
New Basque Cuisine in what many consider to be Madrid's nicest setting,
with a skylight that lets you gaze up at the stars. The tuna mousse with lobster and parsley oil is just one creation. ● Sat lunch, Sun, Aug & public hols. 🍽

	AE			●	
	MC				
	V				

ARCE. Map 5 A5. €€€€
Calle de Augusto Figueroa 32. ¶ 91 522 04 40.
Stylish restaurant serving innovative, creative cuisine. Interesting wine list.
Full of executives at lunchtime; more intimate at night. ● Sat lunch & Sun. 🍽

	AE			●	
	MC				
	V				

JOCKEY. Map 6 D4. €€€€
Calle de Amador de los Ríos 6. ¶ 91 319 10 03.
Among Madrid's top five restaurants, frequented by celebrities, Jockey
offers a seasonal menu. Excellent poultry and game dishes and a superb
wine list. Smart dress only. ● Sat lunch, Sun, Aug & public hols. 🍽 ♿

	AE			●	
	DC				
	MC				
	V				

LA TRAINERA. Map 6 F4. €€€€
Calle de Lagasca 60. ¶ 91 576 80 35.
A narrow, crowded and lively restaurant, specializing exclusively in fresh
seafood. Typical fishing decor and a great ambience. ● Sun & Aug. 🍽

	AE				
	DC				
	MC				
	V				

FURTHER AFIELD

CASA MINGO. Map 3 A1. €
Paseo de la Florida 2. ¶ 91 547 79 18.
Rambunctious, loft-like establishment reminiscent of a German bierkeller,
except that here the drink is Asturian cider. The menu is limited to roast
chicken, salad and braised sausages, but people crowd its long tables.

			●		■

MUSEO DEL JAMÓN €
Calle de Alcalá 155. ¶ 91 431 72 96.
Countless hams hang from the rafters at the "Ham Museum", which
specializes in *jamón serrano* (cured ham). There is a large bar, but meals
are served in the separate dining room. Inexpensive fare in an informal
atmosphere. 🍽

	AE	●	■		
	MC				
	V				

PAULINO €€
Calle de Alonso Cano 34. ¶ 91 441 87 37.
Known as "the Poor Man's Zalacain", this popular restaurant serves creative
dishes at reasonable prices. The food always impresses. ● Sun; Aug. 🍽 ♿

	AE				
	DC				
	MC				
	V				

LA TABERNA DE LA DANIELA €€
Calle del General Pardiñas 21. ¶ 91 575 23 29.
A short but well-chosen menu is offered at this restaurant. At lunchtimes,
only *cocido madrileño (see p155)* is served, or you can choose from a
wide range of *tapas* at the bar. Good home-made desserts. 🍽

	AE	●			
	MC				
	V				

ALBORÁN €€€
Calle de Ponzano 39–41. ¶ 91 399 21 50.
This tastefully decorated restaurant in northwest Madrid offers Andalusian-
style seafood, including *pescaíto frito* (batter-fried fish). ● Sun dinner. 🍽 ♿

	AE			●	
	DC				
	MC				
	V				

For key to symbols see back flap

Price categories for a three-course evening meal for one, including a half-bottle of house wine, tax and service:

€ under 20 euros
€€ 20–30 euros
€€€ 30–40 euros
€€€€ over 40 euros

CREDIT CARDS
Indicates which credit cards are accepted: *AE* American Express; *DC* Diners Club; *MC* MasterCard/Access; *V* VISA.
TAPAS BAR
In addition to the main dining room, there is a bar serving *tapas (see pp30–31)* and *raciones* (larger portions).
FIXED-PRICE MENU
A good-value menu is offered, usually with three courses.
GOOD WINE LIST
Denotes a wide range or specialized selection of wines.
OUTDOOR TABLES
Facilities for eating on a terrace, or in a garden or courtyard.

	CREDIT CARDS	TAPAS BAR	FIXED-PRICE MENU	GOOD WINE LIST	OUTDOOR TABLES
BADEN €€€ Calle General Rodrigo 17. 91 553 87 96. Combining a bustling tapas bar and a cosy restaurant, Baden serves excellent *chuletón de ternera* (veal chop) and the best pizzas in Madrid. 🗏	AE DC MC V	●			
EL BUEY €€€ Calle del General Pardiñas 7–10. 91 431 44 92. A small restaurant specializing in steaks, but fish is always on offer, too. The popular bar serves Ribera del Duero wine and *tapas*. ● Sun dinner. 🗏	AE DC MC V	●	■		
CASA RICARDO €€€ Calle de Fernando El Católico 31. 91 447 61 19. A typical bar serving home-style dishes at a reasonable price. The oxtail soup is delicious as are the baby squid prepared in their ink. ● Sun dinner. 🗏 ♿	DC MC V			●	
DON SANCHO €€€ Calle de Bretón de los Herreros 58. 91 441 37 94. A varied menu is served in this small, pretty dining room in the tranquil Chamberí neighbourhood. ● Sun & Mon dinner, Easter, Aug & public hols. 🗏	AE DC MC V		■		
EL BARRIL DE GOYA €€€€ Calle de Goya 86. 91 578 39 98. Patrons crowd the bar of this popular restaurant, and the dining room, with its fishing motifs and big picture windows, is equally busy. The speciality is fresh fish and seafood of every description. ● Sun dinner. 🗏	AE DC MC V	●			
CABO MAYOR €€€€ Calle de Juan Ramón Jiménez 37. 91 350 87 76. One of Madrid's finest seafood restaurants, with Cantabrian-Navarrese cuisine. Try the delicious pasta and prawn salad or the monkfish with mushrooms. Excellent wines and desserts. ● Sat lunch, Sun & public hols. 🗏	AE DC MC V		■	●	■
COMBARRO €€€€ Calle de la Reina Mercedes 12. 91 554 77 84. The day's offerings are displayed in the window of one of Madrid's best seafood restaurants. Relaxed yet elegant. ● Sun dinner, Easter & Aug. 🗏	AE DC MC V	●			
CURRITO €€€€ Pabellon Vizcaya, Casa del Campo. 91 464 57 04. Traditional Basque specialities – meat and fish grilled over charcoals – are served at this restaurant installed in a pavilion in the Casa del Campo. Large terrace for dining outdoors in warm weather. ● Sun dinner. 🗏	AE DC MC V			●	■
GOIZEKO KABI €€€€ Calle del Comandante Zorita 37. 91 533 01 85. Traditional Basque cuisine in a refined setting. Excellent fresh produce and seafood and delectable desserts. ● Sun; Jul & Aug, Sat lunch. 🗏 ♿	AE DC MC V			●	
EL OLIVO €€€€ Calle del General Gallegos 1. 91 359 15 35. Top Mediterranean cuisine, with olive oil as the underlying culinary theme. The owner will advise you on which of the 40 different olive oils will best accompany your meal. ● Sun, Mon, late Aug & Easter. 🗏	AE DC MC V		■	●	
PEDRO LARUMBE. Map 6 E3. €€€€ Calle de Serrano 61. 91 575 11 12. This elegant, spacious restaurant with a palatial entrance offers creative cuisine. The fish dishes are especially good. ● Sat lunch & Sun. 🗏	AE MC V		■	●	
SACHA €€€€ Calle de Juan Hurtado de Mendoza 11 (entrada posterior). 91 345 59 52. Decorated like a cosy bistro, this restaurant serves traditional specialities such as partridge with rice and mushrooms. ● Sun, Aug & public hols. 🗏 ♿	AE DC MC V			●	■

ZALACAIN   €€€€   AE DC MC V
Calle de Álvarez de Baena 4. ☎ 91 561 48 40.
Considered to be Madrid's finest restaurant, Zalacain has a luxurious
setting, attentive service and above all, delicious Basque-oriented cuisine.
Smart dress only. ● Sat lunch, Sun, Easter, Aug & public hols. 🗐 ♿

BEYOND MADRID

ARANJUEZ: *Casa José.*   €€   AE MC V
Calle Abastos 32. ☎ 91 891 14 88.
A popular restaurant which is well known for its international style of
cooking using the best fresh local ingredients. ● Sun dinner & Mon.

CHINCHÓN: *Mesón de la Virreina.*   €€   AE DC MC V
Plaza Mayor 28. ☎ 91 894 00 15.
Traditional Castilian food, including *sopa castellana* (a garlic soup with
chickpeas) and classic roast lamb, is prepared in this 16th-century
building. The local *anís* makes an excellent *digestif.* 🗐 ♿

LA GRANJA DE SAN ILDEFONSO: *Hilaria.*   €€   AE DC MC V
Carretera Madrid-Valladolid km 124, Valsaín (Segovia). ☎ 921 47 02 92.
This family-run restaurant uses an original recipe for white bean stew.
Good roast suckling lamb and pig. ● Mon & Jun 12-22. 🗐 ♿

PEDRAZA DE LA SIERRA: *Hostería Pintor Zuloaga.*   €€   AE DC MC V
Calle Matadero 1 (Segovia). ☎ 921 50 98 35.
Located in a former Inquisition house, this restaurant serves traditional
Castilian fare such as roast pork and lamb, and hearty stews. ● Tue. 🗐

SAN LORENZO DE EL ESCORIAL: *Taberna La Cueva.*   €€   MC V
Calle San Antón 4. ☎ 91 890 15 16.
Juan de Villanueva, architect of the Prado, designed this 18th-century
inn whose specialities include the *huevos a la cueva* (fried eggs and
ham served in a nest of straw potatoes). ● Mon.

TOLEDO: *Hostal del Cardenal.*   €€   AE DC MC V
Paseo de Recaredo 24. ☎ 925 22 08 62.
Once the summer residence of Cardinal Lorenzana, this 18th-century
palace retains its beautiful garden, enclosed by the city walls. It serves
garlic soup, suckling pig and the famous Toledo *mazapán* (marzipan). 🗐

ARANJUEZ: *Casa Pablo.*   €€€   AE MC V
Calle Almíbar 42. ☎ 91 891 14 51.
A centrally located tavern offering solid home cooking. Try the pheasant
with grapes or the fresh asparagus and strawberries. ● Aug. 🗐 ♿

GUADALAJARA: *Amparito Roca.*   €€€   AE MC V
Calle Toledo 19. ☎ 949 21 46 39.
This pleasantly decorated house offers traditional Spanish cuisine with
innovative touches. Try the venison sirloin served in a mushroom sauce
and the scrambled eggs with potato and salmon. ● Sun & 15-31 Aug. 🗐 ♿

SEGOVIA: *Mesón de Cándido.*   €€€   AE DC MC V
Plaza del Azoguejo 5. ☎ 921 42 81 03.
Don't leave town without visiting Mesón de Cándido, *the* place to eat in
Segovia. The restaurant has good views of the Roman aqueduct and
serves local specialities such as roast lamb and suckling pig. 🗐 ♿

SIGÜENZA: *El Motor.*   €€€   AE DC MC V
Avenida Juan Carlos I 2 (Guadalajara). ☎ 949 39 08 27.
As well as the typical roast suckling pig and lamb you can also try the
fried breadcrumbs *(migas)* or the garlic soup *(sopa castellana).* 🗐 ♿

TOLEDO: *Adolfo.*   €€€   AE DC MC V
Calle de Granada 6. ☎ 925 22 73 21.
Set in the heart of the Jewish quarter, the Adolfo, with its tiles, columns,
antiques and a wonderful 15th-century Mudéjar coffered ceiling, serves game
in winter and fresh trout from the Río Tajo. ● Sun dinner & late Jul. 🗐 ♿

TOLEDO: *La Lumbre.*   €€€   AE DC MC V
Calle Real de Arrabal 3. ☎ 925 22 03 73.
A lovely old house with wooden beams, next to the Puerta de Bisagra.
The meat dishes, such as roast suckling pig and lamb, are especially good,
and there is delicious *manchego* cheesecake for dessert. ● Sun & Jul. 🗐

SHOPPING IN MADRID

FROM SHERRY TO SEAFOOD, the finest goods in Spain have always made their way across the country to the capital. Madrid still lives off that heritage, despite increasing competition from other parts, especially arch rival Barcelona. Many products are basic Castilian commodities – Manchego cheese, olive oil and leather goods – whose quality lies in the excellent raw materials. Since the swinging 1980s, fashion design has flourished in Madrid. New-look, home-grown fashion outlets now dot Madrid's different shopping areas from the city centre to the upmarket district of Salamanca *(see p99)*. The latest street-wear is available in the Chueca area *(see p94)*. There are colourful food markets all over the city, and in the heart of Old Madrid you'll find superb speciality food and wine stores. Don't miss the El Rastro flea market *(see p61)* on Sundays.

The logo of Spain's best known department store

OPENING HOURS

SPANISH SHOPPING HOURS are not like anywhere else in Europe, thanks to Spanish mealtimes. Most shops are open from 10am to 2pm and from 5pm to 8pm, with only department stores staying open during the lunch break. Small shops often close on Saturday afternoons. Sunday opening in Madrid is largely restricted to tourist shops, delicatessens and department stores and to the rush before Christmas until 5 January, eve of the Feast of the Epiphany.

HOW TO PAY

BOTH CASH and credit cards are popular methods of payment in Madrid, whereas cheques are hardly ever accepted. Small shops may sometimes reject credit cards which charge them high commission, so it's always worth double-checking that your card is acceptable. A passport or photo ID may be required when you pay by credit card. Some tourist shops accept payment in US dollars.

VAT EXEMPTION AND TAX

A VALUE-ADDED TAX (IVA) is applied to most goods. The standard rate of 16 per cent is charged on clothes and most other products, while the rate for most foodstuffs is seven per cent. A reduced rate of four per cent is applied to basic foods such as cheese and fruit, as well as printed matter and materials for the disabled. At shops with a "Tax-free for Tourists" sign, non-EU residents can claim tax refunds on all purchases over 90 euros, except food, drink, tobacco, motor bikes, cars and medicines.

SALES

SPANISH SALES ARE a popular institution, taking place in January and July. Beginning after the Feast of the Epiphany on 6 January, the New Year sales go on well into February. In July the summer fashion sales can turn up some real bargains, especially useful as Madrid's hot season often lasts well into September. Look out for signs advertising , *Rebajas, Ofertas* or *Liquidación.*

High fashion on Calle de Serrano, Madrid's smartest shopping street

SHOPPING CENTRES

SHOPPING CENTRES, or *centros comerciales*, have grown rapidly in Madrid. Among the best for upmarket fashion are the **Jardín de Serrano** and **ABC Serrano**, both set in the elegant neighbourhood of Salamanca, where you will also find many specialist luxury shops and the top international designer stores in and around the Calle de Serrano *(see p98)*. If you want to find everything under one roof, go to the huge **La Vaguada** mall on the north side of Madrid.

The department store **El Corte Inglés** is a national institution. Gigantic branches all over the city sell clothes, food, household goods and almost everything else. They offer photo-developing and shoe repair services, too.

Madrid also boasts a number of hypermarkets, mostly located off the M30 ring road.

Entrance to the Museo del Jamón *(see p170)*

Display of hand-painted ceramics in Toledo

MARKETS

THE LEGENDARY **El Rastro** flea market is held on Sundays and public holidays. It is located between the Plaza de Cascorro and streets leading off the Ribera de Curtidores. Do not expect to stumble across a painting by Velázquez, but you will find everything else from valuable antiques to second-hand clothes, jewellery, records, collector items, mountain gear and statues for your garden. This is probably the only market in Madrid where it is possible to knock two-thirds off the starting price. Many shops and stalls in the area are open on weekdays for more relaxed browsing.

Open on Sundays only, the **Mercadillo de Sellos y Monedas** is a small coin, stamp and postcard market held under the arches of the Plaza Mayor. For a browse through old books, visit the **Mercado del Libro**, on the south side of the Real Jardín Botánico (see p84). Both new and second-hand books are sold here. On Sundays the stalls are thronged, but most open on weekdays, too.

ANNUAL FAIRS

FOR MANY MADRILEÑOS, the passing of the year is marked by popular annual fairs, many of them outdoors.

The contemporary art fair **ARCO** takes place in February. Whether you want to buy or just browse, it provides a great opportunity to catch up on the latest trends in the art world. In the week prior to Madrid's Fiestas de San Isidro (see p34), which begin on 15 May, you can buy earthen cookware and wine jugs at the **Feria de Cerámica** in the colourful district of Malasaña (see p103). A sure sign that summer is just around the corner is the arrival of hundreds of book stalls along the leafy avenues of Parque del Retiro (see p77), where publishers and bookshop owners exhibit their wares at the **Feria del Libro** over two weeks, beginning at the end of May.

On the Paseo de Recoletos the **Feria de Artesanos** takes place every December. Craft items from ceramics and jewellery to leather goods, glassware and silks make it ideal for Christmas shopping. Throughout December, the Plaza Mayor is the venue for a traditional Christmas fair, the **Mercado de Artículos Navideños**. Christmas trees are for sale, as well as cork-wood and moss for use in homemade nativity scenes. Stallholders sell figurines, including joke items such as the Catalan *caganers* – bare-bottomed shepherd figures traditionally placed behind the manger.

Sunday morning in the busy El Rastro flea market

What to Buy in Madrid

Traditional fan

IF FLAMENCO FRILLS and kitsch bulls are not to your taste, you can find a satisfying reminder of your visit in many traditional Spanish goods. Strongly scented saffron, matured ewe's cheese or a fruity extra-virgin olive oil all make prized gifts. Leather goods are particularly sought-after. The beautifully crafted Loewe bags are in a league of their own, but most leather, especially shoes, is extremely good value. Traditional crafts, such as woven baskets, are harder to find, but lovely and inexpensive ceramics are widely available. By looking around, you may even pick up an original piece of clothing.

Chulapo Dolls
These typically Spanish dolls with their endearing pout are dressed in the traditional costume of Madrid's castizos (see p105).

Phineas T-shirt
T-shirts make great gifts, and Phineas (see p169) offers a wide range of unique designs.

Leather Handbag
The best bags come from Majorca, and are stocked at Piamonte (see p168), although many other shops sell leather, too.

Mantón de Manila
Classical, beautifully embroidered silk shawls, like this one, are easy to find and come in a wide range of colours.

Saffron (Azafrán)
Hand-picked azafrán comes from the autumn crocus.
Introduced by the Moors, it is the world's most expensive spice.

Queso Manchego
Used in tapas or served with quince jelly (membrillo) at the end of a meal, Manchego cheese also makes an ideal gift. It is widely regarded as Spain's finest cheese.

Turrón
Luxury nougat and almond paste, pressed into almond-shaped shells, comes in a wooden gift box at Casa Mira (see p170).

Barquillera
Filled with wafer biscuits, this old-fashioned cookie (biscuit) tin has a children's roulette game on the lid. Barquilleras are sold in the pastry departments of El Corte Inglés and Mallorca (see p170).

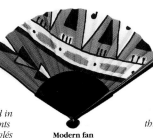

Modern fan

Modern Fan
A wide range of fans, from the traditional delicate lace to colourful, simple modern versions, can be found throughout Madrid.

Traditional Ceramics
The art of hand-painting ceramics with traditional colours and designs continues to thrive in Madrid. The attractive plates and tiles make memorable keepsakes.

Antique ceramic tiles

Decorative ceramic plates

Painted modern candlesticks

Modern Ceramics
Those in search of 20th-century ceramics will not need to look far. As well as traditional designs, Madrid offers a wide range of entirely modern craftwork.

SAUSAGES AND HAMS

Spain has a deep-rooted tradition of pork products, ranging from whole hams to sausages of every shape and size. The annual *matanza*, when pigs were killed and families spent the day preparing food for the months ahead, was an important date on the country calendar. Today, most products are made in a factory. *Jamón serrano* is cured ham, served thinly sliced as a *tapa* or used diced as an ingredient in numerous recipes. The best, and most expensive ham, is *ibérico*, from the small, black-hoofed, free-ranging Iberian pig. Many sausages are seasoned with Spain's favourite spice – paprika; they are called *chorizo*. Those without paprika are called *salchichón*. Other types of sausage are *longaniza* (long, thin sausages), *morcilla* (blood sausage or black pudding, made with rice, onions or potatoes) and *chistorras* (small Basque sausages, often flambéed). *Caña de lomo* is cured pork loin.

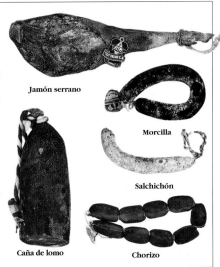

Jamón serrano

Morcilla

Salchichón

Caña de lomo

Chorizo

Fashion and Accessories

S PANIARDS ARE CELEBRATED for their elegance. No woman will leave the house, even if it is simply to go to the market, without dressing impeccably. The most popular styles tend towards classic cuts, with the occasional Baroque flounce. Madrid's cultural boom in the 1980s impacted the fashion world with a look based on sleek, understated design and sophisticated accessories. Footwear and clothing boutiques carry all the well-known international designer labels but, if you want something a little bit different, look out for the Spanish designers.

SHOES

T HE BEST SHOES are made in Mallorca, with classic footwear by Yanko at the very top of the range. Yanko shoes are so soft and comfortable that they feel like slippers. **Bravo** shoe shops carry many top Mallorcan makes, including Yanko, Lotusse and Barratts.

Another Mallorcan export is the young and comfortable **Camper** shoe. Outlets exist all over Madrid, with customer-friendly displays. The **Geltra** chain stocks the Camper brand in addition to its own good quality range of shoes.

For sophisticated designs – and prices – go to **Farrutx**. For a more avant-garde style, it is worth trying the Catalan shoe outlet **Excrupulus Net**.

If you forgot your trainers, or need to get out of rain-soaked shoes cheaply, try the shops along the Calle de Fuencarral, or go to **Los Guerrilleros** in the heart of Madrid's "kilometre 0" – the area around the Puerta del Sol. Jot down the reference number of the shoe in the showcase and you will get efficient service inside.

Brightly coloured espadrilles are sold in most areas but, for an old-world feel, visit **Casa Hernanz** off the Plaza Mayor.

HANDBAGS AND OTHER LEATHER GOODS

T HE ULTIMATE in Spanish bags and leather clothing goes by the prestigious name of **Loewe**. Established over a century ago by a German tanner who settled in Spain, Loewe bags are sold all over the world. At the Loewe shop in Calle de Serrano, you can feast your eyes, if nothing else.

Around the corner you will find **Lotusse** selling wallets, bags and coats, as well as its famous shoes. The Mallorcan connection continues nearby at **Boxcalf**, with an enticing range of quality leather clothing and accessories.

Piamonte, in the Chueca district, has become synonymous with attractive bags at affordable prices. They also have belts and an interesting selection of jewellery.

For a touch of Andalusian chic, see the handbags and belts for sale at **El Caballo**.

Manuel Herrero offers value for money in what feels like a bazaar crammed with leather and suede, visitors and persuasive salespeople.

A delightful outlet for classic gloves is the small, but well-stocked **Guante Varade**.

JEWELLERY

M ADRID IS FULL of small shops, stacked with trays of 18-carat gold studs, chains and bracelets, and grand jewellers – whether you walk down the Gran Vía or Calle de Serrano. Most Spanish women adore gold – the heavier the better – and pearls. Popular, man-made "Majorica" pearls, as well as the cultivated variety, can be found all over Madrid. **Las Perlas** on Gran Vía sells all categories of pearls, starting at good prices.

Del Pino on Calle de Serrano is fun for its variety of costume jewellery across the price range, and the Catalans' innovative **Tous** outlet in Madrid should not be missed.

If you are interested in new creations, visit internationally acclaimed jeweller **Joaquín Berao**. His shop is like a

miniature art gallery devoted to thoughtfully understated and tasteful design.

At **La Oreja de Plata**, designer Chus Burés displays his own work and that of other jewellers he has discovered. **Helena Rohner**, whose silver, bronze and enamel jewellery can be found in **Piamonte** *(see Handbags)*, is also becoming a popular name. You can visit her workshop, but it is best to call first.

WOMEN'S FASHIONS

T HE BEST OF SPANISH and international fashion is located on Calle de Serrano and Calle de José Ortega y Gasset, as well as in adjacent streets. The best place to find the work of young designers is the Chueca district, in and around Calle del Almirante, with shops such as **Ararat**. If you want original "street" fashion, go to **Glam** in busy Calle de Fuencarral, a street full of fun shops for the young.

In the designer category, **Adolfo Domínguez** – doyen of Madrid's minimalist look – and **Roberto Verino** offer excellent value for money. The more eccentric should try **Agatha Ruíz de la Prada**'s unique creations – also for children – in her shop off the Paseo de la Castellana. For the best young designs go to **Mezcla**, and for a combination of designer clothes and leather goods, try **Loewe**, but be prepared for high prices.

Another creation in a league of its own is the traditional **Seseña** cape, exclusive to the Madrid fashion house of the same name which also makes more modern versions.

The chain store **Zara** has become a national phenomenon, offering easy-to-wear clothes for women, men and children at very good prices.

Fine lingerie is part of a Spanish tradition, and lingerie shops – called *corseterías* in the more popular parts of town – are everywhere. A cotton nightdress can be an expensive affair but, for a select choice of sleepwear as well as bed linen, visit ¡Oh **qué luna!** for original and attractive designs.

Not to be forgotten, Spain is big on babies, and **Prenatal** is well worth a visit for expectant women and for mothers with very young children.

MENSWEAR

MEN'S FASHIONS can be found in the same areas of Madrid as women's. The traditional tailored look lives on, but Spanish men also like styles from abroad. You will find that many shops which sell off-the-peg clothes have Italian- or English-sounding names, but only sell home-produced merchandise. Prices and quality vary. For a more

interesting purchase, check out the menswear at **Roberto Verino**, **Adolfo Domínguez** or **Zara** *(see Women's Fashions)*. At the top end, **Loewe**'s store for men has beautiful clothes, adapting fashion trends to its own look. A Loewe silk tie with a Spanish art motif makes a rewarding purchase.

In the Calle del Almirante, **Pedro Morago** has stylish clothes for men on the move. Even though the young and fashionable stars of Spanish cinema and sports shop here, prices are accessible.

Another name to look out for is Antonio Miró and his famous shirts, available in

Gallery, which hosts a range of top international labels.

For casual wear, **Phineas** has become a very popular Madrid label and there are clothes for women, too. Its outlets throughout the city offer quality cottonwear with original designs that come in attractive colours.

When it comes to cotton, a Portuguese label, intriguingly named **Throttleman**, has set up shop in Madrid, offering shirts and fantasy boxer shorts. And for outdoor clothes, which cater for anything between a walk in the park and a safari, go to **Coronel Tapioca** for comfort at a reasonable price.

DIRECTORY

SHOES

Bravo
Calle de Serrano 42.
Map 6 E4.
91 435 27 29.

Camper
Gran Vía 54. **Map** 4 E1.
91 547 52 23.
www.camper.es

Casa Hernanz
Calle de Toledo 18.
Map 4 E3.
91 366 54 50.

Excrupulus Net
Calle del Almirante 7.
Map 5 C5.
91 521 72 44.

Farrutx
Calle de Serrano 7.
Map 8 D1.
91 576 94 93.

Geltra
Gran Vía 33.
Map 4 F1.
91 531 13 53.

Los Guerrilleros
Puerta del Sol 5.
Map 4 F2.
91 521 27 08.

HANDBAGS AND OTHER LEATHER GOODS

Boxcalf
Calle de Jorge Juan 14.
Map 6 E5.
91 435 34 29.

El Caballo
Calle de Lagasca 55.
Map 6 E5.
91 576 40 37.

Guante Varadé
Calle de Serrano 54.
Map 6 E3.
91 575 67 41.

Loewe
Calle de Serrano 26.
Map 6 E4.
91 577 60 56.
www.loewe.es

Lotusse
El Jardín de Serrano,
Calle de Goya 6–8.
Map 6 E4.
91 577 20 14.

Manuel Herrero
Calle de Preciados 7 & 16.
Map 4 F2.
91 521 29 90.

Piamonte
Calle del Marqués de
Monasterio 5. **Map** 5 C5.
91 308 48 62.

JEWELLERY

Del Pino
Calle Ayala 46.
Map 6 E3.
91 435 26 70.

Helena Rohner
Calle del Almendro 4.
Map 4 D3.
91 365 79 06.

Joaquín Berao
Calle del Conde de
Xiquena 13.
Map 5 C5.
91 310 16 20.

La Oreja de Plata
Calle de Jorge Juan 39.
Map 6 F5.
91 576 39 01.

Las Perlas
Gran Vía 33. **Map** 4 E1.
91 521 18 44.

Tous
Calle de Ayala 26.
Map 6 E4.
91 575 53 86.
www.tous.es

WOMEN'S FASHIONS

Adolfo Domínguez
Calle de Serrano 18.
Map 6 E5.
91 577 82 80.

Agatha Ruíz de la Prada
Calle del Marqués de
Riscal 8.
Map 6 D3.
91 310 44 83.

Ararat
Calle del Almirante 10.
Map 5 C5.
91 531 81 56.

Glam
Calle de Fuencarral 35.
Map 7 A1.
91 522 80 54.

Mezcla
Calle de Claudio Coello 81.
Map 6 E3.
91 435 42 03.

¡Oh que luna!
Calle de Ayala 32.
Map 6 F4.
91 431 37 25.

Prenatal
Calle Goya 99.**Map** 7 A1.
91 431 59 30.
www.prenatal.es

Roberto Verino
Calle de Serrano 33.
Map 6 E4.
91 426 04 75.

Seseña
Calle de la Cruz 23.
Map 7 A2.
91 531 68 40.

Zara
ABC Serrano, Calle de
Serrano 61. **Map** 6 E3.
91 575 63 34.

MENSWEAR

Coronel Tapioca
Calle del Carmen 12.
Map 4 F2.
91 531 59 29.

Gallery
Calle de Jorge Juan 17.
Map 6 E5.
91 576 79 31.

Loewe
Calle de Serrano 34.
Map 6 E4.
91 435 30 56.

Pedro Morago
Calle del Almirante 20.
Map 5 C5.
91 521 66 28.

Phineas
Calle Conde de Peñalver 20.
91 576 09 11.

Throttleman
Calle de Ayala 28.
Map 6 E4.
91 577 87 92.

Antiques, Crafts and Gifts

SPAIN'S RICH AND VARIED POPULAR ART makes it relatively easy to pick up an original piece of handicraft. It is often possible to obtain the same item, be it a ceramic mortar or a silk shawl, as an antique, a reproduction or even a stylized update. Genuine articles at good prices can still be found, but many rural crafts are fast disappearing. Fortunately, they do not include the age-old arts of producing Manchego cheese, cured ham and wines. Spain's musical tradition is very much alive, and a CD of flamenco-jazz fusion can be a spellbinding gift.

ANTIQUES

STROLLING DOWN the Calle de Claudio Coello, in elegant Salamanca, you will pass some outstanding antique shops. The streets around are also full of specialist outlets for rare antiques, ranging from 18th-century lacquered furniture at **María Gracia Cavestany**, to 15th-century Flemish paintings at **Theotokopoulos**, or rustic tools at **Collector**. Some of Madrid's top dealers, such as Pedro Alarcón and Luis Carabe, can be found under one roof at the **Centro de Anticuarios**.

Calle del Prado is lined with antique shops crammed with Castilian-style furniture, books, old tiles, religious artifacts and antique jewellery. Shops on neighbouring Calle de las Huertas deal in old prints.

Hidalgo in El Rastro *(see p61)* sells collectors' items, such as keys and corkscrews, while reasonably priced bric-à-brac (including some reproductions) can be found at **La Trastienda de Alcalá**, just northeast of the Parque del Retiro *(see p77)*.

Casa Postal, near Plaza de Cibeles, specializes in old postcards and has a great selection of old signs and posters.

MODERN ART, PRINTS AND PHOTOGRAPHS

WHEN IT COMES TO modern art, new trends and new talent, the galleries around Calle de Claudio Coello are well worth visiting. The **Juan Gris** gallery always has works from established as well as up-and-coming artists. **Juana de Aizpuru**, a relative newcomer, has rapidly become one of the most influential galleries in Madrid. Also well known for promoting young artists are **Fúcares** and **Soledad Lorenzo**. You can find sketches by artists such as Picasso, Chillida, Tàpies and Miró at **Estiarte**. Most galleries are closed on Mondays.

CRAFTS

A WIDE CHOICE of ceramics is offered at **Cántaro**, near the Plaza de España *(see p53)*. Well stocked in regional styles, the shop also carries so-called "extinct" ceramics – pottery which is no longer produced. **El Caballo Cojo**, in Old Madrid, offers a bewildering array of ceramics from the 1960s and 1970s, as well as "extinct" pottery. In all shops, some of the attractive pottery is likely to be Moroccan.

The Spanish are proud of their embroidered linen, but hand-embroidered tablecloths or shawls at ridiculously low prices probably come from China. **Casa Bonet** offers the real thing, but at a premium.

One of the best shops for *mantones* (silk shawls) and linen – hand- and machine-made – is **Borca**, just off the Puerta del Sol *(see p44)*.

Basket shops tend to offer Asian imports, but you will still find traditional wares at **Joaquín Fernández**. And for fine hand-made guitars, visit **Guitarrería F Manzanero**.

BOOKS AND MUSIC

THERE IS AN AMPLE stock of foreign language titles at **Casa del Libro** on Gran Vía. French-owned **FNAC**, nearby, offers a wide choice of books both in English and in other languages. **Booksellers**, a little further afield, has classics but only a limited choice of new books. The second-hand bookstalls of the **Mercado del Libro** behind the Ministerio de Agricultura *(see p84)* are good for cheap paperbacks and, sometimes, rare volumes.

Art books can be found at **Crisol** branches, while one of the best specialist art bookshops is **Gaudí**, near Chueca.

For all types of music, go to the FNAC or **El Corte Inglés** branches in Calle de Preciados or Paseo de la Castellana. Flamenco buffs must drop in to **El Flamenco Vive**.

GIFTS

FOOD GIFTS FROM Madrid are always appreciated, and olive oil or "green gold" from Catalonia to Andalusia is available at **Patrimonio Comunal Olivarero**, a specialist olive oil shop near Chueca. The **El Corte Inglés** Club du Gourmet on the 4th floor of its Calle de Serrano branch also carries a wide selection of olive oil and other typical Spanish produce, such as sherry vinegar.

At **Casa Mira** you can get *turrón* – Spain's traditional Christmas sweet – all year round. An almond speciality, *turrón* comes in a hard or a soft version. For a less sticky, bite-size treat of soft *turrón* pressed into almond-shaped wafer shells, try *almendras imperiales* (imperial almonds).

For assorted cakes in the centre of Madrid go to **Horno de San Onofre**; for a first-class selection of wines visit **Mariano Madrueño**. Various categories of cured ham are available at **Museo del Jamón** outlets. One of the best cheese shops is **La Boulette** inside the Mercado de la Paz, just off Calle de Serrano. **Mallorca**, Madrid's finest delicatessen, carries the very best of foodstuffs to eat in or take away.

El Arco de los Cuchilleros is one of Madrid's most tasteful gift shops, with jewellery, leather goods and ceramics, while **Así**, conveniently located in the city centre, sells all kinds of dolls as well as reasonably priced household goods.

The Spanish share a national passion for cologne, and there are *perfumerías* (toiletry and cosmetic shops) everywhere.

SOUVENIRS

For a superior tourist shop, go to **La Tienda de Madrid**, which is located in Puerta de Toledo market. You will find souvenirs such as *barquilleras* (traditional biscuit or cookie tins), also sold at **El Corte Inglés** pastry shops and **Mallorca** *(see Gifts)*.

Dolls in typical Madrid costume are available at the **Sanatorio de Muñecos**.

Between the Puerta del Sol and Plaza Mayor, especially on Calle Postas, are outlets for religious artifacts. **Palomeque** specializes in postcards and reproductions of religious art.

Almoraima, on the Plaza Mayor, sells a vast range of fans. For a T-shirt that will remind you of your stay, but will not make you feel too touristy, try **El Tintero** in Chueca, which does designs and messages in Spanish.

DIRECTORY

ANTIQUES

Casa Postal
Calle de la Libertad 37.
Map 7 B1.
C 91 532 70 37.

Centro de Anticuarios
Calle de Lagasca 36.
Map 6 E5.

Collector
Calle del Conde de Aranda 18. **Map** 8 E1.
C 91 575 10 74.

Hidalgo
Galerías Piquer, Shop 23
Ribera de Curtidores 29.
Map 4 E5.
C 91 530 56 53.

María Gracia Cavestany
Calle de Jorge Juan 14.
Map 6 E5.
C 91 577 76 32.

Theotokopoulos
Calle de Alcalá 97.
Map 8 E1.
C 91 575 84 66.

La Trastienda de Alcalá
Calle de Alcalá 64.
Map 8 F1.
C 91 576 34 86.

MODERN ART, PRINTS AND PHOTOGRAPHS

Estiarte
Calle de Almagro 44.
Map 5 C3.
C 91 308 15 69.

Fúcares
Calle del Conde de Xiquena 12.
Map 5 C5.
C 91 319 74 02.

Juan Gris
Calle de Villanueva 22.
Map 6 E5.
C 91 575 04 27.
W www.galeriajuangris.com

Juana de Aizpuru
Calle de Barquillo 44.
Map 5 B5.
C 91 310 55 61.

Soledad Lorenzo
Calle de Orfila 5.
Map 5 C4.
C 91 308 28 87.
W www.soledadlorenzo.com

CRAFTS

Borca
Calle del Marqués Viudo de Pontejos 2. **Map** 4 E2.
C 91 532 61 53.

El Caballo Cojo
Calle de Segovia 7.
Map 4 D3.
C 91 366 43 90.

Cántaro
Calle de la Flor Baja 8.
Map 2 D5.
C 91 547 95 14.

Casa Bonet
Calle de Núñez de Balboa 76. **Map** 6 F4.
C 91 575 09 12.

Guitarrería F Manzanero
Calle de Santa Ana 12.
Map 4 D4.
C 91 366 00 47.

Joaquín Fernández
Calle de Claudio Coello 115. **Map** 6 F1.
C 91 575 83 11.

BOOKS AND MUSIC

Booksellers
Calle de José Abascal 48.
C 91 442 79 59.

Casa del Libro
Gran Vía 29. **Map** 4 F1.
C 91 521 21 13.
W www.casadellibro.com

El Corte Inglés
Calle de Preciados 1–3.
Map 4 F2.
C 91 379 80 00.

Crisol
Calle de Serrano 24.
Map 6 E5.
C 91 577 36 74.
W www.crisol.es

El Flamenco Vive
Calle Conde de Lemos 7.
Map 4 D2.
C 91 547 39 17.

FNAC
Calle de Preciados 28.
Map 4 E1.
C 91 595 61 00.
W www.fnac.es

Gaudí
Calle de Argensola 13.
Map 5 C4.
C 91 308 18 29.

GIFTS

El Arco de los Cuchilleros
Plaza Mayor 9. **Map** 4 E2.
C 91 365 26 80.

Así
Gran Vía 47.
Map 4 E1.
C 91 548 28 28.

La Boulette
Mercado de la Paz (Calle de Ayala 28). **Map** 6 E4.
C 91 431 77 25.

Casa Mira
Carrera de San Jerónimo 30. **Map** 7 A2.
C 91 429 88 95.

El Corte Inglés
Calle de Serrano 47.
Map 6 E3.
C 91 432 54 90.

Horno de San Onofre
Calle de San Onofre 3.
Map 7 A1.
C 91 532 90 60.

Mallorca
Calle de Serrano 6.
Map 8 D1.
C 91 577 18 59.

Mariano Madrueño
Calle del Postigo de San Martín 3.
Map 4 E1.
C 91 521 19 55.

Museo del Jamón
Carrera de San Jerónimo 6.
Map 7 A2.
C 91 521 03 46.

Patrimonio Comunal Olivarero
Calle de Mejía Lequerica 1.
Map 5 B4.
C 91 308 05 05.

SOUVENIRS

Almoraima
Plaza Mayor 12.
Map 4 E2.
C 91 365 42 89.

Palomeque
Calle del Arenal 17.
Map 4 E2.
C 91 548 17 20.

Sanatorio de Muñecos
Calle de Preciados 21.
Map 4 E1.
C 91 521 04 47.

La Tienda de Madrid
Mercado Puerta de Toledo, 5th floor.
Map 3 C5.
C 91 364 16 82.

El Tintero
Calle de Gravina 5.
Map 5 B5.
C 91 308 14 18.

ENTERTAINMENT IN MADRID

EW EUROPEAN CITIES take their entertainment as seriously as Madrid. The city is an international mecca for cultural events, putting a great deal of energy into providing its citizens and visitors with the best in traditional and modern entertainment throughout the year. World-famous orchestras, ballets and operas, including Madrid's own *zarzuela*, are daily staples. Dozens of mainstream and alternative theatres offer everything from Spanish Golden Age classics to experimental drama. The country's best flamenco acts bring their southern Spanish art to Madrid's international audiences. Some of Europe's liveliest cafés and bars are found here. The afternoon siesta, once a civilized way to escape the Spanish heat, is now either an excellent remedy for the previous night's revelry, or a way to prepare for the one ahead. Most bars and dance clubs are crowded four nights a week, from Thursday through Sunday, and smaller venues offer jazz, rock, salsa and world music on an almost nightly basis. Be prepared for late nights, however, because most activities begin well after midnight and often continue until after breakfast.

Street performer in Parque del Retiro

Façade of the Teatro Real (see p58), fronted by a statue of Felipe IV

PRACTICAL INFORMATION

THE FIRST STOP for visitors to Madrid should be at one of several tourist information offices, where English will be spoken and free information on events and venues can be obtained. For those interested in exploring Madrid with a professional guide, contact **A.P.I.T.** or **COSITUR**. These agencies supply guides with a comprehensive and intimate knowledge of the city.

Most Spaniards speak some English and are usually willing to help confused foreigners. Unfortunately, however, most of the city's entertainment guides are published exclusively in Spanish. *Lookout* is one informative English-language magazine relied upon by Madrid's expatriate community. Another is *In Madrid*, a free monthly publication that can be found in many bookshops, Irish bars and record shops.

You can also pick up a copy at most embassies and at the tourist information office at **Barajas Airport** *(see p192)*.

Of the Spanish options, the most complete entertainment guide is the weekly *Guía de Ocio*, which hits newsstands and bookstores on Friday and is usually sold out by Sunday. It covers every kind of entertainment on offer.

Madrid's top three daily newspapers – *El Mundo, El País* and *ABC* – have weekly entertainment supplements. These are more geared towards entertainment features, but their listings are broad and sometimes include last-minute events that you may not find in the *Guía de Ocio*. The *El Mundo, El País* and *ABC* supplements appear on Friday, covering information on music, theatre, cinema and books.

BOOKING TICKETS

THE EASIEST WAY to purchase tickets to major events, especially theatre, opera and concerts, is by telephone. **Entradas.com** and **Tel-Entrada** are the two main agents. Both accept VISA and MasterCard. Their services are provided free of charge and your tickets will be waiting for you at the venue's ticket booth.

SEASONS AND TICKETS

WHILE THERE IS never a shortage of top events year-round in Madrid, the main concert and theatre seasons run from September to June. During May's Fiestas de San Isidro *(see p34)* and the Festival de Otoño *(see p36)*, from October to November, the authorities

A full house at the Joy Madrid dance club (see p176)

Children enjoying the adventure playground in the Plaza de Oriente

like to splurge by booking top Spanish and international names in music, theatre and dance. Special events listings can be picked up at tourist offices and at most branches of the Caja Madrid bank.

The **Madrid Rock** record shop and **FNAC** sell most big-venue concert tickets, while the **TEYCI** agency sells tickets for most other events, but charges up to 20 per cent commission.

Another agency that sells tickets for a wide variety of events is **El Corte Inglés**, by telephone, or directly from the stores.

FACILITIES FOR THE DISABLED

To find out about wheelchair accessibility, you are advised to telephone the venue itself. *El País* provides a 1–4 rating for some venues in its daily listing: '1' means totally accessible while '4' indicates considerable difficulty.

Getting to and from events is easier. Each bus route runs several low-level vehicles with a wheelchair symbol. **Radioteléfono Taxi** (91 547 82 00) provides special cars – book well in advance and ask for Eurotaxis. Only the new Metro stations have elevators.

CHILDREN'S ACTIVITIES

There is no shortage of activities in Madrid for visitors with children. To give them some space, head for the Casa de Campo *(see p114).* Simply getting to this park can be fun if you take the highflying **Teleférico** cable car. The park is home to the **Zoo-Aquarium**, the modern **Parque de Atracciones** amusement park, a boating lake and several swimming pools. In the centre of Bourbon Madrid is the popular Parque del Retiro *(see p77)* with magic shows, jugglers, clowns and a lake.

The main children's theatre is **Sala San Pol**, but numerous fringe theatres also hold performances for young people.

Flamenco guitarist in the Parque del Retiro

Relaxing at a street café in the Plaza del Dos de Mayo *(see p103)*

Traditional Entertainment

THE SPANISH TAKE PARTICULAR pride in their cultural heritage, and attending a performance at one of Madrid's theatres, opera houses, music auditoriums or cabarets is one of the best ways of sharing the experience and traditions of Spain. Madrid plays host to a wide variety of classical art performances, which equal the best on offer in other European cities, but it also provides plenty of opportunities for savouring the traditional art forms of the Spanish people. These include the spontaneity of flamenco, the three-act drama of the *corrida* or bullfight *(see p111)*, and *zarzuela*, Madrid's particular version of the Spanish operetta *(see p75)*.

CLASSICAL MUSIC

THE NEWLY RENOVATED **Teatro Real de Madrid** *(see p58)* is probably best known as the home of the city's opera company, but it is also the venue for top national and international classical music concerts.

The two concert halls of the **Auditorio Nacional de Música** also host international classical music performances, along with programmes by the national orchestra, the Orquesta Nacional de España. The Orquesta Nacional is frequently accompanied by Spain's national choir, the Coro Nacional de España.

The **Teatro Monumental** is the main venue for the excellent Orquesta Sinfónica y Coro de RTVE, the orchestra and choir of Spain's state radio and television company. The **Auditorio Conde Duque** also hosts a variety of classical concerts.

OPERA AND ZARZUELA

A VISIT TO THE Spanish capital would not be complete without spending a night at the *zarzuela*, Madrid's own variety of comic opera. The best productions are those staged at the **Teatro de la Zarzuela**. Other venues include the **Teatro Albéniz** and the newly reopened **Teatro Príncipe**. Several other theatres also offer *zarzuela* productions during the summer.

The best place to see national opera, as well as international productions on tour to the city is the **Teatro Real de Madrid**, which is appropriately located next to the Ópera Metro station. The **Teatro Calderón** also hosts some excellent classical and modern opera productions.

DANCE

THERE ARE SEVERAL venues in Madrid that stage performances of classical and modern dance, in addition to those that put on larger flamenco productions. The **Teatro Albéniz** is the main place to see good international dance companies as well as the top national acts. The three other major venues are the **Teatro Madrid**, the **Nuevo Teatro Alcalá** and the **Teatro de la Zarzuela**.

FLAMENCO

A SPONTANEOUS musical art form, flamenco has its roots in the gypsy culture of Andalusia. However, many of the best exponents are now based in the capital.

Flamenco is a late-night art form with shows usually taking place through the evening and into the early hours of the morning. Most venues offer dinner and a show, which may be singing only, or both singing and dancing. Although the familiar rhythmic dancing is often a part of flamenco, the purest form of the art consists of a solo singer accompanied by a guitar.

Casa Patas is still the best place to catch the raw power of genuine flamenco guitar and *cante* singing. Dancing often, but not always, accompanies the singing. Both music and dance can be enjoyed at **Café de Chinitas**. Other venues offering high-quality flamenco performances are **Arco de Cuchilleros**, **Corral de la Morería**, **Candela** and **Torres Bermejas**.

THEATRE

MADRID'S MOST prestigious theatres are the **Teatro de la Comedia** and the **Teatro María Guerrero**. The former is the home of the Compañía Nacional de Teatro Clásico, which stages classic works by Spanish playwrights. The Teatro María Guerrero hosts foreign productions as well as modern drama in Spanish. It has recently been renovated. Many other theatres, including **Teatro Alcázar**, **Teatro Muñoz Seca** and **Teatro Reina Victoria**, also stage drama productions.

As well as drama, Teatro Muñoz Seca and Teatro Reina Victoria also offer comedy productions, as do **Teatro Lara** and **Teatro La Latina**, which specializes in *Madrileño* comedy productions. **Centro Cultural de la Villa** presents popular theatre. Madrid also has a thriving network of alternative venues, most notably **Cuarta Pared**, **Ensayo 100** and **Teatro Alfil**. **Teatro Calderón**, **Teatro Lope de Vega** and **Teatro Nuevo Apolo** often stage musicals.

An enormous range of radical and established Spanish and international theatrical talent gathers in the city during the annual Festival de Otoño *(see p36)*.

BULLFIGHTING

BULLFIGHTING continues to be a popular spectacle in Madrid *(see p111)*, as throughout the country, but it is not for the squeamish. The **Plaza de Toros de Las Ventas** bullring is the most important in the world, and holds *corridas* every Sunday from March through to October. During the May Fiestas de San Isidro *(see p34)* there are fights every day. Each fight is made up of six 15-minute *faenas* of three acts, the last of which ends with the killing of the bull or, on very rare occasions, the matador.

FOOTBALL

WINNERS OF the European Cup on many occasions, **Real Madrid** are the local aristocrats of football. Their Bernabéu stadium, which has a capacity of 105,000, is one of the great theatres of the game. Real Madrid's cross-town rivals are **Atlético de Madrid**. They play at the Vicente Calderón stadium, a smaller and cheaper venue along the Manzanares River. Madrid's third team is **Rayo Vallecano**, who are constantly shifting up and down between the first and second divisions. Tickets are available at the stadiums or through the clubs themselves, but to see the massively popular Real Madrid, you may need to book ahead. Numerous websites offer ticketing services for Real Madrid and other team's games – expect a hefty booking fee. Once in Madrid, try the ticket agents listed on page 173.

Modern Entertainment

Madrid's nightlife starts to rumble at dusk in the city's numerous *tapas* bars and cafés. After a quick bite and yet another *caña* (small glass of beer), you may decide to head off to one of the city's palatial movie houses to see a film, or perhaps you would prefer to hit a lively night spot for a little rock, jazz or salsa to warm up your dancing shoes. The younger *Madrileños*, who may well have to go to school the next day, begin to head for the Metro stations at about 1:30am to catch the last train home, clearing the way for the multitudes of over-20s to take over the dance clubs until daybreak.

Cinema

Spanish cinema has been undergoing a renaissance in recent years as a new crop of film-makers tries to follow in the footsteps of internationally acclaimed film director Pedro Almodóvar, famous for his *Women on the Verge of a Nervous Breakdown (see p104)*.

For those with a grasp of the language, Spanish cinema is a rewarding experience, especially if enjoyed at one of the vast movie houses along Gran Vía *(see p48)*, such as the **Capitol** or **Palacio de la Música**. At the weekends many cinemas have late-night film programmes which begin only after midnight.

For those with no knowledge of Spanish, Hollywood productions and independent films can be seen in their original-language version at **Alphaville**, **Luna**, **Princesa** and **Renoir**. These cinemas have sprung up over the years to cater to Madrid's foreign residents and Spaniards who wish to enjoy productions in their purest form with Spanish subtitles. Films shown in their original version are listed in the film section of newspapers and various listings magazines as *VO (versión original)*.

Cafés and Bars

With such a vast array of cafés and bars in Madrid, you'd think supply would outstrip demand. But Madrid's social life revolves around the city's endless watering holes, which are also great places for people-watching and encounters. The large, historic **Café**

Comercial is a Madrid landmark. Its comfortable turn-of-the-century ambience is authentic and its proximity to the popular night spots in the Bilbao-Malasaña area makes it an excellent meeting point. The **Café del Círculo de Bellas Artes** is a cultural institution overlooking the busy Gran Vía, and the view of the Palacio Real *(see pp54–7)* from the **Café de Oriente** is without equal.

Overlooking the lively Plaza de Santa Ana *(see p47)* are the well established **Cervecería Alemana** and **Cervecería Santa Ana** bars. Two quite different bars can be found in the La Latina district. **El Almendro 13** offers sherry on the crowded first floor and popular Spanish cuisine in the basement. **Café del Nuncio** is an old style café with a beautiful outdoor terrace on an old stone staircase over Calle Segovia. And then, of course, there are the *tabernas (see pp28–9)*, the quintessential ingredient of any visit to Madrid. One of the most popular *tabernas* is **Los Gabrieles**, although **Viva Madrid** draws in a healthy crowd of young *Madrileños* attracted by the nightly activity around the Plaza de Santa Ana. For a more bohemian flavour, try **Casa Carmencita**, famous for its association with writers and artists in the 1920s. **Casa Labra** was the birthplace of the Spanish socialist party in the late 19th century and, as well as its clandestine history, you can savour its tasty *tapas*. For sheer character born from centuries-old history, visit **Casa Alberto**, **La Bola** and

Taberna Antonio Sanchez. The elegant surroundings of the **Taberna Casa Domingo** exude a more modern feel, whereas **Taberna del Foro** actually is modern but has succeeded in recreating an authentic feel of "Old Madrid".

Nightclubs

There is a high price to pay for dancing until dawn at one of Madrid's many nightclubs as entrance fees tend to be expensive. Two that are very much in vogue at the moment are **Kapital** and **Joy Madrid**. For something slightly different, however, you might like to try **Berlín Cabaret** where dance is mixed with cabaret acts.

The roomy and renowned upmarket dance club **Pachá** contrasts with the rest of the music bars in Malasaña, which tend to be reasonably priced but rather claustrophobic. A particular favourite with tourists is the **Villa Rosa** dance club in Old Madrid, or the Madrid de los Austrias. The decorative mosaics of this one-time café are exceptional.

Famous Spanish actor Javier Bardém is the proprietor of the nightclub **El Torero**, where you can dance to Latin and Flamenco style music upstairs, or head downstairs for some funky House music. The club **Samsara** also plays mainly Latin style music. Nightclubs stay open until after 6am.

Rock, Jazz and World Music

For those who would rather seek out good live music, there is no shortage of venues in Madrid. For rock music, **Sala la Riviera** has hosted some internationally famous bands, while **Moby Dick** and **Siroco** are good places to see some of the vibrant local and national talent. **Café Central** is considered the best place to enjoy jazz in a wonderfully elegant setting. The nearby **Popular't** is an excellent venue too. Formerly a pottery shop, it is a relaxed and busy venue. Both the Café Central and Popular't are also near to some of the best Latin music clubs in Madrid, where you can see live bands and dance to the sinuous rhythms of salsa into the early hours of the morning. The much larger **Clamores** hosts a range of musical performers, from jazz and tango to pop and blues.

Honky Tonk holds some of the city's best rock concerts, so keep an eye out for posters advertising forthcoming events.

Needless to say, this partially-covered venue located next to the Manzanares river (*see p114*) is more popular during the warm summer months.

GAY CLUBS

THE HEART OF the gay scene is located in the Chueca district (*see p94*) of central Madrid. **Why Not** is a small

bar that caters mostly to locals and plays music from the 1970s and '80s. There's not much in the way of leather at **New Leather**, but it is still one of the most popular male gay bars in the city. **Ambient** is a lesbian disco bar in the Alonso-Martínez area and, for mixed crowds, **La Lupe** is a favourite hangout that puts on frequent cabaret shows.

DIRECTORY

CINEMA

Alphaville
Calle de Martín de
los Heros 14.
Map 1 A1.
[91 559 38 36.

Capitol
Gran Vía 41. **Map** 4 E1.
[902 33 32 31.

Luna
Calle de la Luna 2.
Map 2 E5.
[91 522 47 52.
[w] www.cinentradas.com

**Palacio de la
Música**
Gran Vía 35.
Map 4 F1.
[902 22 16 22.

Princesa
Princesa 3. **Map** 1 C5.
[91 541 41 00.

Renoir
C/ Martín de los Heros 12.
Map 1 C5.
[91 541 41 00.

CAFÉS AND BARS

El Almendro 13
Calle Almendro 13.
Map 4 D3.
[91 365 42 52.

La Bola
C/ Bola 5.
Map 4 D1.
[91 547 69 30.

Café Comercial
Gta. de Bilbao 7.
Map 2 F3.
[91 521 56 55.

**Café del Círculo de
Bellas Artes**
Calle del Marqués de
Casa Riera 2. **Map** 7 B2.
[91 531 85 03.

Café del Nuncio
Calle Segovia 9.
Map 4 D3.
[91 366 08 53.

Café de Oriente
Plaza de Oriente 2.
Map 3 C2.
[91 541 39 74.

Casa Alberto
Calle de las Huertas 18.
Map 7 A3.
[91 429 93 56.

Casa Carmencita
Calle de la Libertad 16.
Map 7 B1.
[91 521 59 66.

Casa Labra
Calle de Tetuán 12.
Map 4 F2.
[91 531 00 81.

**Cervecería
Alemana**
Plaza de Santa Ana 6.
Map 7 A3.
[91 429 70 33.

**Cervecería Santa
Ana**
Plaza de Santa Ana 10.
Map 7 A3.
[91 429 43 56.

Los Gabrieles
Calle de Echegaray 17.
Map 7 A3.
[91 429 62 61.

**Taberna Antonio
Sanchez**
C/ Mesón de Paredes 13.
Map 4 F5.
[91 539 78 26.

**Taberna Casa
Domingo**
Calle de Alcalá 99.
Map 8 F1.
[91 576 01 37.

Taberna del Foro
Calle de San Andrés 38.
Map 2 F4.
[91 445 37 52.

Viva Madrid
Calle de Manuel
Fernández y González 7.
Map 7 A3.
[91 429 36 40.

NIGHTCLUBS

Berlín Cabaret
Costanilla de San
Pedro 11. **Map** 4 D3.
[91 366 20 34.

El Torero
Calle de la Cruz 26.
Map 4 F3.
[91 523 11 29.

Joy Madrid
Calle del Arenal 11.
Map 4 E2.
[91 366 37 33.

Kapital
Calle del Atocha 125.
Map 7 B4.
[91 420 29 06.

Pachá
Calle de Barceló 11.
Map 5 A4.
[91 447 01 28.

Samsara
Calle de la Cruz 7.
Map 4 F3.
[91 532 39 09.

Villa Rosa
Plaza de Santa Ana 15.
Map 7 A3.
[91 521 36 89.

ROCK, JAZZ AND
WORLD MUSIC

Café Central
Plaza del Angel 10.
Map 7 A3.
[91 369 41 43.

Clamores
Calle de Alburquerque 14.
Map 5 A3.
[91 445 79 38.

Honky Tonk
Calle de Covarrubias 24.
Map 5 B3.
[91 445 68 86.

Moby Dick
Avenida del Brasil 5.
[91 555 76 71.

Populart
Calle de las Huertas 22.
Map 7 A3.
[91 429 84 07.

Sala la Riviera
Paseo de la Virgen
del Puerto.
[91 365 24 15.

Siroco
Calle de San Dimas 3.
Map 2 E4.
[91 593 30 70.

GAY CLUBS

Ambient
Calle de San Mateo 21.
Map 5 A4.
(no telephone).

La Lupe
Calle de Torrecilla del
Leal 12.
Map 7 A4
[91 527 50 19.

New Leather
Calle de Pelayo 42.
Map 5 B5.
[91 308 14 62.

Why Not
Calle de San
Bartolomé 7.
Map 7 A1.
[91 523 05 81.

OUTDOOR ACTIVITIES

A VAST WILDERNESS, ranging from the gentle to the dramatic, lies on the doorstep of Madrid. A scant hour's drive from the city centre will bring you to granite peaks, pine forests, glacial lakes and wild pastureland. Against this backdrop there are endless possibilities for hiking, climbing, horse riding, camping, swimming, skiing or simply finding tranquillity. Stretching across central Spain, the Sierra de Guadarrama and the Sierra de Gredos form a 250-km (155-mile) chain of craggy peaks dipping down to lush

Cycling in Madrid

pastureland, where you can track a mountain stream in spring, ski in winter or picnic in the wilderness in summer. Within Madrid, golf and tennis facilities are on hand, and waterworlds have begun to appear everywhere in response to the hot summers. Beyond Madrid, the area surrounding Toledo is famous for its hunting and, further afield, Cuenca's river gorges and ravines are an ideal setting for adventure sports. Details on all outdoor activities are available at **Comunidad de Madrid Tourist Information** offices.

Enjoying a game of golf in the attractive countryside of El Escorial

GOLF AND TENNIS

M ADRID'S FINEST sports grounds are to be found at the semi-private **Club de Campo**. The entrance fee for non-members is high, but the excellent facilities and lovely setting make it well worth the

A pleasant break from sightseeing at one of Madrid's tennis courts

cost for weary tourists who need a day away from the museums. Tennis, squash and golf are all on offer here. The club also provides designated play areas for children. Tennis courts can be reserved over the telephone, but for golf you must turn up at the club in person. When deciding which day to plan your activities, it is worth bearing in mind that admission prices rise at the weekends.

El Olivar de la Hinojosa is a new golf course that has opened just off the road to Barajas airport *(see p192)*. It accepts reservations over the telephone. At both the Club de Campo and El Olivar you can rent golf equipment.

If you want a game of tennis in the centre of town, you can reserve a court at the **Canal de Isabel II** sports centre. This

modern, attractively designed complex, which is conveniently located in north-central Madrid, boasts excellent facilities as well as a pleasant bar and restaurant. The **Puerta de Hierro** complex, alongside the Río Manzanares *(see p114)*, also has tennis courts.

WALKING AND CYCLING

F OR KEEN WALKERS, there are numerous day hikes within easy access of the city – even if you don't have a car. Just an hour away by train, Cercedilla is an excellent starting point for trails into the Valle de la Fuenfría. One such trail is the old Roman road *(calzada romana)*. Dating from around the 1st century AD, the road once ran over the mountain to Segovia. A tram which links Cercedilla with the area's ski resorts climbs to the Puerto de Navacerrada for more substantial trails higher up.

Further east, the regional park which encompasses Manzanares el Real *(see p126)* leads into a valley of fast-flowing streams and pools, climbing sharply to the source of the Río Manzanares. The valley tends to attract large numbers of picnickers – one good reason for an early start.

Because only limited roadside bicycle trails are available, many cyclists opt for mountain biking instead. **Karacol Sport** near Atocha Station *(see p85)* rents bicycles which can then be taken by train to Cercedilla. For other destinations, check

An ideal site for birdwatching and walking outside the city

with RENFE first *(see p196)*. In addition to organizing walks, **Sport Natura** and other specialist outlets provide bikes and transport at weekends to areas such as the Sierra Pobre, east of the Guadarrama.

Remember to take sensible precautions when walking or cycling in the intense Spanish summer heat. It is essential to wear a hat and a high-factor suncream and to take an adequate supply of water with you. Walkers venturing into high-mountain areas should always check the weather forecast first, as conditions here can change very rapidly.

HORSE RIDING

THE SIERRAS and *cañadas* (old sheep trails) surrounding Madrid are ideal for horse riding. Spaghetti westerns were once filmed in this wild region of the country. At the **Club de Campo**, on the edge of the city, horses can be hired for rides through Madrid's expansive Casa de Campo *(see p114)*. You can also hire a steed by the hour or even for the day at **El Potril**.

Centro Equestre Alameda del Pardo is situated in the village of El Pardo about 5 km northwest of Madrid and offers routes through the extensive forest surrounding the famous Palacio de El Pardo *(see p134)*.

High up on the route from Cercedilla to the Puerto de Navacerrada, set back from the tram line, **Picadero los Ciruelos** also offers a wide choice of day horse riding routes or even longer outings. In the rugged Sierra Pobre near Buitrago del Lozoya, **Rutas Equestres Sierra Norte** organizes routes from Braojos de la Sierra, which is accessible by direct bus once a day from Madrid.

For an overnight stay or longer stays, the Sierra de Gredos offers superb horse riding set against imposing peaks. You can hire horses at **Turismo Ecuestre Almanzor**, down the road from the Parador Nacional de Gredos. Further along, **Gredos Rutas a Caballo (GRAC)** also organizes day- or week-long outings. During holiday periods, especially Easter week, you should book your accommodation well in advance. Also make sure the riding centre is open on the day you plan to go, and specify your riding level.

Rugged terrain of the sierras – perfect for horse riding

Skiing at the popular resort of the Puerto de Navacerrada

SKIING

IN A YEAR of good snowfall, skiing through pine trees under an azure sky can be a glorious experience. The most popular resort near Madrid is the **Puerto de Navacerrada**. It has 15 slopes and a daunting chairlift up to the "Bola del Mundo" at 2,200 m (7,200 ft). Further away, **Valdesquí** offers better snow conditions and 24 slopes, while **La Pinilla** in the Segovia region is probably the least crowded. All the equipment you need, including skis, snowboards and sleds, can be rented at the resorts.

On weekends during the skiing season, the route to the Puerto de Navacerrada tends to be congested with traffic. Avoid driving if you can and take the tram from Cercedilla. A reliable source of information is **ATUDEM** (Asociación Turística de Estaciones de Esquí y Montaña), a group that specializes in alpine skiing and will provide details on any of the resorts.

MOUNTAINEERING AND CLIMBING

SOME PERFECT DROPS for novice climbers can be found at La Pedriza de Manzanares, as well as at La Cabrera at the eastern end of the Guadarrama mountains. Patones, in the Sierra Pobre, offers ideal rock

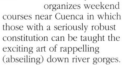

Climbing at Escalada en Patones

faces. For the experienced mountaineer, the huge granite needles and walls in the Sierra de Gredos present a greater challenge. Information on courses and guides is available at the **Federación Madrileña de Montañismo**. **Club Ibérico de Expediciones** organises four-wheel drive (4WD) trips out of Madrid for weekends. They take care of the accommodation and the food and also offer tuition in driving the 4WD off-road vehicles. A company called **Gente Viajera** organizes weekend courses near Cuenca in which those with a seriously robust constitution can be taught the exciting art of rappelling (abseiling) down river gorges.

SHOOTING

LIKE THE REST OF Spain, the rugged terrain surrounding Madrid is ideal for hunting. But, unless you are fortunate enough to hunt on one of the many private estates, you will not find much game in the remaining free shooting zones. The best option is to go to Toledo or Ciudad Real, both of which are rich in game, from birds to wild boar and deer. To avoid hassles for permits, contact **Cacerías Ibéricas** in advance. They will do the paperwork, organize the outing and provide equipment. **Viajes Marsans** will do everything except provide your equipment.

WATER SPORTS

MADRID'S SIZZLINGLY hot summers make watering holes a dire necessity. There is a splendid swimming pool at the **Club de Campo** although, in spite of its great size, it can be uncomfortably full on a hot day. The sports complex at **Puerta de Hierro** has a huge, neck-deep basin just for cooling off, as well as a proper lane pool for swimmers. By far the best pool in Madrid is the **Centro de Natación M-86**, but it is only open to the public from June to the end of August. The **Canal de Isabel II** sports complex, which is also conveniently situated in town, has a much-appreciated outdoor pool, as well as an Olympic-size indoor

One of the reservoirs on the outskirts of Madrid – ideal for canoeing

Causing a splash outside Madrid

pool and a children's pool. There are also a number of large reservoirs outside Madrid, which are perfect for sailing, windsurfing and canoeing.

Contact **Sport Natura**, which provides equipment and transport at weekends to its centre at Embalse del Atazar near El Berrueco.

THEME PARKS

NEARLY 500 ANIMALS run wild at **Safari Madrid** outside Aldea del Fresno, making this a great outing for children. There is also a daily show of birds of prey. A nearby added attraction is the park and beach along the Alberche river.

Aquópolis, a 40-minute drive from the city, is Madrid's most complete waterworld, with slides and innumerable

other water features. Bring a picnic, and enjoy a day out for the family. Free buses leave from the Plaza de España.

Another waterworld, the **Aquamadrid** in San Fernando de Henares, boasts a huge pool with a water chute and waves.

The thrilling **Parque de Atracciones** (see p114) has the latest stomach-churning rides from roller coasters to vertical drops, as well as all the old favourites. There is also a zone for small children. A new **Warner Bros. Park** in Madrid has roller-coaster rides and recreations of film sets and a Hollywood Boulevard.

DIRECTORY

Comunidad de Madrid Tourist Information
Calle del Duque de Medinaceli 2, Madrid.
Map 7 B3.
☎ 91 429 49 51.
ⓦ www.madrid.org/turismo

GOLF AND TENNIS

Canal de Isabel II
Avenida de Filipinas 54, Madrid.
☎ 91 533 17 91.

Club de Campo
Carretera de Castilla, km 2, Madrid.
☎ 91 550 20 18 (tennis).
☎ 91 550 20 27 (water sports).
☎ 91 550 20 10 (riding school).

El Olivar de la Hinojosa
Campo de las Naciones, Avenida de Dublin, Madrid.
☎ 91 721 18 89.

Puerta de Hierro
Carretera de El Pardo, km 1, Madrid.
☎ 91 316 15 47.

WALKING AND CYCLING

Karacol Sport
Calle de Tortosa 8, Madrid.
Map 7 C5.
☎ 91 539 96 33.

Sport Natura
Avenida Donostiarra 4 posterior, Madrid.
☎ 91 403 61 61.

HORSE RIDING

Centro Ecuestre Alameda del Pardo
Carretera Fuencarral, km 2.3, El Pardo.
☎ 91 372 09 58.

Club de Campo
See Golf and Tennis.

El Potril
Avenida de las Caudalosas, Brunete.
☎ 91 816 42 91.

Gredos Rutas a Caballo (GRAC)
Calle Trigueras 4, Hoyos del Espino (Avila).
☎ 920 34 90 85.

Picadero los Ciruelos
Camino los Ciruelos 30, Carretera Camorritos, Cercedilla.
☎ 91 852 07 67.

Rutas Ecuestres Sierra Norte
Calle Generalísimo 13, Braojos de la Sierra.
☎ 91 868 09 44.

Turismo Ecuestre Almanzor
Barajas de Gredos, Navarredonda de Gredos (Avila).
☎ 920 34 80 47.

SKIING

ATUDEM
Calle del Padre Damián 43, 2nd Floor 26, Madrid.
☎ 91 359 75 26.

La Pinilla
☎ 921 55 03 04.

Puerto de Navacerrada
☎ 91 852 33 02.

Valdesquí
☎ 91 852 39 41.

MOUNTAINEERING AND CLIMBING

Federación Madrileña de Montañismo
Calle del Ferrocarril 22, 1st Floor, Madrid.
☎ 91 527 38 01.

Club Ibérico de Expediciones
Avenida Complutense 16 Camarma de Esteruelas.
☎ 606 72 94 21.

Gente Viajera
Calle de Santa Alicia 19, Madrid.
☎ 91 478 01 11.

SHOOTING

Cacerías Ibéricas
Calle de San Pedro el Verde 49.3, Toledo.
☎ 925 21 25 52.

Viajes Marsans
Gran Vía 84, Madrid.
Map 4 E1.
☎ 91 559 87 59.

WATER SPORTS

Canal de Isabel II
See Golf and Tennis.

Club de Campo
See Golf and Tennis.

Centro de Natación M-86
Calle de José Martínez de Velasco 3, Madrid.
☎ 91 409 53 51.

Puerta de Hierro
See Golf and Tennis.

Sport Natura
See Walking and Cycling.

THEME PARKS

Aquamadrid
Carretera N-II, km 15.5, San Fernando de Henares.
☎ 91 673 10 13.

Aquópolis
Avenida de la Dehesa, Villanueva de la Cañada.
☎ 91 815 69 11.

Parque de Atracciones
Casa de Campo, Madrid.
☎ 91 463 29 00.

Safari Madrid
N-V Salida 32, Aldea del Fresno.
☎ 91 862 23 14.

Warner Bros. Park
Carretera M-301, km 15.5, San Martin de la Vega.
☎ 91 808 76 00.

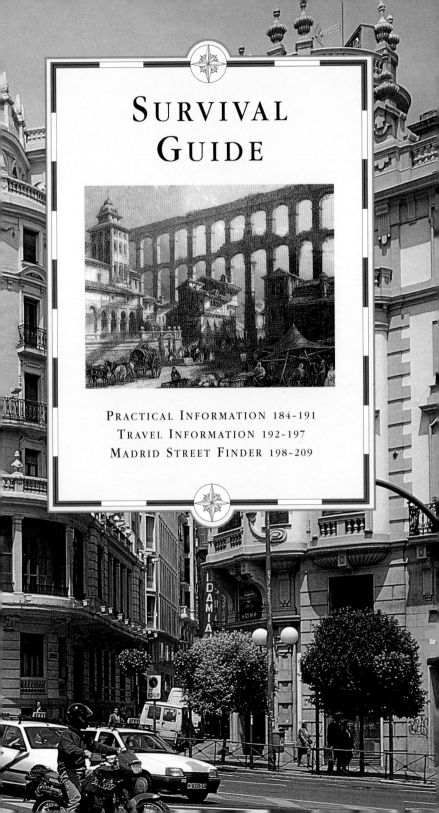

SURVIVAL
GUIDE

PRACTICAL INFORMATION

PAIN HAS FINALLY begun to market itself beyond the attractions of its coastline, and now has a solid tourist infrastructure. In Madrid there are national tourist offices, while the smaller towns have regional offices. All offer help with finding accommodation, restaurants and activities in their area. One of Madrid's best offices is at Calle del Duque de Medinaceli.

Old street sign

August is Spain's vacation (holiday) period, during which many businesses close. Roads are very busy at the beginning and end of the month. Find out in advance whether your visit coincides with Madrid's many fiestas because, although these are attractions, they often entail widespread closures. It is a good idea to plan leisurely lunches, as most of Spain stops from 2pm to 5pm.

LANGUAGE

SPAIN'S OFFICIAL LANGUAGE is *castellano* (Castilian). It is spoken by everyone and is certainly the language you will experience most frequently in Madrid. There are three main regional languages – *català* (Catalonia), *euskera* (Basque country) and *gallego* (Galicia). Places that deal with tourists usually employ at least one English-speaker.

MANNERS

MADRILEÑOS are a warm, open, spirited people who are justly proud of their city. Drawn to the capital from all parts of the country, they have brought with them a strong and varied cultural tradition. As a result, this lively city teems with culture and the arts.

It is common for the Spanish to greet and say goodbye to strangers at bus stops and in elevators (lifts), shops and other public places. They often talk to people they do not know. People shake hands when introduced and subsequently whenever they meet. Women usually kiss on both cheeks when they meet; friends and family members embrace or kiss. In bars or restaurants, it is unusual to sit at someone else's table.

VISAS AND PASSPORTS

VISAS ARE NOT required by citizens of most EU countries but it is wise to check entry requirements before you go. A list is available from Spanish embassies, which specifies 35 other countries, including Canada, Australia and the US, whose nationals do not need a visa for visits of less than 90 days. For an extension, apply to the *Gobierno Civil* (a local government office) with proof of employment or of sufficient funds to cover a long stay. Visitors from all other countries need a visa. British visitors can no longer travel on a Visitor's Passport and must have a full passport.

TAX-FREE GOODS AND CUSTOMS INFORMATION

NON-EU RESIDENTS can reclaim IVA (VAT) on single items worth over 90 euros and bought in shops displaying a "Tax-free for Tourists" sign. Food, drink, tobacco, cars, motorcycles and medicines are exempt. You pay the full price and ask the sales assistant for a *formulario* (tax exemption form). When you leave Spain, ask customs to stamp your *formulario* (this must be within six months of purchase). You will receive the refund by mail or as a credit on your credit card account.

Branches of Spain's Banco Exterior at Madrid's Barajas Airport give refunds on *formularios* that have been stamped by customs.

Sign indicating tax-free goods

TOURIST INFORMATION

MADRID AND ALL MAJOR historic towns in the vicinity have *oficinas de turismo* (tourist information offices). On arrival, it is worth visiting the tourist office at **Barajas Airport**'s international terminal (Terminal One) where there is also a hotel reservation desk and a RENFE *(see p192)* desk offering information on rail travel. Tourist information offices provide maps of the town, transport details, lists of hotels (including rural retreats)

MADRID TIME

Madrid is one hour ahead of Greenwich Mean Time (GMT) and 6 hours ahead of Eastern Standard Time (EST). Spain uses the 24-hour clock, so 1pm = 13:00 hours.

City and Country	Hours ahead or behind Spain	City and Country	Hours ahead or behind Spain
Athens (Greece)	+ 1	Moscow (Russia)	+ 2
Auckland (New Zealand)	+ 11	New York (US)	– 6
Bangkok (Thailand)	+ 6	Paris (France)	0
Berlin (Germany)	0	Perth (Australia)	+ 7
Cape Town (South Africa)	+ 1	Rome (Italy)	0
Chicago (US)	– 7	Sydney (Australia)	+ 9
Dublin (Ireland)	– 1	Tokyo (Japan)	+ 8
Hong Kong (China)	+ 7	Toronto (Canada)	– 6
London (UK)	– 1	Vancouver (Canada)	– 9
Los Angeles (US)	– 9	Washington DC (US)	– 6

◁ **The start of Madrid's sweeping Gran Vía with its relentless flow of traffic**

and restaurants. They also provide information on local sights, activities and special events. They are usually open Monday to Friday from 8am or 9am until 7 or 8pm, and on Saturday from 9am until 1pm. They are closed on Sundays.

OPENING HOURS

Most museums and monuments close daily from 2pm to 5pm, as well as Sunday afternoons and all day Monday. Major art museums do not close over lunch. Churches have more restricted opening hours; some open only for services.

FACILITIES FOR THE DISABLED

Spain's national association for the disabled, **Confederación Coordinadora Estatal de Minusválidos Físicos de España (COCEMFE)**, operates Servi-COCEMFE – a tour company which publishes guides to disabled facilities in Spain and can help plan a vacation (holiday) to your requirements.

Tourist information offices and the social services supply information on local conditions and facilities. Metro maps and other information in Braille are available from the Spanish national organization for the blind, **Organización Nacional de Ciegos (ONCE)**. If you prefer to let someone else do the work, the Spanish travel agent **Viajes 2000** specializes in vacations for the disabled. In the United States, the **Society for the Advancement of Travel for the Handicapped (SATH)** publishes the useful *ACCESS to Travel* magazine which deals with destinations, attractions, accommodation, transportation and other information for disabled people.

COCEMFE sign for disabled access

STUDENT INFORMATION

Holders of the International Student Identity Card (ISIC) are entitled to benefits, such as discounts on travel and reduced admission to museums and galleries. Information is available from all international student organizations and, in

Students in Madrid

Madrid, from the government-run youth information centre, **Centro de Información Juvenil (CIJ)**. One company that specializes in student travel is **Turismo y Viajes Educativos (TIVE)**.

ELECTRICAL ADAPTOR

Spain's electricity supply is 220 volts, but the 125-volt system still operates in some old buildings. Plugs for both have two round pins.

A three-tier, standard travel converter will enable you to use appliances from abroad on both supplies. Hair dryers, however, should be used only with 220-volt sockets.

DIRECTORY

EMBASSIES

Australia
Plaza del Descubridor Diego de Ordás 3, 2nd floor,
C/ de Santa Engracia 120.
☎ 91 441 93 00.
ⓦ www.embaustralia.es

Canada
Calle de Núñez de Balboa 35. **Map** 6 F4.
☎ 91 423 32 50.
ⓦ www.canada-es.org

New Zealand
Plaza de la Lealtad 2, 3rd Floor. **Map** 7 C2.
☎ 91 523 02 26.

South Africa
Calle de Claudio Coello 91, 6°. **Map** 6 E2.
☎ 91 436 37 80.

Republic of Ireland
Paseo de la Castellana 46, 4th floor. **Map** 6 E2.
☎ 91 436 40 93.

United Kingdom
Calle de Fernando El Santo 16. **Map** 5 C4.
☎ 91 700 82 00.
ⓦ www.ukinspain.com

United States
Calle de Serrano 75.
Map 6 E2.
☎ 91 587 22 00.
ⓦ www.embusa.es

TOURIST OFFICES IN MADRID

Municipal Tourist Office
Plaza Mayor 3. **Map** 4 E3.
☎ 91 366 54 77

Comunidad de Madrid Offices
C/ del Duque de Medinaceli 2. **Map** 7 B3.
☎ 91 429 31 77.

Barajas Airport
Terminal 1 (International).
☎ 91 305 86 56.

Estación de Chamartín
☎ 91 315 99 76.

Mercado Puerta de Toledo
Ronda de Toledo 1.
☎ 91 364 18 76.

SPANISH TOURIST OFFICES ABROAD

Australia
Level 24, 31 Market Street, Sydney, NSW 2000
☎ (612) 926 12433.

United Kingdom
22–23 Manchester Square, London W1U 3PX.
☎ (020) 7486 8077.
ⓦ www.uk.tourspain.es

United States
666 Fifth Avenue, New York, NY 10103.
☎ (212) 265 8822.
ⓦ www.okspain.org

ORGANIZATIONS FOR DISABLED TRAVELLERS

Viajes 2000
Paseo de la Castellana 228.
☎ 91 323 10 29.

COCEMFE
Calle de Luis Cabrera 63.
☎ 91 744 36 00.

ONCE
Centro Bibliográfico Cultural - Braille,
Calle de La Coruña 18.
☎ 91 589 42 00.

SATH
347 Fifth Avenue, Suite 610
New York, NY 10016.
☎ (212) 447 7284.

STUDENT ORGANIZATIONS

CIJ
Gran Vía 10. **Map** 7 B1.
☎ 91 720 11 82.
ⓦ www.madrid.org/inforjoven

TIVE
Calle de Fernando el Católico 88. **Map** 1 B1.
☎ 91 543 74 12.
ⓦ www.madrid.org/juventud/tive.htm

Personal Security and Health

IN MADRID, AS IN OTHER cities with a high concentration of tourists, you should take steps to guard against theft. Carry credit cards, money and a photocopy of your passport in a money belt, and never leave anything visible in your car when you park it. If you lose your documents, contact your embassy *(see p185)* and the police. If you are unwell, there will always be a local pharmacy *(farmacia)* open. In Spain, pharmacists are qualified to advise and sometimes even to prescribe.

Spanish pharmacy sign

IN AN EMERGENCY

THE NEW TELEPHONE number for all emergency services is 112. Depending on the nature of the problem you have, ask for *policía* (police), *ambulancia* (ambulance) or *bomberos* (fire brigade).

In cases of medical emergency, hospitals will accept admissions to the *urgencias* (casualty department).

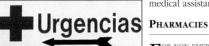

Sign identifying a *Cruz Roja* (Red Cross) emergency treatment centre

MEDICAL TREATMENT

ANY EU NATIONAL who becomes ill in Madrid is entitled to Spanish social security cover. To be able to claim for medical treatment, UK citizens must obtain Form E111 from the Department of Health or from a post office before travelling. This form must be given to anyone who treats you, so take several copies. The accompanying booklet, *Health Advice for Travellers*, explains what health care you are entitled to, and where and how to claim. Not all treatments are covered by Form E111, so you are also advised to arrange private medical insurance before travelling.

If you want private health care, ask at your hotel, embassy or tourist office for the name of a doctor. If necessary, ask for an English-speaker.

Visitors from the US should check with their insurance companies before leaving home to be sure they are covered if medical care is needed. Many medical facilities require payment for treatment in full at the time of service. Get an itemized bill to submit to your insurance company. In some cases, insurance companies require you to provide an official translation before they reimburse you. Travellers may wish to take out extra private travel insurance for emergency hospital care, doctors' fees and repatriation. Have your policy at hand when requesting medical assistance.

PHARMACIES

FOR NON-EMERGENCIES, a pharmacist *(farmacéutico)* can advise and, at times, prescribe without a doctor's consultation. Some medicines available only on prescription at home may be sold over the counter in Spain. The *farmacia* sign is an illuminated green cross. The addresses of those open at night or at weekends are displayed in the windows of all the local pharmacies or may be found in local newspapers.

PERSONAL SECURITY

ALTHOUGH VIOLENT CRIME is rare in Madrid, it is wise to take sensible precautions when out and about, as you would in any city with which you are unfamiliar.

To guard against theft, wear your purse, bag or camera strapped across your body, not on your shoulder, and always keep your possessions in sight, especially at the airport.

At night, avoid walking alone in poorly lit areas and, if possible, take a taxi back to your lodgings late at night.

SPANISH POLICE

THERE ARE ESSENTIALLY three types of police in Spain. The first is the *Guardia Civil* (paramilitary Civil Guard) who mainly police rural areas, country roads, highways and state buildings and take part in anti-terrorist operations. Their uniform is olive green in colour, but their black patent leather tricorns, for which they are renowned, are now donned only on ceremonial occasions.

The *Policía Nacional* wear a blue uniform and they deal mainly with national security, terrorism and major crime in towns with a population of more than 30,000. They also police immigration, work permits and residence documents. There is a special female department in Puerta del Sol which has been set up specifically to deal with crimes perpetrated against women.

The third and final branch of the Spanish police force is the *Policía Municipal*. They are involved for the most part with traffic regulation, the imposition of fines and the policing of local communities.

Guardia Civil   Policía Municipal

DIRECTORY

EMERGENCY SERVICES

Police *(Policía)*
📞 *091*

Ambulance *(Ambulancia)*

Fire Brigade *(Bomberos)*
📞 *112 for ambulance or fire.*

Red Cross *(Cruz Roja)*
📞 *91 522 22 22.*
🌐 *www.cruzroja.es*

LEGAL ASSISTANCE

SOME INSURANCE POLICIES cover legal costs – after an accident, for instance. If you are not covered, telephone your embassy. They should be able to provide you with a list of bilingual lawyers.

If you are arrested, you have the right to telephone your embassy. The *Colegio de Abogados* (Lawyers' Association) can also inform you where best to obtain legal advice or representation.

If you require an interpreter, it is best to consult either your embassy *(see p185)* or the *Páginas Amarillas* (Yellow Pages) telephone directory under *Traductores* (Translators) or *Intérpretes* (Interpreters). Both *Traductores Oficiales* and *Traductores Jurados* are qualified to translate legal and official documents.

PUBLIC CONVENIENCES

PUBLIC PAY-TOILETS have sprung up on some streets in Madrid but, on the whole, public conveniences are rare. Most people walk into a bar or café, a department store or a hotel and ask for *los servicios*, although it would be preferable to be a customer. On highways (motorways), there are toilets at service stations. Women often have to ask for the key *(la llave)*. Always carry toilet tissue with you as it is often not provided.

PERSONAL PROPERTY

VACATION (HOLIDAY) insurance is there to protect you financially in the event of the loss or theft of your property,

Patrol car of the Policía Nacional, Spain's main urban police force

Cruz Roja **(Red Cross) ambulance**

Spanish fire engine

but it is always advisable to take preventative measures – by making use of hotel safes, for example, and playing down the obvious tourist image.

It should not be necessary to carry large sums of money with you, as Spain has more ATMs (cashpoints) than any other country in Europe, and they take EuroCard and all major credit cards. If you have more than one card, do not carry them together. Travellers' cheques are another option, but you will need your passport with you to cash them.

If you discover a loss or theft, report it to the local *comisaría* (police station). To claim insurance you must do this immediately, as many companies give you only 24 hours. You must make a *denuncia* (formal written statement) to the police and obtain a copy to give to your insurers. The process can take some time.

If you lose your passport, your embassy can supply a replacement but cannot provide financial assistance.

Sometimes lost property is found and handed in. If this is the case, it will probably end up at Madrid's main post office in the Plaza de Cibeles or at your embassy, so it is worth checking these two places.

OUTDOOR HAZARDS

SPAIN IS PREY in summer to forest fires fanned by winds and fuelled by bone-dry vegetation. Avoid fire hazards by extinguishing cigarettes in car ashtrays and taking empty bottles away with you.

The sign *coto de caza* in woodland areas identifies a hunting reserve where you must follow the country code. *Toro bravo* means fighting bull – do not approach. A *camino particular* sign indicates a private driveway.

If climbing or hiking, go properly equipped and tell someone when you expect to return. You can also keep in touch by cellular (mobile) phones, which work in most parts of the country.

Banking and Local Currency

Y OU MAY ENTER SPAIN with any amount of money, but if you intend to export more than 6,000 euros, you should declare it. Traveller's cheques may be exchanged at banks, *cajas de cambio* (foreign currency exchanges), some hotels and some shops. Banks generally offer the best exchange rates. The cheapest exchange may be offered on your credit or debit card, which you can use in cash dispensers (automated teller machines, ATMs) displaying the appropriate sign.

24-hour cash dispenser (ATM)

BANKING HOURS

A LTHOUGH SPANISH BANKS are beginning to extend their opening hours throughout the country, expect extended hours only at the large central branches in the city centre.

As a general rule, banks are open from 8am to 2pm on weekdays. Some are also open until 1pm on Saturdays, except in the month of August when most are closed on Saturdays.

Foreign currency exchange

CHANGING MONEY

M OST BANKS HAVE a foreign exchange desk with the sign *Cambio* or *Extranjero*. Always take your passport as ID to effect any transaction.

You can draw up to 300 euros on major credit cards at a bank. If you bank with **Barclays Bank** or **Citibank** it is possible to cash a cheque in the usual way at one of their branches in Spain.

Foreign currency exchange offices (bureaux de change), with the sign *Caja de Cambio* or "Change", invariably charge higher rates of commission than banks, but are often open outside normal hours. They are easy to find in the popular tourist areas.

Cajas de Ahorro (savings banks) also exchange money. They open from 8:30am to 2pm on weekdays and also on Thursday afternoons from 4:30pm to 7:45pm.

CHEQUES AND CARDS

T RAVELLER'S CHEQUES can be purchased at **American Express** (AmEx), **Travelex** or your bank. All are accepted in Spain. If you exchange American Express cheques at an AmEx office, commission is not charged.

Banks require 24 hours' notice to cash cheques larger than 3,000 euros. If you draw more than 600 euros on traveller's cheques, you may be asked to show the purchase certificate.

The most widely accepted card in Spain is the **VISA** card, although **MasterCard** (**Access**)/**Eurocard** and American Express are also useful currency. The major banks will allow cash with-drawals on credit cards. All cash dispensers accept most foreign cards, although the level of commission charged on your withdrawal will depend on your own bank.

When you pay with a card, cashiers will usually pass it through a card reading machine. In shops you will always be asked for additional photo ID. As leaving your passport in the hotel safe is preferable, make sure you have an alternative original document on hand (photocopies will rarely do) such as a driver's license.

As is common throughout Europe, cards are not always accepted in some smaller bars and restaurants. Checking first will avoid unnecessary embarrassment.

CASH DISPENSERS

I F YOUR CARD is linked to your home bank account, you can use it with your PIN to withdraw money from cash dispensers. Nearly all take VISA or MasterCard (Access). Cards with Cirrus or Maestro logos can also be widely used in cash machines.

When you enter your PIN, instructions are displayed in English, French, German and Spanish. Many dispensers are inside buildings so customers must swipe their card through a door-entry system.

THE EURO

INTRODUCTION OF the single European currency, the euro, has taken place in 12 of the 15 member states of the EU. Austria, Belgium, Finland, France, Germany, Greece, Ireland, Italy, Luxembourg, The Netherlands, Portugal and Spain chose to join the new currency; the UK, Denmark and Sweden stayed out, with an option to review the decision. The euro was introduced on 1 January 1999, but only for banking purposes. Notes and coins came into circulation on 1 January 2002. After a transition period allowing the use of both national currencies and the euro, Spain's own currency, the peseta, was completely phased out by March 2002. All euro notes and coins can be used anywhere within the participating member states.

Bank Notes

Euro bank notes have seven denominations. The 5-euro note (grey in colour) is the smallest, followed by the 10-euro note (pink), 20-euro note (blue), 50-euro note (orange), 100-euro note (green), 200-euro note (yellow) and 500-euro note (purple). All notes show the 12 stars of the European Union.

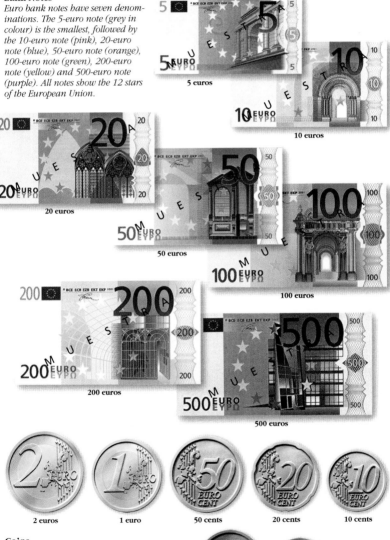

5 euros

10 euros

20 euros

50 euros

100 euros

200 euros

500 euros

2 euros

1 euro

50 cents

20 cents

10 cents

Coins

The euro has eight coin denominations: 2 euros and 1 euro (silver and gold); 50 cents, 20 cents and 10 cents (gold); and 5 cents, 2 cents and 1 cent (bronze). The reverse (number) side of euros are the same in all Euro-zone countries, but the front is different in each state.

5 cents

2 cents

1 cent

Communications

**Sign for shops
selling stamps**

THE SPANISH TELECOMMUNICATIONS company, Telefónica, was digitized in
1995 and 1998 saw the end of the state
monopoly. Most public telephones operate with a card or coins. International
calls are expensive. The postal service
(correos) is identified by a crown insig-
nia in red or white on a yellow background. Registered
mail and telegrams can be sent from *correos* offices; they
also sell stamps, as do state-run *estancos* (tobacconists).
Madrid also has an increasing number of internet cafés.

Telefónica

Logo of the Spanish telecom system

TELEPHONING IN SPAIN

As well as public telephone
boxes *(cabinas)*, there are
nearly always payphones in
bars. Both types take coins.
There will be a high minimum connection charge,
especially for international
calls. Phonecards can be
bought at newsstands and
estancos. Some phones are
equipped with multilingual
electronic instruction displays.

There are also public
telephone offices called
locutorios where you can
make a call and pay for it
afterwards. The cheapest are
those run by Telefónica;
private *locutorios*, often found
in shops, cost more. Calls from
a *cabina* or a *locutorio* can
cost as much as 35 per cent
more than calls made from a
private phone in someone's
home. Calls from hotels can
also be expensive.

There are four charge bands
for international calls: EU
countries; non-EU European
countries and Northwest Africa;
North and South America; and
the rest of the world.

Collect calls within the EU
may be dialled directly, but
most others must be made
through the operator.

The first digit in each area
code is 9. For example,
Madrid's code is 91. To call

USING A COIN AND CARD TELEPHONE

1 Lift the receiver, and wait for
the dialling tone and for the
display to show *Inserte monedas o
tarjeta*.

2 Insert either coins *(monedas)*
or a card *(tarjeta)*.

3 Key in the number firmly, but
not too fast – Spanish phones
prefer you to pause between
digits.

4 As you press the digits, the
number you are dialling will
appear on the display. You will
also be able to see how much
money or how many units are
left and when to insert more
coins.

5 When your call is
finished, replace the
receiver. The phonecard
will then re-emerge
automatically or any
excess coins will
be returned.

Spanish phonecard

USEFUL SPANISH DIALLING CODES

- To call another province, first dial the area
  code (beginning with 9, e.g. Barcelona 93).
  Area codes are listed in the A-K phone
  book or obtained from directory enquiries.
- Use area codes for calls within a province.
- To make an international call, dial 00, wait
  for the tone, then dial the country code, the
  area code and the number. Country codes
  are: UK 44; Eire 353; US and Canada 1; New
  Zealand 64; Australia 61; South Africa 27.
- If calling Spain from another country, dial
  that country's international access code, the
  code for Spain (34) and the full area code.

- For operator/directory service, dial 11818.
- For international directories, dial 11825.
- To make a collect (reversed-charge) call
  within the EU, dial 900 99 00 followed
  by the country code; to the US or
  Canada, dial 900 99 00 followed by 11
  or 15 respectively. Numbers for other
  countries can be found in the front of
  the A-K telephone directory under
  Modalidades del Servicio Internacional.
- To report technical faults, dial 1002.
- The speaking clock is on 093, the weather
  on 807 17 03 08, wake-up calls on 096.

Madrid from abroad, first dial your country's international access code, then Spain's country code (34), and then Madrid's area code (91).

City telephone numbers generally have seven digits, while those in smaller towns have six digits only.

MAIL (POSTAL SERVICE)

THE POSTAL SERVICE *(correos)* in Spain can be rather slow. Urgent or important items can be sent by *urgente* (express) or *certificado* (registered) mail, although to be sure of fast delivery it is wise to use a private courier.

Mail can be registered and telegrams sent from all *correos* offices. Stamps for letters and postcards can be bought from an *estanco* (tobacconist). Postal rates fall into four price bands: the EU; the rest of Europe; the USA; and the rest of the world. Parcels have to be weighed and stamped at a post office and must be securely tied with string or a charge may be made to have them sealed by a clerk.

The main *correos* offices open 8am–9pm from Monday to Friday and 9am–7pm on Saturday. Branches in the suburbs of cities and in smaller towns and villages open from 9am–2pm Monday to Friday and from 9am–1pm on Saturday.

Standard issue stamps

ADDRESSES AND LETTERS

IN SPANISH ADDRESSES the house number follows the name of the street. The floor of an apartment block is indicated by the number which appears after the hyphen. Therefore, 4-2° means an apartment on the second floor of number

four. All postcodes have five digits, with the first two standing for the province.

If you mail your letters at a central post office they are usually likely to arrive more quickly than if you were to mail them in a local mailbox *(buzón)*. Cities have yellow pillar boxes; towns and villages normally have small, wall-mounted mailboxes.

Poste restante letters should be addressed care of the *Lista de Correos* and the town. You will be able to collect them from main post offices.

To send and receive money by mail ask for a *giro postal*. When dealing with business-es in Spain, it is always quicker and more convenient to phone or fax. The mail tends to be used only as a last resort. Fax facilities are available in some *locutorios*, in hotels and in many private shops. Look for a *telefax* sign.

TELEVISION AND RADIO

TELEVISIÓN ESPAÑOLA is Spain's state television company, which broadcasts two channels by the names of TVE1 and TVE2.

Several of the autonomous regions have their own television stations. Madrid's is called Telemadrid and is a useful source of local news.

There are three national independent television stations in Spain: Antena 3, Tele-5 (Telecinco) and Canal+ (Canal Plus). Unfortunately, there are some Canal+ programmes which you will only be able to receive if you pay a subscription for a station decoder.

Most foreign films shown on Spanish television (and in cinemas) are dubbed. Subtitled films will appear in listings as *V.O. (versión original)*.

The Satellite channels CNN, Eurosport and Cinemanía can be received throughout Spain.

The state radio station, Radio Nacional de España, has four channels. Radio 2 and 3 play music, while Radio 1 and 5 broadcast news programmes.

NEWSPAPERS AND MAGAZINES

MOST OF THE KIOSKS around Puerta del Sol, Gran Vía, Calle de Alcalá and Paseo de la Castellana stock foreign newspapers and periodicals. English newspapers available on the day of publication are the *International Herald Tribune*, the *Financial Times* and *The Guardian Europe*. Many other English-language and European titles are sold, usually a day after publication. *The European* newspaper and popular weekly current affairs magazines, such as *Time, Newsweek* and *The Economist*, are readily available throughout Madrid.

The most widely read of the Spanish newspapers, in descending number of sales, are *Marca, El País, El Mundo* and *ABC. Marca* is a sports newspaper while *El Mundo* is aimed at a younger market than the others, which cover international news in more depth.

The main weekly listings magazines for arts and events are the *Guía del Ocio*, which appears on Fridays; *Metrópoli*, free in *El Mundo* on Fridays; *Tentaciones*, free with *El País*, on Fridays *(see p172)*; and the magazine *Salir Salir* on Fridays.

Local newspapers in Spanish can be a useful source of detailed information about events throughout the region.

Publications in English edited in Madrid are *Guidepost*, with business and general information; *In Madrid*, free each month and available in pubs, bookshops and record shops; and *Lookout*, with articles about Spanish life.

Spanish daily papers

Spanish mailbox

TRAVEL INFORMATION

SPANISH ROAD AND RAIL LINKS were improved for the Expo in Seville and the Olympics in Barcelona in 1992, and Madrid, with its central location, is probably one of the easiest places in Spain to get to. The city is also a good starting point for trips to other destinations, whether Spanish, European or international.

Sign for the airport

While Barajas Airport, one of Europe's busiest, caters for domestic and European travel, it is also one of the main gateways to South America. By road, there are seven main points of entry to Madrid, and its train stations offer regular services to many European cities, as well as high-speed links with destinations all over Spain.

FLYING TO MADRID

BARAJAS AIRPORT is served by dozens of international airlines and charter companies. **Iberia**, the national carrier, has daily flights linking all Western European capitals except Dublin, and once- or twice-weekly flights to the capitals of Eastern Europe. **Air Europa** and **Spanair** also fly between London and Madrid. **British Airways** and **EasyJet** are the only UK airlines to offer direct scheduled flights. **Virgin** offers a service via Brussels.

US airlines **Continental** and **Delta Air Lines** link Madrid to New York, while **American Airlines** links Madrid to Miami. Iberia now flies direct to New York, Montréal and Toronto.

GETTING TO AND FROM THE AIRPORT

IT TAKES ABOUT 20 minutes by taxi or bus to reach the city centre from Barajas Airport. The airport bus departs from Terminal 1 and goes to Plaza de Colón. Taxis should cost no more than 25 euros. It takes a mere 12 minutes on the Metro to reach the central station of Nuevos Ministerios, where numerous airlines have check-in facilities.

Buses to the airport go from Plaza de Colón via Calle de Velázquez (returning via Calle de Serrano) and Avenida de América. They run every 12 minutes between 4:45am and 1:30am and the journey costs around 2.5 euros.

AIR FARES

AIR FARES TO MADRID vary throughout the year. They are generally at their highest in the summer months. Special deals for weekend breaks in the city are often offered during winter and may include a number of nights at a hotel with vouchers to visit the sights. Iberia and British Airways invariably have some cheap return-flight deals on offer throughout the year. Air Europa and Spanair also have some very competitive deals.

DOMESTIC FLIGHTS

IBERIA OPERATES a frequent shuttle service *(puente aéreo)* between Madrid and Barcelona. It flies every

Self-ticketing machine

quarter of an hour and passengers can buy tickets just 15 minutes prior to departure.

Air Europa and Spanair also have scheduled services between Madrid and Barcelona. **Air Nostrum**, Spanair and Air Europa operate flights between Madrid and the regional capitals and, even though they are not quite as frequent as the *puente aéreo*, their prices tend to be slightly lower. As a rule, the earlier you can book a flight, the greater will be your discount. To benefit from the cheapest tickets, you must book at least one week in advance.

ARRIVING BY TRAIN

THE SPANISH national rail network, **RENFE** (*Red Nacional de Ferrocarriles Españoles*), has two long-distance train stations in Madrid – **Atocha** (*see p85*) south of the centre and **Chamartín** in the northwest. Atocha receives trains from Portugal and the south and west of Spain, as well as the high-speed AVE trains from Seville, Córdoba, Zaragoza and Lleida. Those coming from France or northern and eastern Spain go to Chamartín station. Since the two stations are linked by a tunnel under the city, some trains stop at both stations and often the intermediate stations, Nuevos Ministerios and Recoletos.

The new AVE service between Madrid and Lleida via Guadalajara and Zaragoza

National carrier, Iberia, connecting Spain with the rest of Europe

Atocha station, one of Madrid's first glass and wrought-iron structures

is scheduled to extend to Barcelona and the French border by 2006. This will open the door to a high-speed rail line linking Madrid and Barcelona with similar lines in France and the rest of the European Union network.

There are also TALGO expresses, which use both the AVE and European tracks, and slower, long-distance *(largo recorrido)* trains. TALGO high-speed services mean that it is now possible to travel between the main cities extremely quickly.

Overnight sleeper trains arrive from Lisbon, Paris and parts of Spain. Cars can be loaded in advance to travel with the train. Bicycles can be carried only in the sleeping compartments of these trains and must be dismantled and packaged up, or unpackaged on regional trains, but only during non-peak periods.

ARRIVING BY CAR

MANY PEOPLE DRIVE to Spain via the French highways (motorways). From the UK there are also car ferries from Plymouth to Santander and from Portsmouth to Bilbao.

From whichever direction you approach Madrid, make sure you are able to identify your highway (motorway) turn-off by its street name. Madrid has two major ring roads, the outer M40 and the inner M30. If you need to cross the city, it is advisable

Typical road signs in Madrid

to take one of the two and get as close as possible to your destination before turning off. All highways (motorways) lead to the M30 but most do not continue into the city.

For information on Spanish driving law, see p195.

ARRIVING BY BUS

TRAVELLING BY BUS (coach) is usually a relatively cheap form of travel and, in Spain, it can quite often be a quicker way to get around than trains, especially from destinations such as the costas (coast). Buses offer travellers a modern airline-style service on fast highways. **Eurolines** buses operate regular services throughout Europe.

There are three main long-distance bus stations in Madrid. The **Estación Sur de Autobuses**, situated just southeast of the city centre, serves the whole of Spain. The second is **Terminal Auto-Res**, which operates services to Valencia, eastern Spain, Lisbon and northwest Spain. And the third, **Terminal Continental-Auto**, is located north of the city centre. Buses from this station serve towns in northern Spain and Toledo.

The transport interchange at Calle de Méndez Alvaro also provides convenient access to the city buses, the Metro and to regional trains.

DIRECTORY		

AIRPORT

Barajas Airport Information
- 91 305 83 43.
- w www.aena.es

IBERIA

Flights
- 902 40 05 00 (Spain).
- (0845) 601 2854 (UK).
- (800) 772 4642 (US).
- w www.iberia.com

OTHER AIRLINES

Air Europa
- 902 40 15 01.
- w www.air-europa.com

Air Nostrum
- 902 20 02 22.

American Airlines
- 902 11 55 70 (Spain).
- (817) 267 1151 (US).
- w www.aa.com

British Airways
- 902 11 13 33 (Spain).
- (08457) 773 3377 (UK).
- w www.britishairways.com

Continental
- 91 559 27 10 (Spain).
- (281) 821 2100 (US).
- w www.continental.com

Delta Air Lines
- 91 749 66 30 (Spain).
- (800) 241 4141 (US).
- w www.delta.com

EasyJet
- 902 29 99 92 (Spain).
- w www.easyjet.com

Spanair
- 902 13 14 15 (Spain).
- w www.spanair.com

Virgin
- 900 46 76 12 (Spain).
- (01293) 616 161 (UK).
- w www.virgin-express.com

TRAINS

Atocha
Plaza del Emperador Carlos V. **Map** 7 C5.
- 902 24 02 02.

Chamartín
Calle de Agustin de Foxá.
- 902 24 02 02.

RENFE
Calle de Alcalá 44. **Map** 7 B1.
- 902 24 02 02.
- w www.renfe.es

BUS STATIONS AND COMPANIES

Estación Sur de Autobuses
Calle de Méndez Alvaro, Esquina Calle de la Retama.
- 91 468 42 00.

Eurolines
- 91 506 33 60 (Madrid).
- (020) 7730 8235 (UK).
- w www.eurolines.es

Terminal Auto-Res
Calle Fernández Shaw 1.
- 902 02 09 99.
- w www.auto-res.net

Terminal Continental-Auto
Avenida de América 9.
- 91 745 63 00.
- 902 33 04 00 (tickets).

Getting Around Madrid

MOST OF THE TOURIST SIGHTS are clustered together in the centre of Madrid within walking distance of each other. There are also other interesting attractions further afield, and you will have to decide how to get there. Plan your day in advance, bearing in mind that some museums and shops close between 2pm and 5pm, and try to cover one area at a time. The Metro is by far the best way to travel around Madrid because the trains are quick and clean. However, if you have more time and prefer to see where you are going, the city bus service is excellent, and there is no shortage of taxis in Madrid if you don't mind spending a bit extra.

Sightseeing in one of the city's bright red buses outside the Puerta de Toledo

GETTING AROUND BY BUS

BUSES ARE AN excellent way to see the city. If you plan to make a number of bus trips, it is best to buy a *Metrobus* – a ten-trip ticket good for buses and the Metro. It costs around 5-6 euros, so is better value than tickets bought individually. *Bonobuses* are available at *estancos* (tobacconists), news kiosks and the **EMT** booths in Plaza de Colón, Plaza de Cibeles, Plaza del Callao, Plaza de Manuel Becerra and Puerta del Sol. These booths and tourist information offices offer large maps and details of bus and Metro services and regional trains. Bus stop signs display the bus numbers and

also their basic routes. Either pay the driver or put your *Metrobus* ticket in the machine behind him or her. Request a stop by pressing a button next to the exit doors at the rear.

People in wheelchairs can board buses displaying the words *piso bajo* (low floor), which means that the rear exit is close to the ground and wheelchairs can enter and exit there.

Some useful bus routes: 2 crosses central Madrid east to west; 5 starts at Puerta del Sol, going northwest to Chamartín railway station via Plaza de Cibeles; 27 travels from north to south the length of the Paseo de la Castellana from Plaza de Castilla to Glorieta de Embajadores via Paseo del Prado and Calle de Atocha; C makes a circuit around Madrid via Calle de Atocha.

Day buses run from 6am until 11:30pm. Twenty night buses, or *buhos* (owls), run every half an hour between midnight and 3am and then each hour until 6am. All leave from the Plaza de Cibeles.

THE METRO

THE METRO IS the quickest, cheapest and easiest way to travel around Madrid, avoiding the madness of the city's traffic at street level. Many of the main Metro stations have shops and bars, and Retiro station even boasts an art gallery.

The Metro is open from 6am to 1:30am and consists of over 200 stations which are linked by 12 colour-coded lines plus the Ópera-Príncipe Pío link. A *Metrobus* ticket for ten trips on either the Metro or bus can be bought at any of the stations. For a comprehensive map of the Metro system, see the inside back cover of this book.

New Metro extensions now provide fast and convenient links with the IFEMA Parque Ferial exhibition centre as well as Barajas Airport.

Sign for a Metro station

TAXIS

MADRID HAS some 15,000 taxis, identifiable by the red diagonal stripe on the door. If they are available, the green light on the roof will be illuminated and a card in the window will say *"libre"*.

Within Madrid's city limits, including the airport, taxis are obliged to turn on their meters once hired. The initial charge is about 1.5 euros, but there are various additional charges, including fees for the airport, each piece of luggage, a dog (except guide dogs), IFEMA Parque Ferial and leaving from a train station between 11pm and 6am Saturdays, Sundays and public holidays.

You can order a cab by telephone through **Radio Taxi** or **Radioteléfono Taxi**. For a car specially adapted for the disabled, call Radioteléfono Taxi and ask for Eurotaxis.

City taxis with their logo and official numbers

Organized coach trips with Juliá Travel, one way to see the sights

BUS TOURS

A SIGHTSEEING SERVICE is operated by **Madrid Vision**, whose double-decker buses are equipped with multilingual headphone commentaries. There are 14 points along the route where you can get on or off, and it is possible to use the buses all day. The bus tours run all year round.

Juliá Travel also offers a variety of bus trips around the city, which can include visits to a *corrida* or bullfight *(see p111)* or an evening flamenco performance *(see p174)*.

DRIVING

I N SPAIN YOU MUST CARRY a valid driver's licence with you when driving, as well as your insurance documents. If you are not an EU citizen, it is essential to have an international driver's licence. In the United States, these are available through the AAA.

Driving around Madrid is quite an experience for the uninitiated as *Madrileños* tend to drive aggressively. Signs are often misleading or missing altogether, service stations are few and parking is usually difficult. Read the map before setting off, but watch out for one-way systems, tunnels and overpasses (flyovers). In rush hour, traffic hardly moves and the M30 inner ring road often comes to a standstill. If you get lost while driving, hail a taxi, shout the address and follow the driver.

In urban areas the speed limit is 50 km/h (31 mph), while it is 100 km/h (62 mph) on main roads and 120 km/h (75 mph) on highways (motorways).

CAR RENTAL (HIRE)

T O RENT A CAR in Spain you should have an international driver's licence (if you are an EU citizen your ordinary licence is usually sufficient) and be over 21 years of age. You can pay using cash, credit card or traveller's cheques.

On the ground floor of Barajas Airport's International Terminal 1 are various car rental firms, including **Avis**, **Europcar**, **Hertz** and **National Atesa**. Cars can also be rented at Atocha and Chamartín railway stations. You are strongly advised to take out full insurance, and air-conditioning is recommended.

In the city, your hotel or a travel agent will be able to arrange car rental for you.

Some of the leading car rental agencies operating in Spain

PARKING

P ARKING IN MADRID is difficult, so you may want to select a hotel with parking facilities. There are also underground parking garages (car parks) which charge by the hour. A green sign saying *"libre"* means that space is still available; a red sign saying *"completo"* means the car park is full.

Parking illegally can result in being towed away, with a fine of 180 euros to recover your vehicle. In the city centre green and blue lines on the road denote different parking zones. Green zones are for residents, although non-residents can park for one hour. Blue zones offer non residents two hours parking. Tickets must be purchased from appropriately coloured machines. When parking, lock your doors and do not leave anything of value in your car. If you must leave items in the car, stow them in the boot (trunk).

No parking at any time of the day

CYCLING

R IDING A BICYCLE around Madrid in weekday traffic is dangerous. Only on Sundays and public holidays can cycling in Madrid be fun. **Karacol Sport SA** near Atocha train station rents bikes.

Travelling Outside Madrid

Logo of the Spanish national railways

THE MAIN SITES around Madrid can each be visited in a day but, if you plan to visit several, you might like to consider staying outside Madrid, at a hotel or at one of an increasing number of rural hostelries. The most convenient way to travel is by car, but trains are also very easy to use with services to all the main historic towns and cities. Even Córdoba, Seville, Lleida and Valencia are accessible using the AVE and Alaris high-speed trains which afford superb views of the countryside. Tour companies offer coach trips to Toledo, El Escorial and Segovia. A trip usually includes the main sites and a basic meal. If you intend to use a scheduled bus service, use the most direct, as some buses stop at every village.

AVE trains at Atocha station

TRAIN SERVICES

MADRID IS SERVED by six types of train: *cercanías* (commuter), *regional* (local) *largo recorrido* (long-distance), TALGO (long-distance express), Alaris (to Valencia) and AVE (high-speed link to Ciudad Real, Puertollano, Córdoba, Seville, Guadalajara, Zaragoza, Calatayud and Lleida).

There are frequent services to Alcalá de Henares and Guadalajara on the *cercanías* C-2 from Chamartín, Nuevos Ministerios, Recoletos and Atocha. *Cercanías* leave from Atocha to Aranjuez every half an hour. During weekends from mid-April to mid-July and mid-September to mid-October, a special Strawberry Train *(Tren de las Fresas)*, pulled by a steam engine, serves Aranjuez from Atocha. Strawberries are included and you must book in advance. To Puerto Navacerrada and the ski

resorts, take *cercanías* C-8b from Atocha to Cercedilla and then change to *cercanías* C-9. Use C-8a for San Lorenzo de El Escorial, and C-8b or the *regional* from Atocha station for Segovia. Sigüenza is served by *regional* trains from Chamartín, with three or four trains a day. Toledo is served by *regional* trains from Atocha. Trains run every two hours.

TICKETS AND FARES

INFORMATION AND train tickets can be obtained at **RENFE** offices and stations, or from travel agents. Rail fares depend on the speed and quality of the train; obviously, therefore, TALGO, Alaris and AVE trains are the most expensive.

Bicycles can be taken only on *regional* trains on weekends and public holidays and at specified non-peak times in the week. *Largo recorrido* and TALGO trains will take them if dismantled and kept in the sleeping compartments.

Fares rise on weekends and public holidays. Children, aged four to 11, get a 40 per cent discount, while students, aged 12 to 25, get a 20 per cent discount. Return tickets are valid for 15 days and carry the same discounts. For long journeys, RENFE may offer special rates on certain days. **Iberrail** also offers economical rail-plus-hotel deals. For a one-way journey, ask for *ida* and for a return, ask for *ida y vuelta*.

TAKING YOUR OWN CAR

A GREEN CARD and a bail bond from a motor insurance company are needed to extend your comprehensive cover to Spain. In the UK, the RAC, AA and Europ Assistance offer rescue and recovery policies with European coverage.

By law you must always carry with you your vehicle's registration document, a valid insurance certificate and your driving licence. Always be able to show a passport or a national ID card, and display a country of registration sticker on the rear of the vehicle.

The headlights of right-hand-drive vehicles must be adjusted. This can be done with stickers sold at ferry ports or on ferries. You risk on-the-spot fines if you do not carry a red warning triangle, spare light bulbs and a first-aid kit.

Driving along a mountain road through Spain's spectacular countryside

A filling station run by a leading chain with branches throughout Spain

In winter you should carry chains if you intend to drive in mountain areas. In summer, take drinking water if you are travelling in a remote area.

Spain's fastest roads are its *autopistas,* usually highways (motorways) with tolls *(peajes)*. *Autovías* are similar but have no tolls. The *carretera nacional* is Spain's network of main roads prefixed by "N".

Madrid is served by six main *autovías*, numbered NI to NVI (or A6), which fan out in different directions, and one *autopista*, N401, which goes to Toledo. In addition, there are two ring roads with links between the NI–NVI and the N401. The inner ring road is the M30 and the outer one, with direct access to and from the airport, is the M40.

For road and traffic information in Spanish call the toll-free number for **Información de Tráfico de Carreteras**.

BUYING FUEL

I N SPAIN *gasolina* (gas/petrol) and *gasóleo* (diesel) are sold by the litre. *Gasolina sin plomo* (unleaded gas/petrol) is available everywhere.

SPEED LIMITS AND FINES

S PEED LIMITS in Spain for cars without trailers are: 120 km/h (75 mph) on *autopistas* (toll highways/motorways); 100 km/h (62 mph) on *autovías* (non-toll highways/motorways); 90 km/h (56 mph) on *carreteras nacionales* (main roads) and *carreteras comarcales* (secondary roads); 50 km/h (30 mph) in built-up areas. There are instant fines of 6 euros for every kilometre over the limit. Tests and fines for drinking and driving are increasingly common.

TOUR BUSES AND LOCAL BUSES

B Y FAR THE easiest and most relaxing way to visit the sights is by tour bus. Madrid's main tour bus company, **Juliá Travel** *(see p195)*, will take direct bookings. **Pullmantur** tours have to be booked at a travel agency. **Mundo Joven** also gives guided tours but they tend to be in Spanish.

Major towns and many villages are served by local buses. Buses for the following destinations depart from **Estación Sur de Autobuses**, south of the city centre (metro station Méndez Álvaro). Aranjuez is served by **Autocares Samar**, San Martín de Valdeiglesias by **Autocares Cevesa**, Segovia by **La Sepulvedana**, Sigüenza by **Floravilla** (6pm departure only) and Toledo by **Continental-Auto**.

Alcalá de Henares is served by **Continental-Auto** (corner of Calle María de Molina/Avenida de América), Chinchón by **La Veloz** (Plaza de Conde Casal), Manzanares el Real by **Hijos de J Colmenarejo** (Plaza de Castilla), Puerto de Navacerrada by **Larrea SA** (Metro Moncloa), San Lorenzo de El Escorial by **Autocares Herranz** (Metro Moncloa).

Buses can be quicker than trains. **Enatcar** operates a competitively priced service from the costas, for example.

Spanish touring bus, a quick and convenient way to see the sights

DIRECTORY

TRAIN SERVICES

Iberrail
C 91 571 66 92.
W www.iberrail.es

RENFE
C 902 24 02 02.
W www.renfe.es

TRAFFIC INFORMATION

Información de Tráfico de Carreteras
C 900 12 35 05.
W www.dgt.es

CAR RESCUE SERVICE

RACE
Calle General Perón 32.
C 902 12 04 41.
W www.race.net

TOUR BUSES AND LOCAL BUSES

Autocares Cevesa
C 91 539 31 32.

Autocares Herranz
C 91 890 41 22.

Autocares Samar
C 91 468 48 39.

Continental-Auto
Avenida América station.
C 91 745 63 00.
W www.continental-auto.es

Enatcar-Alsa
Estación Sur de Autobuses.
C 902 42 22 42.
W www.enatcar.es

Floravilla
C 91 530 88 29.

Hijos de J Colmenarejo
C 91 845 00 51.

Larrea SA
C 91 392 03 96.

Mundo Joven
C 91 521 86 01.

Pullmantur
C 91 556 11 14.

La Sepulvedana
C 91 530 48 00.
W www.lasepulvedana.es

La Veloz
C 91 409 76 02.

MADRID STREET FINDER

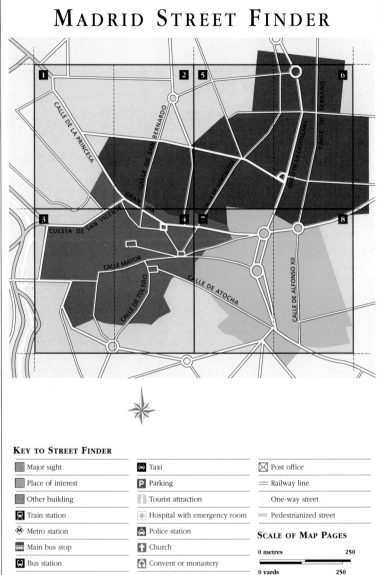

KEY TO STREET FINDER

⬛ Major sight	🚖 Taxi	⊠ Post office
⬛ Place of interest	🅿 Parking	═ Railway line
⬛ Other building	🛈 Tourist attraction	One-way street
🚆 Train station	✚ Hospital with emergency room	Pedestrianized street
Ⓜ Metro station	🚓 Police station	
🚌 Main bus stop	✝ Church	**SCALE OF MAP PAGES**
🚌 Bus station	Convent or monastery	

0 metres   250

0 yards   250

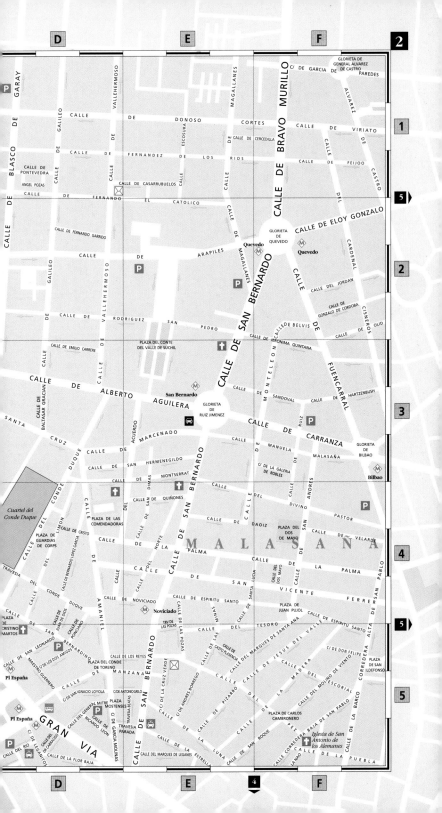

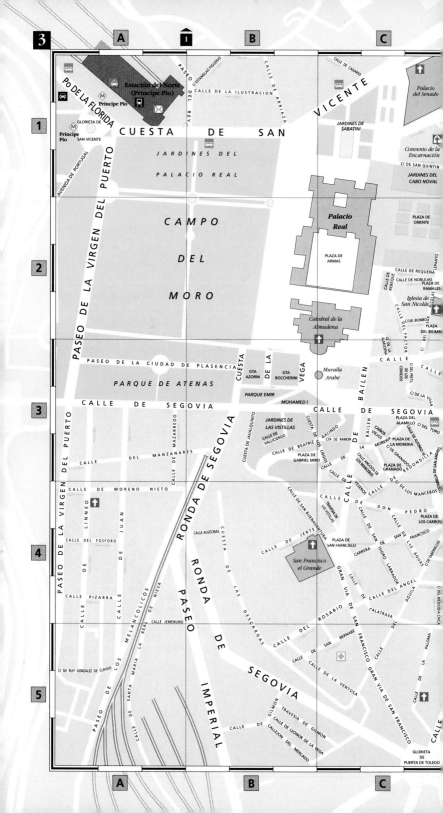

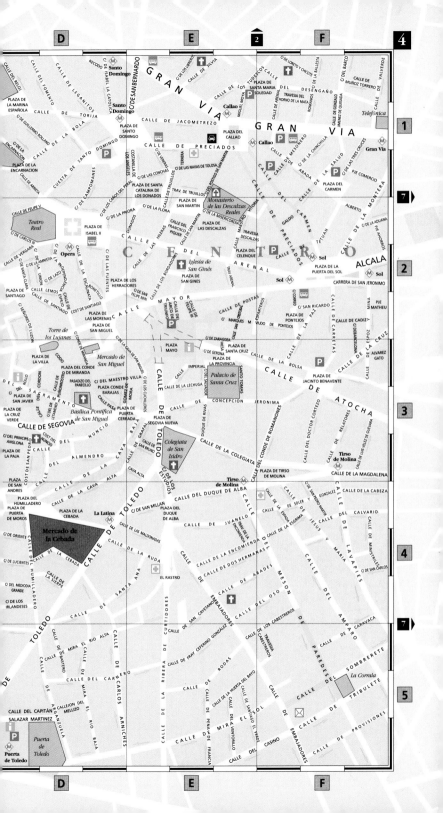

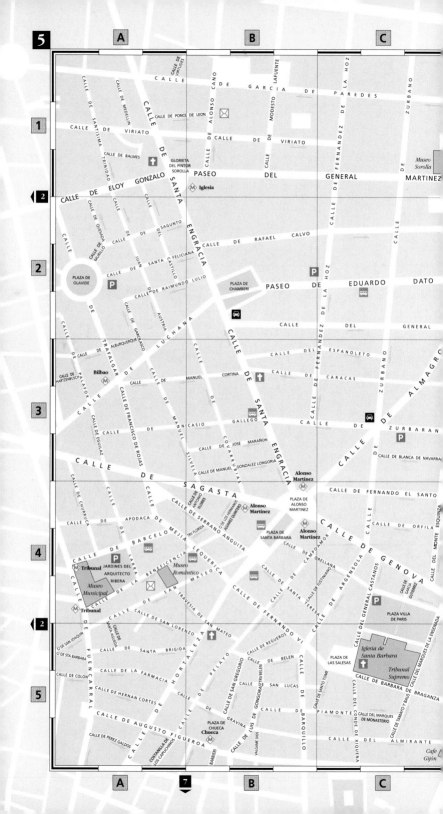

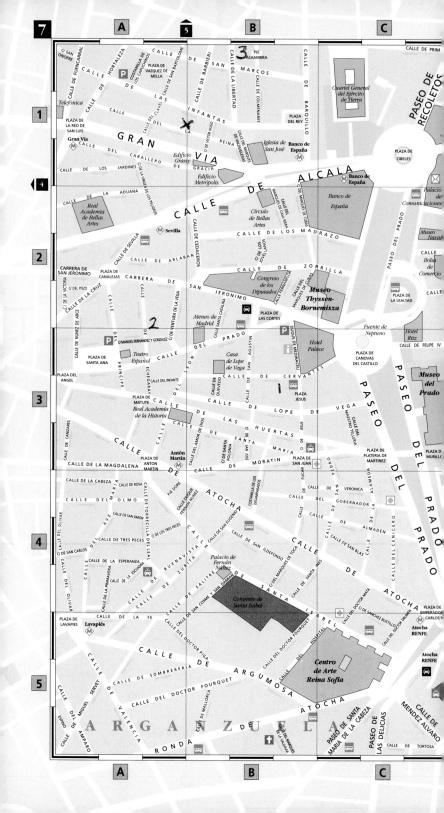

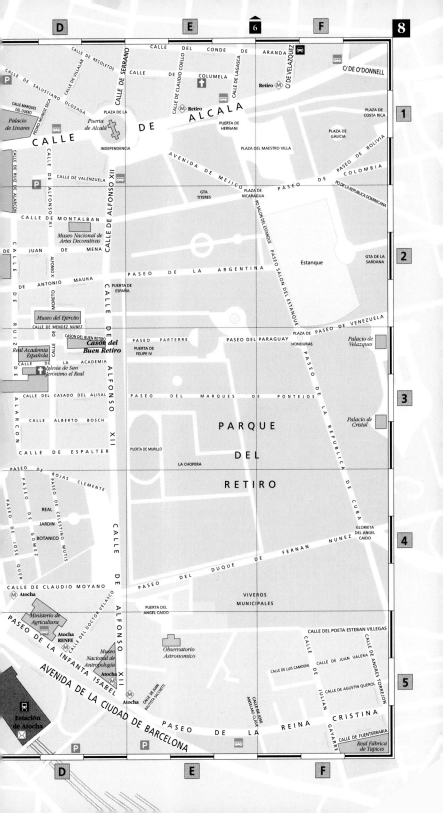

1

CALLE DEL CONDE DE ARANDA

CALLE DE RECOLETOS

CALLE DE SALUSTIANO OLOZAGA

CALLE MARQUES DEL DUERO

CALLE DE VILLALAR

CALLE DE SERRANO

CALLE

CALLE DE CLAUDIO COELLO

CALLE DE LAGASCA

C/ DE VELAZQUEZ

C/ DE O'DONNELL

Palacio de Linares

PLAZA DE LA

Puerta de Alcalá

COLUMELA

Retiro Ⓜ

PLAZA DE COSTA RICA

CALLE DE ALCALÁ

CALLE

DE

Ⓜ Retiro

PUERTA DE HERNANI

PLAZA DE GALICIA

INDEPENDENCIA

DE

AVENIDA DE MEJICO

PLAZA DEL MAESTRO VILLA

PASEO DE BOLIVIA

CALLE DE RUIZ DE ALARCON

CALLE DE ALFONSO XII

CALLE DE VALENZUELA

PASEO

DE

COLOMBIA

PO. DE LA REPUBLICA DOMINICANA

2

CALLE DE MONTALBAN

CALLE DE ALFONSO XII

GTA TITERES

PLAZA DE NICARAGUA

PO. SALON DEL ESTANQUE

Museo Nacional de Artes Decorativas

DE CALLE JUAN DE MENA

ALFONSO X

MAURA

PASEO DE LA ARGENTINA

PASEO SALON DEL ESTANQUE

Estanque

GTA DE LA SARDANA

DE CALLE

MORETO

ANTONIO

PUERTA DE ESPAÑA

Museo del Ejército

CALLE DE MENDEZ NUÑEZ

3

CALLE RUIZ DE

CASON DEL BUEN RETIRO

Cason del Buen Retiro

PASEO PARTERRE

PUERTA DE FELIPE IV

PASEO DEL PARAGUAY

PLAZA DE HONDURAS

PASEO DE VENEZUELA

Palacio de Velazques

Real Academia Española

CALLE DE LA ACADEMIA

Iglesia de San Jerónimo el Real

DE ALFONSO XII

PASEO DE LA REPUBLICA DE CUBA

DE ALARCON

CALLE DEL CASADO DEL ALISAL

PASEO DEL MARQUES DE PONTEJOS

Palacio de Cristal

CALLE ALBERTO BOSCH

PARQUE

CALLE DE ESPALTER

PUERTA DE MURILLO

LA CHOPERA

DEL

4

PASEO DE ROJAS CLEMENTE

PASEO DE CELESTINO

REAL

RETIRO

PASEO DE JOSE GOMEZ

PASEO DE GOMEZ QUER

JARDIN BOTANICO

MUTIS

CALLE DE

ALFONSO

GLORIETA DEL ANGEL CAIDO

PASEO DEL DUQUE DE FERNAN NUÑEZ

CALLE DE CLAUDIO MOYANO

Ⓜ Atocha

XII

VIVEROS MUNICIPALES

5

PASEO DE LA INFANTA ISABEL

Ministerio de Agricultura

Atocha RENFE

CALLE DE DOCTOR VELASCO

PUERTA DEL ANGEL CAIDO

CALLE DEL POETA ESTEBAN VILLEGAS

CALLE DE ANDRES TORRECON

Ⓜ Atocha

Museo Nacional de Antropología

Observatorio Astronomico

CALLE DE LUIS CAMOENS

CALLE DE JUAN VALERA

CALLE DE AGUSTIN QUEROL

DE CALLE

AVENIDA DE LA CIUDAD DE BARCELONA

Ⓜ Atocha

CALLE DE JUAN BAUTISTA SACCHETTI

ALFONSO XII

CALLE DE JOSE ANSELMO CLAVE

CALLE DE JULIAN GAYARRE

CRISTINA

Estación de Atocha

PASEO

DE

LA

REINA

CALLE DE FUENTERRABIA

Real Fábrica de Tapices

D E F

General Index

Acknowledgments

DORLING KINDERSLEY would like to thank the following people whose contributions and assistance have made the preparation of this book possible.

CONTRIBUTORS

ADAM HOPKINS is an indefatigable travel writer and author of *Spanish Journeys: A Portrait of Spain*.

MARK LITTLE, an American who grew up in Spain, is a freelance writer based in southern Spain. For many years he was the editor of *Lookout* magazine.

EDWARD OWEN has been, for many years, a foreign correspondent based in Madrid, contributing to *The Times* and *The Express* in London and *Time Magazine* among other publications.

JAMES RUSSO, a freelance journalist, is also a staff writer for Spain's state news agency, EFE. He has lived in Spain since the 1980s.

KATHY WHITE is a freelance journalist who has contributed to *The Christian Science Monitor* and *Newsweek*. She also worked for the French Service of the BBC and was foreign desk assistant at Channel 4 News.

DESIGN AND EDITORIAL ASSISTANCE

Special thanks to Hilary Bird for preparing the index, Juan Fernández for providing feedback on the content of the guide, Joy Fitzsimmons for visualizing the artworks, Elly King for the final design check, ERA Maptech for creating the maps, Graphical Innovations for outputting the text film, Barbara Minton for support from DK Publishing, Inc., Roberto Rama and Cristina Barrallo for fact checking, Mary Sutherland for providing feedback on the Survival Guide, Tom Prentice, Mani Ramaswamy, Zoë Ross and Lynda Warrington for editorial assistance and Stewart Wild for proofreading. Project assistance given by Fay Franklin, Annette Jacobs, Vivien Crump, Gillian Allen, Douglas Amrine, Joanne Blackmore, Monica Allende and Pamela Shiels.

PHOTOGRAPHY PERMISSIONS

© Patrimonio Nacional, Madrid: Monasterio de las Descalzas Reales; El Escorial; La Granja de San Ildefonso; Palacio Real; Palacio Real Aranjuez; Palacio de Fernán Núñez propriedad de Renfe Sede de la Fundación de los Ferrocarriles Españoles.

Dorling Kindersley would like to thank all the cathedrals, churches, museums, restaurants, hotels, shops, galleries, and other sights too numerous to thank individually.

PICTURE CREDITS

t=top; tl=top left; tlc=top left centre; tc=top centre; trc=top right centre; tr=top right; cla=centre left above; ca=centre above; cra=centre right above; cl=centre left; c=centre; cr=centre right; clb=centre left below; cb=centre below; crb=centre right below; bl=bottom left; b=bottom; bc=bottom centre; bcl=bottom centre left; br=bottom right; d=detail

Works of art have been reproduced with the permission of the following copyright holders:

Gernika Picasso © Succession Picasso/DACS 1999 87br; *Lugar de Encument* Chillida © DACS 1999 99c; *Mosaic* Miró © ADAGP, PARIS and DACS, London 1999 107t, front cover c.

The publisher would like to thank the following individuals, companies and picture libraries for their kind permission to reproduce their photographs:

ACE PHOTO: Bill Wassman 172b; AISA, Barcelona: 7inset, 14cb, 17b, 21bl, 21bc, *Retrato de Camilo Jose Cela* Alvaro Delgado © DACS 1999 26t, 27t, 56c, 76b, 80t, 82t, 83b, *La Tertulia del Café de Pombo* Jose Gutiérrez Solana © DACS 1999 87t, 104b; MAX ALEXANDER: 118; MUSEO ARQUEOLÓGICO NACIONAL, Madrid: 96, 97.

BRIDGEMAN PICTURE LIBRARY: *The Adoration of the Shepherds* El Greco 80ca, *The Annunciation* Fra Angelico 80cb, *The Clothed Maja* Goya 81t, *The Naked Maja* Goya 81ca, *The Three Graces* Rubens 81cb, *The Martyrdom of St Philip* Jose Ribera 81b, *St Dominic of Silos Enthroned as Abbot* Bermejo 82c, *Children at the Beach* Sorolla © DACS 1999 83t.

JOE CORNISH: 128c; COVER: Quim Llenas 27b; Matias Nieto 37c; EL DESEO: 104tr; AGENCIA EFE, Madrid: 35b, 36b.

EUROPEAN COMMISSION: 189; MARY EVANS PICTURE LIBRARY: 14b, 117inset, 143inset, 183inset.

FUNDACIÓN LÁZARO GALDIANO: 25t, 100/101; HULTON GETTY: 139b; GODO FOTOS: 131b; ROBERT HARDING PICTURE LIBRARY: James Strachan 53tr, 115t; P. Robinson 40

IMAGES COLOUR LIBRARY: A.G.E. Fotostock 23tr, 111cra; Horizon 111c; INDEX, Barcelona: 13b, 14c, 16b, 18b, 20ca, 20cbl, 21tl, 21tc, 21br, 26c, 26b, 27c; NICK INMAN: 187c, 193t.

ANTHONY KING: 76t.

ARXIU MAS, Barcelona: 10b; MUSEO DEL PRADO, Madrid: 80b; MUSEO THYSSEN BORNEMISZA, Madrid: 23cr, 70tr; *Harlequin with Mirror,* Picasso © Succession Picasso/DACS 1999 70cl; 70bl; *Portrait of Baron Thyssen-Bornemisza* © Lucian Freud 70bc; 71tl, 71cra, 71crb; *Autumn Landscape in Oldenburg*, Karl Schmidt-Rottluff © DACS 1999 71bl; 72 (3), 73 (2).

NATURPRESS, Madrid: 178b; J.L. González Grande 179b; A. Ibannñez & Fco González 180c; Diana Kvaternik 23bc; W Kvaternik-R. Olivas 2/3, 36c, 178c, 180t, 181t; Luis Olivas 34b; Petro Retamar 180b; Carlos Vegas 35c; Jaime Villanueva 1, 19c, 23ca, 34c, 113t, 178t; MUSEO NAVAL, Madrid: 65br.

ORONOZ, Madrid: 13t, 14t, 15t, 15c, 15b, 17c, 19t, 20tl, 20tr, 20cr, 24t, 24c, 24b, 47b, 56t, 56b, 57t, 57c, 57b, 67b, 75ca, 75b, 82b, 83c, *Portrait II* Miró © ADAGP, PARIS and DACS, London 1999 86t, *Woman in Blue* Picasso © Succession Picasso/DACS 1999 86ca, 102b, 103b, 111cla, 124, 125.

PRISMA, Barcelona: 12, 16t, 16c, 18t, 18c, 21tr, 21clb, 60b.

CENTRO DE ARTE REINA SOFIA, Madrid: *Retrato de Josette* Juan Gris © ADAGP, PARIS and DACS, London 1999 25b; *Landscape in Cadaqués* Dalí © Salvador Dalí – Foundation Gala – Salvador Dalí/DACS 1999 86c, 86b; *Toki-Egin* (*Homenaje a San-Juan de la Cruz*), 1952 Eduardo Chillida © DACS 2002 87bl; *Guitarra ante el Mar* Juan Gris © ADAGP, PARIS and DACS, London 1999 88t; *El Profeta* Pablo Gargallo © ADAGP, PARIS and DACS, London 1999 88c; *Minotauromaquia* Picasso © Succession Picasso/DACS 1999 88b; *Muchacha en la Ventana* Dalí © Salvador Dalí – Foundation Gala – Salvador Dalí/DACS 1999 89t; *Toda la Ciudad Habla de Ello* Eduardo Arroyo © DACS 1999 89b.

6 TOROS 6 magazine: 111cr.

M ANGELES SANCHEZ: 35t, 105b; Juan Carlos Martínez Zafra 52b; ARCHIVO DEL SENADO: Oronoz 53b; SCIENCE PHOTO LIBRARY: Geospace 8; STOCKPHOTOS: Marcelo Brodsky 34t; TONY STONE: 164b.

PETER WILSON: 38; WORLD PICTURES: 165c.

JACKET: Front - DK PICTURE LIBRARY: c, bc; GETTY IMAGES: Jon Bradley bl; PETER WILSON: main image. Back - ROBERT HARDING PICTURE LIBRARY: G. R. Richardson bl; Phil Robinson t. Spine - PETER WILSON.

FRONT END PAPER: All special photography except MAX ALEXANDER tr.

All other images © DORLING KINDERSLEY. For further information see www.DKimages.com

Phrase Book

IN AN EMERGENCY

Help!	¡Socorro!	soh-**koh**-roh
Stop!	¡Pare!	**pah**-reh
Call a doctor!	¡Llame a un médico!	**yah**-meh ah oon **meh**-dee-koh
Call an ambulance!	¡Llame a una ambulancia!	**yah**-meh ah **oonah** ahm-boo-**lahn**-thee-ah
Call the police!	¡Llame a la policía!	**yah**-meh ah lah poh-lee-**thee**-ah
Call the fire brigade!	¡Llame a los bomberos!	**yah**-meh ah lohs bohm-**beh**-rohs
Where is the nearest telephone?	¿Dónde está el teléfono más próximo?	**dohn**-deh ehs-**tah** ehl teh-**leh**-foh-noh **mahs prohx**-ee-moh
Where is the nearest hospital?	¿Dónde está el hospital más próximo?	**dohn**-deh ehs-**tah** ehl ohs-pee-**tahl mahs prohx**-ee-moh

COMMUNICATION ESSENTIALS

Yes	Sí	see
No	No	noh
Please	Por favor	pohr fah-**vohr**
Thank you	Gracias	**grah**-thee-ahs
Excuse me	Perdone	pehr-**doh**-neh
Hello	Hola	**oh**-lah
Goodbye	Adiós	ah-dee-**ohs**
Good night	Buenas noches	**bweh**-nahs **noh**-chehs
Morning	La mañana	lah mah-**nyah**-nah
Afternoon	La tarde	lah **tahr**-deh
Evening	La tarde	lah **tahr**-deh
Yesterday	Ayer	ah-**yehr**
Today	Hoy	oy
Tomorrow	Mañana	mah-**nya**-nah
Here	Aquí	ah-**kee**
There	Allí	ah-**yee**
What?	¿Qué?	keh
When?	¿Cuándo?	**kwahn**-doh
Why?	¿Por qué?	pohr-**keh**
Where?	¿Dónde?	**dohn**-deh

USEFUL PHRASES

How are you?	¿Cómo está usted?	**koh**-moh ehs-**tah** oos-**tehd**
Very well, thank you.	Muy bien, gracias.	mwee bee-**ehn grah**-thee-ahs
Pleased to meet you.	Encantado de conocerle.	ehn-kahn-**tah**-doh deh koh-noh-**thehr**-leh
See you soon.	Hasta pronto.	ahs-tah **prohn**-toh
That's fine.	Está bien.	ehs-**tah** bee-**ehn**
Where is/are ...?	¿Dónde está/están ...?	**dohn**-deh ehs-**tah**/ehs-**tahn**
How far is it to ...?	Cuántos metros/ kilómetros hay de aquí a ...?	**kwahn**-tohs **meh**-trohs/kee-**loh**-meh-trohs **eye** deh ah-**kee** ah
Which way to ...?	¿Por dónde se va a ...?	pohr **dohn**-deh seh **bah** ah
Do you speak English?	¿Habla inglés?	**ah**-blah een-**glehs**
I don't understand	No comprendo	noh kohm-**prehn**-doh
Could you speak more slowly please?	¿Puede hablar más despacio por favor?	pweh-deh ah-**blahr mahs** dehs-pah-thee-oh pohr fah-**vohr**
I'm sorry.	Lo siento.	loh see-**ehn**-toh

USEFUL WORDS

big	grande	**grahn**-deh
small	pequeño	peh-**keh**-nyoh
hot	caliente	kah-lee-**ehn**-teh
cold	frío	**free**-oh
good	bueno	**bweh**-noh
bad	malo	**mah**-loh
enough	bastante	bahs-**tahn**-teh
well	bien	bee-**ehn**
open	abierto	ah-bee-**ehr**-toh
closed	cerrado	thehr-**rah**-doh
left	izquierda	eeth-key-**ehr**-dah
right	derecha	deh-**reh**-chah
straight on	todo recto	toh-doh **rehk**-toh
near	cerca	**thehr**-kah
far	lejos	**leh**-hohs
up	arriba	ah-**ree**-bah
down	abajo	ah-**bah**-hoh
early	temprano	tehm-**prah**-noh
late	tarde	**tahr**-deh
entrance	entrada	ehn-**trah**-dah
exit	salida	sah-**lee**-dah
toilet	lavabos, servicios	lah-**vah**-bohs sehr-**bee**-thee-ohs
more	más	mahs
less	menos	**meh**-nohs

SHOPPING

How much does this cost?	¿Cuánto cuesta esto?	**kwahn**-toh **kwehs**-tah **ehs**-toh
I would like ...	Me gustaría ...	meh goos-ta-**ree**-ah
Do you have?	¿Tienen?	tee-**yeh**-nehn
I'm just looking.	Sólo estoy mirando, gracias.	**soh**-loh ehs-**toy** mee-**rahn**-doh **grah**-thee-ahs
Do you take credit cards?	¿Aceptan tarjetas de crédito?	ah-**thehp**-tahn tahr-**heh**-tahs deh **kreh**-dee-toh
What time do you open?	¿A qué hora abren?	ah keh oh-rah **ah**-brehn
What time do you close?	¿A qué hora cierran?	ah keh oh-rah thee-**ehr**-rahn
This one.	Éste	**ehs**-teh
That one.	Ése	**eh**-seh
expensive	caro	**kahr**-oh
cheap	barato	bah-**rah**-toh
size, clothes	talla	**tah**-yah
size, shoes	número	**noo**-mehr-oh
white	blanco	**blahn**-koh
black	negro	**neh**-groh
red	rojo	**roh**-hoh
yellow	amarillo	ah-mah-**ree**-yoh
green	verde	**behr**-deh
blue	azul	ah-**thool**
antiques shop	la tienda de antigüedades	lah tee-**ehn**-dah deh ahn-tee-gweh-**dah**-dehs
bakery	la panadería	lah pah-nah-deh-**ree**-ah
bank	el banco	ehl **bahn**-koh
book shop	la librería	lah lee-breh-**ree**-ah
butcher's	la carnicería	lah kahr-nee-theh-**ree**-ah
cake shop	la pastelería	lah pahs-teh-leh-**ree**-ah
chemist's	la farmacia	lah fahr-**mah**-thee-ah
fishmonger's	la pescadería	lah pehs-kah-deh-**ree**-ah
greengrocer's	la frutería	lah froo-teh-**ree**-ah
grocer's	la tienda de comestibles	lah tee-**yehn**-dah deh koh-mehs-**tee**-blehs
hairdresser's	la peluquería	lah peh-loo-keh-**ree**-ah
market	el mercado	ehl mehr-**kah**-doh
newsagent's	el kiosko de prensa	ehl kee-**ohs**-koh deh **prehn**-sah
post office	la oficina de correos	lah oh-fee-**thee**-nah deh kohr-**reh**-ohs
shoe shop	la zapatería	lah thah-pah-teh-**ree**-ah
supermarket	el supermercado	ehl soo-pehr-mehr-**kah**-doh
tobacconist	el estanco	ehl ehs-**tahn**-koh
travel agency	la agencia de viajes	lah ah-**hehn**-thee-ah deh bee-**ah**-hehs

SIGHTSEEING

art gallery	el museo de arte	ehl moo-**seh**-oh deh **ahr**-teh
cathedral	la catedral	lah kah-teh-**drahl**
church	la iglesia	lah ee-**gleh**-see-ah
	la basílica	lah bah-**see**-lee-kah
garden	el jardín	ehl hahr-**deen**
library	la biblioteca	lah bee-blee-oh-**teh**-kah
museum	el museo	ehl moo-**seh**-oh
tourist information office	la oficina de turismo	lah oh-fee-**thee** nah deh too-**rees**-moh
town hall	el ayuntamiento	ehl ah-yoon-tah-mee-**ehn**-toh
closed for holiday	cerrado por vacaciones	thehr-**rah**-doh pohr bah-kah-thee-**oh**-nehs
bus station	la estación de autobuses	lah ehs-tah-thee-**ohn** deh owtoh-**boo**-sehs
railway station	la estación de trenes	lah ehs-tah-thee-**ohn** deh **treh**-nehs

STAYING IN A HOTEL

Do you have a vacant room?	¿Tiene una habitación libre?	tee-**eh**-neh **oo**-nah ah-bee-tah-thee-**ohn** lee-breh
double room	habitación doble	ah-bee-tah-thee-**ohn doh**-bleh
with double bed	con cama de matrimonio	kohn **kah**-mah deh mah-tree-**moh**-nee-oh
twin room	habitación con dos camas	ah-bee-tah-thee-**ohn** kohn dohs **kah**-mahs
single room	habitación individual	ah-bee-tah-thee-**ohn** een-dee-vee-doo-**ahl**
room with a bath	habitación con baño	ah-bee-tah-thee-**ohn** kohn bah-nyoh
shower	ducha	**doo**-chah
porter	el botones	ehl boh-**toh**-nehs
key	la llave	lah **yah**-veh
I have a reservation.	Tengo una habitación reservada.	tehn-goh **oo**-na ah-bee-tah-thee-**ohn** reh-sehr-**bah**-dah

EATING OUT

Have you got a table for . . .?	¿Tiene mesa para . . .?	tee-**eh**-neh meh-sah pah-**rah**
I want to reserve a table.	Quiero reservar una mesa.	kee-eh-roh reh-sehr-**bahr oo**-nah **meh**-sah
The bill please.	La cuenta por favor.	lah **kwehn**-tah pohr fah-**vohr**
I am a vegetarian	Soy vegetariano/a	soy beh-heh-tah-ree-**ah**-no/na
waitress/ waiter	camarera/ camarero	kah-mah-**reh**-rah kah-mah-**reh**-roh
menu	la carta	lah **kahr**-tah
fixed-price menu	menú del día	meh-**noo** dehl **dee**-ah
wine list	la carta de vinos	lah **kahr**-tah deh **bee**-nohs
glass	un vaso	oon **bah**-soh
bottle	una botella	oo-nah boh-**teh**-yah
knife	un cuchillo	oon koo-**chee**-yoh
fork	un tenedor	oon teh-neh-**dohr**
spoon	una cuchara	oo-nah koo-**chah**-rah
breakfast	el desayuno	ehl deh-sah-**yoo**-noh
lunch	la comida/ el almuerzo	lah koh-**mee**-dah/ ehl ahl-**mwehr**-thoh
dinner	la cena	lah **theh**-nah
main course	el primer plato	ehl pree-**mehr plah**-toh
starters	los entremeses	lohs ehn-treh-**meh**-sehs
dish of the day	el plato del día	ehl **plah**-toh dehl **dee**-ah
coffee	el café	ehl kah-**feh**
rare (meat)	poco hecho	**poh**-koh **eh**-choh
medium	medio hecho	**meh**-dee-oh **eh**-choh
well done	muy hecho	mwee **eh**-choh

MENU DECODER

al horno	ahl **ohr**-noh	baked
asado	ah-**sah**-doh	roast
el aceite	ah-**thee-eh**-teh	oil
las aceitunas	ah-theh-**toon**-ahs	olives
el agua mineral	**ah**-gwa mee-neh-**rahl**	mineral water
sin gas/con gas	seen gas/kohn gas	still/sparkling
el ajo	**ah**-hoh	garlic
el arroz	ahr-**rohth**	rice
el azúcar	ah-**thoo**-kahr	sugar
la carne	**kahr**-neh	meat
la cebolla	theh-**boh**-yah	onion
el cerdo	**therh**-doh	pork
la cerveza	thehr-**beh**-thah	beer
el chocolate	choh-koh-**lah**-teh	chocolate
el chorizo	choh-**ree**-thoh	spicy sausage
el cordero	kohr-**deh**-roh	lamb
el fiambre	fee-**ahm**-breh	cold meat
frito	**free**-toh	fried
la fruta	**froo**-tah	fruit
los frutos secos	**froo**-tohs **seh**-kohs	nuts
las gambas	**gahm**-bahs	prawns
el helado	eh-**lah**-doh	ice cream
el huevo	oo-**eh**-voh	egg
el jamón serrano	hah-**mohn** sehr-**rah**-noh	cured ham
el jerez	heh-**rehz**	sherry

la langosta	lahn-**gohs**-tah	lobster
la leche	**leh**-cheh	milk
el limón	lee-**mohn**	lemon
la limonada	lee-moh-**nah**-dah	lemonade
la mantequilla	mahn-tch-**kee**-yah	butter
la manzana	mahn-**thah**-nah	apple
los mariscos	mah-**rees**-kohs	seafood
la menestra	meh-**nehs**-trah	vegetable stew
la naranja	nah-**rahn**-hah	orange
el pan	pahn	bread
el pastel	pahs-**tehl**	cake
las patatas	pah-**tah**-tahs	potatoes
el pescado	pehs-**kah**-doh	fish
la pimienta	pee-mee-**yehn**-tah	pepper
el plátano	**plah**-tah-noh	banana
el pollo	**poh**-yoh	chicken
el postre	**pohs**-treh	dessert
el queso	**keh**-soh	cheese
la sal	sahl	salt
las salchichas	sahl-**chee**-chahs	sausages
la salsa	**sahl**-sah	sauce
seco	**seh**-koh	dry
el solomillo	soh-loh-**mee**-yoh	sirloin
la sopa	**soh**-pah	soup
la tarta	**tahr**-tah	pie/cake
el té	teh	tea
la ternera	tehr-**neh**-rah	beef
las tostadas	tohs-**tah**-dahs	toast
el vinagre	bee-**nah**-greh	vinegar
el vino blanco	**bee**-noh **blahn**-koh	white wine
el vino rosado	**bee**-noh roh-**sah**-doh	rosé wine
el vino tinto	**bee**-noh **teen**-toh	red wine

NUMBERS

0	cero	**theh**-roh
1	uno	**oo**-noh
2	dos	dohs
3	tres	trehs
4	cuatro	**kwa**-troh
5	cinco	**theen**-koh
6	seis	says
7	siete	**see**-eh-teh
8	ocho	**oh**-choh
9	nueve	**nweh**-veh
10	diez	dee-**ehth**
11	once	**ohn**-theh
12	doce	**doh**-theh
13	trece	**treh**-theh
14	catorce	kah-**tohr**-theh
15	quince	**keen**-theh
16	dieciséis	dee-eh-thee-**seh-ees**
17	diecisiete	dee-eh-thee-see-**eh**-teh
18	dieciocho	dee-eh-thee-**oh**-choh
19	diecinueve	dee-eh-thee-**nweh**-veh
20	veinte	**beh**-een-teh
21	veintiuno	beh-een-tee-**oo**-noh
22	veintidós	beh-een-tee-**dohs**
30	treinta	**treh**-een-tah
31	treinta y uno	treh-een-tah ee **oo**-noh
40	cuarenta	kwah-**rehn**-tah
50	cincuenta	theen-**kwehn**-tah
60	sesenta	seh-**sehn**-tah
70	setenta	seh-**tehn**-tah
80	ochenta	oh-**chehn**-tah
90	noventa	noh-**vehn**-tah
100	cien	thee-**ehn**
101	ciento uno	thee-**ehn**-toh **oo**-noh
102	ciento dos	thee-**ehn**-toh dohs
200	doscientos	dohs-thee-**ehn**-tohs
500	quinientos	khee-nee-**ehn**-tohs
700	setecientos	seh-teh-thee-**ehn**-tohs
900	novecientos	noh-veh-thee-**ehn** tohs
1,000	mil	meel
1,001	mil uno	meel **oo**-noh

TIME

one minute	un minuto	oon mee-**noo**-toh
one hour	una hora	oo-na **oh**-rah
half an hour	media hora	**meh**-dee-a **oh**-rah
Monday	lunes	**loo**-nehs
Tuesday	martes	**mahr**-tehs
Wednesday	miércoles	mee-**ehr**-koh-lehs
Thursday	jueves	hoo-**weh**-vehs
Friday	viernes	bee-**ehr**-nehs
Saturday	sábado	**sah**-bah-doh
Sunday	domingo	doh-**meen**-goh

EYEWITNESS TRAVEL INSURANCE

FOR PEACE OF MIND ABROAD, WE'VE GOT IT COVERED

 DK INSURANCE PROVIDES YOU WITH QUALITY WORLDWIDE INSURANCE COVER

For an instant quote
go to **www.dk.com/travel-insurance**

MADRID TRANSPORT MAP

Madrid's metro runs from 6am–1:30am daily. Its 11 lines are identified by number and colour, both in the stations and on the trains. Platform signs display the next station and connecting lines. Visitors should note that on the platforms, indicator boards show the time elapsed since the last train, not how long to the next train. A fixed-price ticket *(billete)* will take you anywhere on the system, although a ten-trip ticket *(metrobus)* is much better value for money.

The metro lines are linked with the RENFE train stations: Chamartín, Atocha and Norte (Príncipe Pío), which has a fast line from Ópera. *Largo recorrido* (long-distance) and *cercanías* (suburban) trains leave from these stations. A monthly travel pass can be used on the metro, suburban trains and buses. An additional line (MetroSur), which covers southern suburbs of Madrid, runs from Puerta del Sur on line 10.